RESPONSIBILITY IN
MODERN RELIGIOUS ETHICS

Responsibility in Modern Religious Ethics

BY

ALBERT R. JONSEN

Foreword by James M. Gustafson

CORPUS BOOKS

Washington / Cleveland

CORPUS PUBLICATIONS

EDITORIAL OFFICE
1330 Massachusetts Ave., N.W.
Washington, D.C. 20005

SALES & DISTRIBUTION
2231 West 110th Street
Cleveland, Ohio 44102

Copyright © 1968 by Albert R. Jonsen, S.J.

Library of Congress Catalog Card Number: 68–25761

First Printing 1968

PRINTED IN THE UNITED STATES OF AMERICA

Foreword

The idea of responsibility is a fundamental one in ethics. The literature which addresses the idea, either directly or obliquely, is vast if one includes the writings of philosophers, theologians, novelists, psychotherapists, and many others. It has come into prominence in religious ethics in the past two decades. The four Christian thinkers who are central to Father Jonsen's work have each been important for the explications that they have given to the idea, the ways in which they have related it to a wider context of religious life and ideas, and to other issues in philosophy.

I shall not recapitulate the analysis which the text of this book provides. Nor shall I here display in rhetoric my satisfaction with it, and my aspirations for it as a basis for further explorations and constructive efforts. Father Jonsen was the first Roman Catholic to enroll in and to complete the doctoral program in Christian ethics in the Department of Religious Studies of Yale University. The publication of a book based on his dissertation is, of course, a matter for rejoicing on the part of us who shared in his education during his years at Yale. My high esteem for Father Jonsen, and my deep affection for him have come through many hours in seminars and outside of them, and also through the work he did for me as an assistant in instruction in my course in Christian Ethics for Divinity School students.

There is an ecumenical maturity to this study which suggests that we are moving into a new way of writing religious ethics. The central issue is neither Catholic nor Protestant, but human. The analysis is not basically a defense of a thesis which comes from either of the two traditions. Rather, Jonsen studies the ways in which a substantial and important problem is handled principally by four important Christian thinkers. His final constructive proposals show a way in which thinking about responsibility can go, whether those who pursue it are Catholics or Protestants. Indeed, his generation of students is the first who have been well schooled both in their own tradition and in another, and thus are better prepared to do genuinely ecumenical Christian ethics than are any of us educated in earlier decades. The issues of ethics will in the future be addressed as concerns for Christian theologians, who will be informed by their own and others' historical loyalties. Their work will be judged in the public domain in terms of its contribution to problems we all face in theological ethics, rather than in terms of a defense of an entrenched historical bias.

The idea of responsibility is particularly open to ecumenical thought. It is much in the literature of the philosophers at this time. Some of that literature, but by no means all of it, can be explored through Jonsen's citations. Austrian, English, and American philosophers have had to make a case for their reluctance to give up a notion of responsibility for one's moral actions against their own thrusts of positivism, and determinism. Many essays and chapters of books have dealt with precise and detailed aspects of the age-old issue of freedom and determinism, and largely for the sake of preserving a case for moral responsibility. Highly sophisticated accounts of the nature of human actions have been developed, dealing with the propriety of speaking of "causes" of action, with motives, character, and intentions. The human sciences of psychology, whether Freudian or experimentalist behaviorism, social psychology, cultural anthropology, and sociology have all given both evidences and general theories about the determination of human action which add data to the rethinking of moral responsibility.

The existential and phenomenological philosophers are also addressing the issue. Sartre's concept of freedom alone has provoked a large body of critical literature. Paul Ricoeur's analysis of the voluntary and the involuntary, and his phenomenology of choice and action parallels in its central concerns many essays written by contemporary Anglo-American philosophers, though the mode of thinking about the questions is radically different. Unfortunately there is scant evidence in the citations of philosophers in the two dominant streams of close attention to the efforts of the other to clarify and resolve common questions about the nature of action, freedom and responsibility, and other related matters.

Since the idea of responsibility is so central to the questions of moral action, whether addressed by philosophers or theologians, it becomes one of the fruitful common concerns which make discourse between these types of thinkers possible and fruitful. Much of the concern overlaps these two fields. Jonsen's work itself indicates some of the ways in which the works of one can be used to the beneficial clarification of the works of the other. Theological writers of ethics are at least as likely to find insight into issues that require clarification and resolution from H. L. A. Hart or Richard Brandt as they are from theological writings. It is the issues which require our most sophisticated intellectual attention that move theologians into the writings of philosophers on the question of responsibility, not a desire to find Catholic or Protestant thinkers who might prop up some pre-conceived bias we have on the matter.

The concept of responsibility is one addressed by both theologians and philosophers; the experience of being responsible and of having to assess one's own or other's responsibility functions to join the life of religion and the life of morality. When it is lived and interpreted in the context of man's relation not only to himself and his neighbor, but also in the context of his relation to God, the dimensions of responsible existence are enlarged. In the religious understanding of moral experience, one is responsible not only for one's acts in terms of accountability to oneself or to one's community; one is accountable to the giver and ruler of life. The scope of the discourse is vastly enlarged, for it seeks to understand how a life of responsibility to God is to be lived, what it implies for one's relations with his neighbors, near and distant.

But in religious ethics we are not dealing only with ideas about God and the inferences about human moral responsibility that can properly be derived from these ideas; we are dealing with a personal relationship between sons and their Father, between those who have received the gifts of life and of newness of life and the gracious Giver, between feeble and self-centered men and One who is himself self-giving love. Because of this religious context, it has been the theologians who have reminded us that to be responsible is to respond, and not merely to be accountable; it is to answer a vocation, and not merely to be answerable. Men are called to respond to what God in his grace is doing for them; they are accountable to him for the life they live in that response. Religious faith and devotion and moral seriousness are depicted in the inextricable confluence they have for members of the Christian community in the idea of responsibility.

The idea of responsibility is one that brings Catholic and Protestant thinkers together. It may provide a different way for us to come together than would the ideas of natural law, or sanctification, precisely because of the newness of its centrality in religious ethical thinking. There is less history to be defended, less dogma imbedded in official documents, less ruttedness in our minds and habits of thought. Thus there is more focus on the intrinsic possibilities of a relatively fresh notion in religious ethics. Father Jonsen's quotation from Martin Buber, at the front of his book, reminds us that contributions to a fresh appropriation of the significance of the idea have come also from Judaism. It is worth noting that the four writers who are central to this book were developing their ideas of responsibility independent of each other; Father Johann's use of H. Richard Niebuhr's reflections come after he had developed the idea with a great deal of care in his short and pregnant "Philosopher's Notebook" pieces in *America*.

An understanding of moral responsibility is crucial for the participation of the Christian community in the moral life we share with all men. Theologians can learn many nuances of its meaning from the sensitive portrayals of dramatists and film producers, from physicians and advocates, from civil rights leaders and protestors against war, from conscientious business men and college students. The breakdown of many traditional moral customs and codes not only makes heavier demands on the moral responsibilities of individuals, but heightens in many the seriousness with which they take their participation in the human community. There are signs of a new moral seriousness, a rebirth of concern for personal integrity, a sensitivity to the profound needs of the oppressed, an indignation against injustice and needless suffering. New possibilities for the human community are coming into being; an understanding of the nature of moral responsibility will make a contribution to their fulfillment.

All of this is not to say that one can build a whole ethics on the back of one term, responsibility. It needs to be related to many other terms in discourse such as justice and power; it needs to be seen in relation to many other facets in human life, such as law and economics and politics. Nor is all this to recommend that other questions of ethics be left unattended while we all probe further the questions that are evoked by the idea of responsibility. There is a plurality of vocations among writers in ethics, just as there is a plurality of vocations among all morally responsible men in the world. But since responsibility is so central to all moral experience, and the general idea of it functions to link so many particular ideas with each other, we can be pleased to have this study of Father Jonsen's, and can anticipate further studies by him, and/or others.

Finally, a more personal word. Through no merit of my own, but by good fortune, I have had the privilege of having three of the four major figures in this book as personal friends and intellectual companions: H. R. Niebuhr, Bernhard Haering, and Robert Johann. They have all, as has Bonhoeffer, been my teachers. I have also learned from Father Jonsen, and from his interpretation of these men. I hope the readers of Father Jonsen's book will find the four main subjects of the book and Father Jonsen himself to be their intellectual companions in thinking about Christian Ethics.

JAMES M. GUSTAFSON
Professor of Christian Ethics

Yale University

Preface

Responsibility comes from *respondere,* to respond, to answer, the dictionaries tell us. So, say some moralists, we call that man responsible who answers for himself and for what he does. Responsibility means accepting as one's own the consequences, good or evil, of one's acts. No, say other moralists, rather we call that man responsible who responds, who is responsive to others and their needs. Responsibility means sensitivity to the call which others make upon one. This book is an attempt to thread our way through these assertions, an exploration into the ethics and the theology which lie behind them. But, although we may succeed in distinguishing various strands in the idea of responsibility and isolating distinct patterns, in the last analysis we must *be* responsible in both ways.

This is certainly true in the case of an author: he must bear the responsibility for his words and he must be sensitive to those others who have helped him write those words. It seems that we are able to be our own man, to stand on our own, only when surrounded by other men and supported by their response. If the ethics of responsibility which these pages describe seems to depreciate somewhat the venerable tradition and task of guardian angels, it certainly puts in their place the teachers, colleagues and friends whose interest and help aid in making and keeping us responsible.

Thus, I wish first of all to acknowledge the wise guidance

of my teacher, Professor James Gustafson of Yale University. He not only offers direction and advice, but presents an admirable example of the responsible teacher. I am indebted to the interest of two men whom I make bold to discuss in this book, Fr. Bernhard Haering and Fr. Robert Johann. I appreciate very much the helpful criticism of Professors William Christian and David Little of Yale, and of Fr. Joseph Fuchs of the Gregorian University. Finally, to many confreres, colleagues, and friends, and to one in particular, who responded with interest and encouragement and so are in part responsible for this book, my deep appreciation and gratitude.

Table of Contents

RESPONSIBILITY IN
MODERN RELIGIOUS ETHICS

1

The Language of Responsibility

The language of morality is fickle. The words with which one generation will praise or blame, commend or condemn, sound dull or even comic to their children. "Propriety," "piety," "prudence," for example, once commanded respect as standards of moral excellence. In a culture which values creativity, innovation and daring, they merely evoke images of the past: the proper victorian and the introverted puritan. Even the word "virtue" which inherits an etymological pedigree of strength, manliness and virtuosity, has become a pale specter of its former self.

However, when certain words lose their commendatory force, other words appear to take their place in the lexicon of morality. "Responsibility" is one of these new arrivals. "The responsible man" is replacing "the respectable man," "responsibility" replaces "obedience" as contemporary ideals. The word "responsibility" itself has undergone a significant shift of meaning which indicates the new role it plays in the language of contemporary morals. Our purpose in this book is to document the evolution of "responsibility" and its cognates and to attempt to elucidate its meaning. We will limit ourselves to a particular sector of modern moral thought—religious, more particularly Christian, ethics. We do so because Christian ethics presents an especially interesting example of the introduction and evolution of the concept of responsibility. We also

limit ourselves to Christian ethics because, despite the great
variety of presentations, it is a definite universe of thought,
with certain common problems and presuppositions. We shall
attempt to see how the idea of responsibility takes shape in
this universe.

This study will open with a survey of some of the Christian
ethical literature in which the term "responsibility" is prominently displayed. This literature consists of several official
church documents, some of the recent literature on "responsible
parenthood" and the writings of the popular phenomenon
called "Christian situation ethics." This survey will indicate
that some confusion exists about the precise meaning and use
of "responsibility." In particular, it will reveal the confusion
which arises when several areas of ethical discourse, which
should be treated separately, are confounded.

The third chapter departs for a while from the universe
of Christian religious ethics. It turns to the literature of moral
philosophy, ancient and modern. It abstracts from that literature two basic "patterns of responsibility." These patterns
are the sets of ideas and issues which moral philosophers have
linked together when they discuss moral responsibility. I call
the two basic patterns "attribution of responsibility" and "appropriation of responsibility." The former deals with the problem of justly assigning praise and blame for behavior; the
latter with the agent's own acknowledgment of his actions.
The purpose of this chapter is not to set up norms for the
criticism of the religious use of the term "responsibility."
Rather it is to set out a clear instance of definite and precise
meaning and usage in order to compare the similarities and
differences between philosophers and theologians.

The fourth chapter will examine the efforts of four authors
to employ the term responsibility in a significant way in a
Christian religious ethic. By *religious* ethic I simply mean any
methodological treatment of the moral life within an explicit
affirmation of the relevance of God; by *Christian* religious
ethic, I mean the further affirmation of the relevance of Christ

and Christian revelation for human morality. We shall ask these authors for a definition of responsibility in its religious sense and for an explanation of how the term can be used within the context of a religious ethic. These authors are representative: two are Roman Catholics, two are Protestant; two are European and two are American; two are theologians, two call themselves Christian philosophers. They are Bernhard Haering, Dietrich Bonhoeffer, H. Richard Niebuhr and Robert O. Johann. We will also attend briefly to some statements of Karl Barth, less for the purpose of analysis than for the purpose of illustrating the problems and peculiarities of the religious use of the concept of responsibility.

"Responsibility" is a new arrival in moral discourse in two senses. It is both a new word in the western languages, being only some three centuries old, and it has also, quite recently, taken on a new meaning. It is somewhat surprising to learn that so familiar a word has so short a history. It begins to appear in French, English and German only in the seventeenth century. For example, one of its earliest appearances is in Pascal's *Lettres Provinciales* (1656), where Pascal has the Jesuit superior say, "our whole Society takes responsibility for a book written by any one of our members." The word has its philosophical debut in David Hume's *Treatise of Human Nature* (1740): "actions may be blameable . . . but the person not responsible for them." It is from the beginning used in political literature, as exemplified in Alexander Hamilton's *Federalist Papers* (1787): "Responsibility in order to be reasonable must be limited to objects within the power of the responsible body."

The word appears occasionally, then, in philosophical and political literature as a synonym for accountability, imputability, liability. It was not firmly established in its own right until the British philosopher, F. H. Bradley, gave it currency in his essay, "The Vulgar Notion of Responsibility and its Connection with the Theories of Free Will and Determinism" (1876). Seven

years later, the French philosopher, Lucien Levy-Bruhl, published his study of the problem of freedom in the light of the
Kantian problematic, *L'Idée de Responsabilité*. Since the late
19th century, then, the word "responsibility" has been part of
the vocabulary of philosophical ethics. We shall examine its
meaning in that discipline in the third chapter.

But there is a second way in which responsibility is a new
arrival in moral discourse. The great Jewish thinker, Martin
Buber, called for "the idea of responsibility . . . to be brought
back from the province of specialized ethics into that of lived
life." His desire seems to have been fulfilled. Whereas in
specialized ethics responsibility has a definite and limited
meaning, in recent years the word has become current in
common language with a somewhat different meaning.

Although we intend to study the philosophical meaning
carefully later in this book, we might, in order to understand
Buber's suggestion, look briefly at the definition proposed in
an authoritative source, the philosophical dictionary of the
French Society of Philosophy.

> Responsibility means (1) the moral obligation, sometimes
> sanctioned by law, to repair the harm done to another; (2) the
> situation of a conscious agent with regard to those actions
> which he has really willed to perform. It consists in his being
> able to offer motives for these acts to any reasonable person
> and in his being obligated to incur praise or blame for them
> according to the nature and value of these motives . . . It is
> the solidarity of the human person with his actions, the prior
> condition of all real and juridical obligation.[1]

This, then, is the problem of responsibility which "specialized
ethics" has discussed. Long before the word itself was introduced into ethics, philosophers meditated and argued about
the manner in which a man could be considered the author of
his actions. At the very dawn of western philosophy, Heraclitus
proclaimed that it was a man's formed character, not some external force, which constituted his fate. Since then, philosophers
have debated the issues of fate and freedom, character and

causality, motivation and intention, the justification of praise and blame, punishment and reward. The question of responsibility has always been, in moral philosophy, a question about the necessary and sufficient conditions which must exist if a man is truly to be called the author of his actions and justly to be praised or blamed for them.

Buber, however, has suggested that the idea of responsibility be moved out of its carefully designed niche in specialized ethics into lived life. Today the word appears with increasing frequency in the popular press, in periodical articles, in political speeches, in every sort of moral exhortation. It is used not only by philosophers but by preachers and parents as a strong term of moral approbation and as a criterion for policy and behavior. Political scientists discuss how forms of "responsible government" may be implemented. Psychiatrists and psychologists interest themselves in the formation of the "responsible personality." Sociologists describe the "responsible participant in the responsible society." The president of the United States says, "you have to do what is responsible . . . if you sit in this place." A college textbook, consisting of a wide variety of readings described as "the insights of the humanities" is entitled *The Responsible Man*.

This expanding use of responsibility and its cognates goes far beyond the classical philosophical usage (although, as we shall see, it has definite affinities with it). When the responsible man is praised, when responsible decision is encouraged, when responsibility is proposed as a major ethical criterion, authors are not merely describing the necessary and sufficient conditions for ascribing praise and blame. They are exhorting men to live in a certain manner, to adopt a certain stance toward life and their role in it. They are shaping, with the help of this word, a new ideal of moral behavior. The responsible man is not merely one who is able to perform good actions; he is, in fact, the good man. His goodness consists precisely in his responsibility. This is responsibility in "lived life."

While this word is becoming current in all forms of moral

exhortation and discussion, it appears with surprising frequency in the literature of Christian morality. I say with surprising frequency because Christian morality has generally been depicted (rightly or wrongly) as a morality of law, authority and obligation. The morality of responsibility, as we shall see, is designed to incorporate these very elements into a wider and radically different conception of the moral life— one in which freedom, personal conscience and individual initiative predominate. Thus the appearance of responsibility in this literature would seem to indicate the emergence of a new, or if not new, renewed form of Christian ethics.

In popular essays, theological treatises and ecclesiastical pronouncements, the words "responsible Christian," or "Christian responsibility," "responsible decision," and "responsible freedom," are used to express the appropriate attitudes or characteristics of the Christian person and his Church. The important Constitution on the Church in the Modern World of Vatican II proclaims: "We are witnesses of the birth of a new humanism, one in which man is defined first of all by his responsibility toward his brothers and toward history."[2]

Obviously, if a word is used frequently in a variety of contexts by many authors, a precise, univocal definition cannot be expected. However if the word begins to function in some particularly important way, for example as a term of special commendation in moral discourse, it becomes worthwhile to determine as accurately as possible its connotations and denotations. This is even more urgent if the authors begin to employ the word in such technical literature as serious treatises in ethics.

It is my contention that in much of the Christian moral literature the meaning of the term "responsibility" is vague and its use unstable. This might be attributed partly to the fact that some of the prominent theologians who espouse its use wish to subordinate the established usage of moral philosophy to a "properly religious sense." For example, Emil Brunner, who was one of the first theologians to make prominent use of the term, wrote,

> It is of the very essence of faith in the Word of God that man always understands himself as existing in responsibility and in indissoluble relation to a "Thou." Man never learns what a "Thou" really means save when he understands what responsibility means and this means nowhere save in the word of God.[3]

Bernhard Haering, whose work we shall examine later in detail, writes, "the object and purpose of moral theology is not involved in the philosophical analysis of 'responsibility' nor in the explanation of the term."[4] It will be necessary to determine whether there is a properly religious sense for the term "responsibility" and, if so, what it might be.

However, the lack of clarity and instability of usage can also be attributed to the fact that many authors have eagerly adopted the term into their ethical discussions without making careful distinction between its "religious meaning," its philosophical meaning, and its popular connotations. The result has been a melange of meanings drawn from distinct areas of discourse; consequently the word's theological and ethical clarity is worn away.

This book, then, is first and foremost an essay in clarification. It attempts to find, first among the moral philosophers and then among the religious moralists, some agreement about the proper meaning and use of the concept of responsibility. Since the religious moralists are explicitly dedicated to the task of establishing an *ethic of responsibility*, it is among them that we shall see most clearly the emerging new meaning, the responsibility of "lived life." Our concern is principally with the Christian literature; we have not, therefore, searched the non-religious literature for the secular counterpart of this emerging meaning.

This concern involves more than the clarification of the

meaning and use of responsibility. It also seeks to read beneath that meaning and use the direction which Christian ethics seems to be taking today. We have deliberately chosen to speak of *Christian* ethics and to draw upon both Catholic and Protestant sources. We are convinced that all Christians are experiencing in a very similar way the pressure of the needs and ideals of the contemporary world. Their representative theologians are being challenged by very similar problems and are beginning to read and speak with each other about them. Perhaps the deepest meaning of the ecumenical movement is not so much that Christians of various traditions come to understand each other and share with each other, but rather that they begin to become aware together of the challenge posed to Christianity itself and of their common resources to meet that challenge.

The Christian ethic of responsibility which our four major authors describe is one example of this community of challenge and response. These four, quite unrelated personally or doctrinally, move toward a basic stance which is strikingly similar. They do so because each has experienced, in his own unique way, a similar problem. Each will express that problem and his response to it in the terms proper to his own history and theological tradition, but each draws upon the common resources of the Christian faith and world view. Consequently, their responses converge in a striking manifestation of unintended ecumenism.

Thus, we wish to clarify the meaning of responsibility in Christian ethics and to uncover the trends which the adoption of this concept intimates for Christian ethics. We shall conclude with some thoughts in the final chapter about the prospects of a Christian ethic which follows these trends. Such thoughts are tentative because a trend, like a tornado, may swerve from its predicted path. Yet because we are dealing with ideas rather than the weather, perhaps the prediction itself may help to direct the path. Further, the projection of an ethic of responsibility involves calling up a crowd of metaphysical and theological questions as yet unanswered. They are unanswered, of course, because they have not yet been fully recognized nor fully faced. The looming prospect of a problem is no reason to avoid the path: if we cannot now answer it the experience of living with it may suggest answers, or at least better questions.

The ethic of responsibility which our authors initiate is yet unfinished, its final shape quite undetermined. Still, its beginnings are promising. It seems to have great potential for growth. Its growth will, we hope, contribute to the growth of Christians as persons and as disciples of Jesus Christ.

2

Current Christian Ethical Literature

TWO FORMAL STATEMENTS

Two statements, issued by official ecclesiastical bodies, will provide our first examples of the use of the term "responsibility" in Christian ethical literature. The first is a statement of the World Council of Churches, entitled "The Responsible Society." The second is the annual message of the Roman Catholic hierarchy of the United States for 1960, entitled "On Individual Responsibility."

The World Council of Churches, in its First Assembly at Amsterdam in 1948, proposed that the goal of Christian social action should be "The Responsible Society." The Amsterdam Report states:

> Man is created and called to be a free being, responsible before God and to his neighbor. Any tendencies in State and society to deprive man of the possibility of acting responsibly are a denial of God's intention for man and his work of salvation. A responsible society is one where freedom is the freedom of men who acknowledge responsibility to justice and public order, and where those who hold political authority and economic power are responsible for its exercise to God and the people whose welfare is affected by it . . . For a society to be responsible under modern conditions it is required that the people have freedom to control, to criticize and to change their government, that power be made responsible to law and tradition and be distributed as widely as possible through the community.[1]

This brief paragraph, which has served as the basis for a continuing study of The Responsible Society by the World Council, is directed principally to social and political issues. The intention of its framers was to state "positive social goals toward which Christians should work . . . and ethical criteria to help Christians in their efforts to reshape the existing social order."[2]

This passage uses "responsibility" in a sense which is familiar to political science. To call a democratic government responsible means that it must answer to the electorate for its actions and that it must exercise its power with regard for its legal and moral obligations. Presumably, a responsible society would be one in which there was a responsible form of government, that is, one which was subject to the control and criticism of the people as a whole.

However, the passage goes beyond this political conception. It bases political responsibility on the theological affirmation that God has created and called man to be free and responsible. Denial of political responsibility is said to be a denial of "God's intention for man and his work of salvation." Furthermore, political authorities are not only responsible to legal and moral norms and to their people, but also "to God."

When a Christian theologian uses language like "created and called," he usually wishes to express something about the very nature of man or about man's essential condition before God. God as creator forms man and as redeemer assigns him a destiny within the plan of his eternal love. Thus, in some sense, "created and called to be free and responsible," states that the nature of man and his relationship to God the creator and redeemer must be described as freedom and responsibility.

There is one sense in which Christian theology has traditionally described man's nature and condition as freedom and responsibility. Man is said to be free, that is, his life and eternal destiny are placed by God in his hands: by accepting or refusing God's grace he determines his salvation or damnation. Man is said to be responsible, that is, he must account for each of his free actions before God, the judge of the living and the dead. Final judgment is rendered on the basis of man's disposal of his own life.

Christian theology has also insisted that a crucial feature of that accounting involved a man's relationships with his fellow men. His free and responsible nature has implications for his social life. These implications have been variously described, but a central theme in most of the formulations has been obedience and duty. A man is accountable before God for his obedience. His obedience is measured by the divine commandments and by the legitimate commands of civil authorities. Thus, man's nature and essential condition is one of accountability to God for his observance of the divine, natural, and positive law.

The passage quoted does not fit easily into these traditional interpretations. It seems to imply that man's nature and essential situation before God involve the social behavior and forms described in political language as "responsible." Precisely how the theological affirmation involves the political affirmation is not clear. Is the former intended as the reason justifying the latter? Is the latter intended as an inference from the former? Does it make a difference to describe the relation between God and political life in terms of responsibility rather than obedience?

Either there is no essential connection between theological responsibility and political responsibility, or this connection is left implicit, or theological responsibility means something other than tradition has taught. Further, it must be asked how such a statement provides concrete social goals which are specifically Christian. Political responsibility describes a form of government. If that form proves useful and acceptable, then it is available to all men who desire the best form of society. Is there any reason to call the establishment of this form a "Christian" social goal?

Again, how is "responsibility" an ethical criterion? In the political sense, it is indeed a standard whereby a democratic government can be judged, but it must be filled out by specification of the definite moral, legal, and cultural norms which the government must respect. In the traditional theological sense, man's accountability must be spelled out in terms of the commands and duties which guide a man to eternal salvation. Responsibility is less an ethical criterion than a suggestion that such criteria do exist and that a man will bear the burden of ignoring them or win the reward of observing them.

In sum, the use of the term responsibility is not entirely clear in this passage. It is possible to affirm man's responsibility before God; it is possible to affirm the desirability of political responsibility. However, one should not assume that the connection between them is evident. The traditional theological meaning of responsibility states something about man's nature and essential condition. The political sense of responsibility states something about a contingent form of government and social organization. Both of these senses at least suggest something about the character of the human beings who must exercise this responsibility to God and in society. But it is not at all clear that the character of responsibility before God and that of responsibility in society can be described in the same terms.

Thus, the passage contains at least two clear senses of responsibility, the theological and the political, and suggests a third, in reference to the character of people who live in situations of theological and political responsibility. The theological refers to man's nature and essential condition; the political to a form of social organization and activity; the character to a quality or attribute of persons. It is, we think, necessary to differentiate clearly between these before it is possible to indicate their relationship.

In 1960, the American Roman Catholic hierarchy entitled its annual statement "On Individual Responsibility." The key passage in that statement reads:

Personal responsibility . . . presupposes the acceptance of one's dignity as a son of God in whatever environment he may be placed and the acknowledgment of binding moral law. It requires the free and deliberate acceptance of one's obligations in the position he occupies in the family, in the church, in the corporation, in labor unions, in the community, in the nation. It demands the rule of conscience, not self-satisfaction. It recognizes that every deliberate action of the human person has a relationship to his creator and His purpose in creating the world. . . . It is the solemn profession that every product of his mind and hand is to serve that high purpose. As a man, bearing the image of his creator, he is the brother of every other human person. His noblest work is to bring his fellow man the blessings of the destiny intended for him by God. It must be emphasized especially in these times, that the freedom innate in man as well as the social nature he enjoys demands as a correlative the fullest personal responsibility.[3]

The statement seems to mean: man, created by God with freedom (that is, the ability to choose between right and wrong) is also, in virtue of God's purpose in creation and redemption, under the obligation of God's law. This law is expressed in man's nature and in his state in life, and is manifested through conscience. Man must be aware of these facts about himself and act in accordance with this awareness. To do so is to be responsible. Responsibility might also be called "conscientiousness," or awareness and respect for one's duties and the inclination to act in accord with the various norms dictated by conscience conformed to the moral law.

Bishops, unlike professional ethicians, do not seem to be adverse to mixing with abandon indicatives and imperatives. The statement quoted rests on some indicatives which might be called theological propositions: man's dignity as a son of God, *imago Dei*, brother of all men, the relation of all human action to God, and the existence of a moral law. There are as well a number of imperatives: accept obligations, act according to conscience, serve God's purpose, minister to the brethren.

"Personal responsibility" sums up the union of these theological facts and ethical commands. It appears to be an attitude which that man will adopt who acknowledges these facts and who is aware of the imperatives which are associated with them.

There is little here to justify the substitution of "responsible" for the more conventional "obedient," "dutiful," or "conscientious."

However, the final sentence hints at a possible reason for the bishops' choice of words. They write, "it must be emphasized especially in these times, that the freedom innate in man as well as the social nature he enjoys demands as a correlative the fullest personal responsibility." As we shall see in the chapter on moral philosophy, most moral philosophers have maintained either that the responsibility of man implied his freedom or that his freedom implied his responsibility. The bishops are not interested in the metaphysics of this question. When they say, "especially in these times," they seem to refer to the vast expansion of personal autonomy in contemporary culture. They wish to stress that this emancipation of men from many previously unquestioned sources of authority does not absolve from the moral obligations inherent in his human nature and in his Christian faith. In this sense, "responsibility" designates the general moral attitude which a man should have in a situation in which precise commands and rules are no longer obvious. While the obedient man stands before certain clear obligations, the responsible man has greater autonomy and less definite obligations. Nonetheless, the bishops' statement shows little originality other than a substitution of "responsible" for "obedient." It does not hint at how the theological affirmations might be connected with the imperatives; nor does it explain why these indicatives and imperatives ought to be summed up in the word "responsibility."

As might be expected, neither of these formal "churchly" statements represents an astonishing breakthrough in language or doctrine. In both the term "responsibility" is introduced into a familiar framework of Christian doctrine. In this light, responsibility might be defined as the condition of a free being under obligation, a being whose freedom and obligation are both due to his creation and vocation by God. Precisely in what this condition consists or how it might be described in detail are left undeveloped. It is suggested that this responsibility before God has certain implications for personal morality and for the social order, but how these implications are extracted from the theological doctrine is unexplained. Finally, responsibility apparently describes an attitude or quality of character which those created and called to responsibility should possess. Thus, we see three possible areas of meaning for responsibility: as a theological affirmation about the nature and essential condition, of man, as the designation of certain forms of social and personal morality, as the description of a moral attitude or quality inherent in persons.

RESPONSIBLE PARENTHOOD

The voluminous literature on family planning, an issue which has agitated many Christian denominations, offers another example for further analysis of the use of the terms "responsibility" and "responsible." It has become fashionable to speak of "responsible parenthood" instead of "birth control" or "planned parenthood." The term has appeared in several statements of policy: that of the Nederlandse Hervormde Kirk in 1952, of the Augustana Evangelical Lutheran in 1954, of the United Lutheran Church in the United States in 1956. But the most important of these statements are the Resolutions of the Lambeth Conference in 1958 and the Constitution on the Church in the Modern World of Vatican Council II in 1965.

Resolutions 113 and 115 of the Lambeth Conference read:

> The Conference affirms that marriage is a vocation to holiness, through which men and women may share in the love and creative purpose of God. . . . Christians need always to remember that sexual love is not an end in itself nor a means to self-

gratification, and that self-discipline and restraint are essential conditions of the responsible freedom of marriage and family planning. . . . The Conference believes that the responsibility of deciding upon the number and frequency of children has been laid by God upon the consciences of parents everywhere; that this planning, in such ways as are mutually acceptable to husband and wife in Christian conscience, is a right and important factor in Christian family life and should be the result of positive choice before God. Such responsible parenthood, built on obedience to all the duties of marriage, requires a wise stewardship of the resources and abilities of the family as well as a thoughtful consideration of the varying population needs and problems of society and the claims of future generations.[4]

The statement of Vatican II declares:

Parents should regard as their proper mission the task of transmitting human life and educating those to whom it has been transmitted. They should realize that they are thereby cooperators with the love of God the Creator and are, so to speak, the interpreters of that love. Thus they will fulfill their task with human and Christian responsibility. With docile reverence toward God, they will come to the right decision by common counsel and effort. They will thoughtfully take into account both their own welfare and that of their children . . . for this accounting they will reckon with both the material and the spiritual conditions of the times and of their state in life. Finally, they will consult the interests of the family group, of temporal society, and of the Church herself. The parents themselves should ultimately make this judgment, in the sight of God. But in their manner of acting spouses should be aware that they cannot proceed arbitrarily. They must be governed according to a conscience dutifully conformed to the divine law itself, and should be submissive toward the Church's teaching office, which authentically interprets that law in the light of the gospel. . . . Therefore when there is question of harmonizing love with the responsible transmission of life . . . sons of the Church may not undertake methods of regulating procreation which are found blameworthy by the teaching authority of the Church in its unfolding of the divine law.[5]

Both of these texts urge Christian couples toward "responsible parenthood" and "responsible transmission of life." Both make this recommendation within the framework of common Christian understanding of marriage as a state of life, divinely ordained, in which a man and a woman share in the creative purpose and love of God by their own mutual love and by the procreation and education of children. Given this teaching, both texts affirm that "responsible parenthood" and "human and Christian responsibility" require a decision based on certain considerations.

The decision is one which will determine "the frequency and number of children," "the size of family." The considerations which bear upon this decision concern the welfare of the family itself as well as the wider needs and problems of the culture and the society. In both statements, "obedience to all the duties of marriage" and "conformity to the divine law" are enjoined on the Christian couple. The point of divergence, as is well known, concerns the "ways" or "methods" of family regulation.

Lambeth, relying on the more extensive statement of the Conference of 1930, which declared the moral legitimacy of all methods of contraceptive control, simply requires that the method chosen should be "mutually acceptable to husband and wife in Christian conscience." Vatican II, however, citing in a footnote the declarations of *Casti Connubii* of Pius XI (1930) and the Allocution to Midwives of Pius XII (1951), asserts that there are methods which are "blameworthy" insofar as they do not conform to "objective norms, based on the nature of the human person and his acts."[6]

Thus, although the statements presuppose a different view of the divine law and the manner of its promulgation, both make it clear that the responsible decision must respect that law to the extent that it is known. It is at this point, however, that the term "responsibility" seems to add a new note to the more traditional terms, such as obedience and duty. Insofar as the divine law ordains nothing definite, the moral

decision calls for the use of the full range of human deliberation. The number and frequency of children and, in Lambeth,
the ways of regulation, are not determined exactly by divine
law. They can only be determined by husband and wife considering carefully the multiple factors of their personal and
social situation in light of the Christian view of man and
marriage.

Responsibility, then, seems to add to the notion of obedience the notion of deliberate consideration. Responsible
decision requires not only determinate norms which ought to
be obeyed, but also a range of indeterminate possibilities open
to free choice on the basis of discrimination and reflection. For
Lambeth these free possibilities are the number and frequency
of children and the ways of regulation; for Vatican II they
are the number and frequency of children and those ways of
regulation not opposed to objective divine law.

Thus, it appears that when these two statements advise
"responsible parenthood," or "responsible transmission of life,"
they recommend that a Christian couple 1) acknowledge and
obey the law of God and the Christian teaching on marriage,
2) be aware of the multiple individual and social factors
which bear on the size and composition of a family, 3) apply
to their personal situation a thoughtful consideration of these
multiple factors in a decision about the appropriate time and
method for procreation or prevention thereof.

The responsible parent would so act; such a course of
deliberation, decision and action would constitute responsible
parenthood, human and Christian responsibility.

A Protestant expert on the population problem, Richard
Fagley, discusses responsible parenthood in a manner which
highlights the difference between Lambeth and Vatican II. He
argues that, because *henosis* ("oneness"), not procreation, is
the primary end of marriage, "the decision in regard to procreation is a free ethical decision insofar as husband and wife
are concerned." A "free ethical decision" is one which is not

directly governed by a definite ethical rule. Such decisions are "made responsible" by seeking advice and by prayerful consideration of the multiple factors of personal and familial situation. He continues:

> [if] the husband and wife, who are charged to be responsible parents . . . decide that procreation should be deferred, then they have a positive moral obligation to prevent conception, and the choice of means is a secondary and derivative consideration. Motives rather than methods constitute the primary moral issue. The licit character of any method is based on the presupposition that the contraceptive intent is morally valid in the concrete circumstances . . . what is right or wrong depends on the needs and gifts of the particular couple, including the degree of effectiveness required for their situation. The methods, as methods, are morally neutral.[7]

Fagley's remarks on the importance of intention and motive contrast strikingly with the warning of Vatican II that "when there is question of harmonizing conjugal love with the responsible transmission of life, the moral aspect of any procedure does not depend solely on sincere intentions or on an evaluation of motives, but must be determined by objective standards . . . based on the nature of the person and his acts."[8]

However, if one maintains, on the grounds of some general ethical theory, that methods of regulation are morally neutral, it is most reasonable to say that motives, rather than methods, constitute the primary moral issue. (This is, indeed, the original and unperverted meaning of the phrase, "the end determines or justifies the means," that is, those means which are morally neutral.) If the intention is to regulate one's family in the most reasonable way, if the motives which urge a couple to follow this intention—motives carefully examined and considered— are in conformity with the fundamental Christian teachings on marriage, and if there is no convincing ethical argument for a distinction between various methods of regulation, then it appears that the morality of a decision rests principally on the honesty and carefulness with which the moral intention and motives are related to the factual situation. In fact, "positive moral obligation," according to Fagley, arises from such a decision. The term "responsible decision" is a suitable one to describe the act which draws together the basic commitment to a Christian view of marriage, motives tested against this view, the factual circumstances of the couple's life, and which then issues in a course of action.

Finally, we should note a point which is made in the so-called Mansfield Report, issued by a study commission convoked by the World Council of Churches and the International Missionary Council. This report affirms that "the knowledge of the relation of sexual love to procreation process gives to the couple the power, and therefore the responsibility, to lift the begetting of children out of the realm of biological accident or 'fate' into the realm of personal decision."[9] Parents now have the "responsibility of choice based on knowledge." Responsibility is seen as the consequence of power, that is, of the ability to control a process or the relation between acts and their consequences.

Certainly, man could have no obligation to control his reproduction, even though he might realize the need of control, before he knew how such control might be achieved (apart from abstinence). But when he does attain such knowledge, and is able to exert control, he is faced, by the very fact that such control will be exercised by his free choice, with the obligation of using both the knowledge and the ability in a moral way. Part of what is meant generally by "in a moral way" is that behavior is governed by the properly human activities of deliberation and decision and that deliberation and decision have reference to some norm. In other words, the "moral" is opposed to the merely arbitrary, the capricious, the irrational and indeliberate. Thus, the very fact that man gains an ability to control some area of his existence, seems to imply that this area is assumed into the sphere of his moral obligations. The word "responsibility" is used to describe this "assumption" of a certain area of human behavior into the sphere of moral obligation. Used in this way, responsibility is almost synonymous with "morality," if by morality one means a manner of conduct in which free decisions are made in the light of some norms, rather than capriciously or arbitrarily.

Most Roman Catholic theologians who employ the term "responsible parenthood" have been influenced in their interpretation by the remarks of Pius XII. In 1951 he affirmed for the first time in an official way that Catholics might licitly use the "rhythm method" for family planning. However, a couple must have "serious motives" for avoiding conception. These motives "are not rarely present in the so-called 'indications,' medical, eugenic, economic, or social."[10]

Theologians have generally interpreted the phrase "responsible parenthood" in terms of the deliberation required to assess the seriousness of the motives which would justify family planning. For example, Father Felix Cardegna defines responsible parenthood as:

> wanting to have as many children as a couple can bring into the world, raise, educate in a human and Christian way. . . . This decision must be made by considering the human factors, like the health of the mother or child, the psychological state of the mother, income, housing, education; Christian factors like faith, belief in the ultimate destiny of heaven, not soft living, love and its perpetuation through children.[11]

Cardegna then proceeds to a lengthy and closely-reasoned consideration of how this decision can be executed without infringing on the objective moral law.

Some theologians, however, see more in the term responsible parenthood than simply deliberation about the "indications" justifying the limitation of offspring. They find in it a stress upon the importance of personal decision with regard to the whole disposition of the marriage. For example, Father Charles Curran takes up the question of the hierarchy and urgency of values. He writes:

Theologians and pastors must pay more than lip service to the moral principle of responsible parenthood. There are times when the health of the mother and the good of a family demand that the mother not become pregnant for the present. Under certain conditions, it would be a greater evil to risk a pregnancy than to use contraceptives. Justice and charity toward the wife and family prevail over chastity and control of sexuality. Although artificial contraception is considered objectively wrong, there are times when even objectively speaking it is the lesser of two moral evils.[12]

In the quotation from Cardegna, the "principle of responsible parenthood" directs the deliberation about the motives for family planning; contraception, however, is clearly ruled out by the objective moral law. In the quotation from Curran, the principle of responsible parenthood directs deliberation about the morality of contraception itself in a situation of conflict of values.

Finally, some few theologians, while admitting the place of deliberation about the "indications," will translate the language of responsibility into the language of obedience. For example, Msgr. George Kelly writes:

The modern married Christian, by virtue of his knowledge, may regulate the relationship between marriage and fertility. . . . The dutiful married couple may or may not procreate often. This is their thoughtful and personal decision. But for what they do, why they do it, how it is done, they answer to almighty God. . . . True responsibility begins with the acknowledgment that marriage was created by God for children as much as for mutual happiness. . . . God has plans for every family. He leaves them a wide range of free choice. He expects them to be motivated by generosity, hope, morality, even asceticism. He will be satisfied as long as his children do not frustrate his positive will by sinful acts. . . . Contraception is the real irresponsibility.[13]

The theologians cited and many of their confreres have accepted the term responsibility into their vocabulary, but they offer a spectrum of interpretations. To be responsible is to exercise rational control over sexuality and procreation, but a control which accords with objective moral law. All Roman Catholic theologians would agree to this. For some few, however, responsibility refers principally to the observance of the divine law which prohibits certain methods of regulation. For others, perhaps the majority, responsibility means the contrary of heedless and arbitrary reproduction: it means to plan rather than not to plan. Responsible planning means thoughtful deliberation about the applicability of the "indications" to one's personal and family situation. Finally, certain authors insist that the term implies much more; that it refers to the necessity of deliberation about the very moral norms themselves, of discrimination between the various moral values which are relevant in the life of the couple at a particular time and in particular circumstances. For these authors, the moral law itself must be matter for personal deliberation: not whether there is a law which rules over human behavior, but whether and how it applies in individual personal circumstances.

If we look for any common factor in the variety of uses to which the term responsibility is put, we find that, in both Catholic and Protestant discussions, the realm of moral phenomena to which the term is applied appears to include 1) those elements of human life over which it is possible to exercise control of some sort, and 2) in which there is considerable moral indeterminacy, that is, no precise moral rule. Protestants and Catholics alike refer to the fact that due to modern scientific knowledge, man is now able to control his reproduction. Previously, conception was simply a matter of chance; for Christians, of divine providence. One cannot be responsible for that which lies beyond his calculation and choice. But now, precisely because we can calculate and choose the time and circumstances of conception, we have become responsible for it. Responsibility deals, then, only with those elements over which human knowledge, choice, and physical capacity can exercise control.

These elements can be called physically indeterminate insofar as they can be controlled and changed by human intervention. However, they are also indeterminate in the moral sense, that is, it is not *prima facie* clear what course of action would be the right one. Considerable deliberation is required to determine the right course. This deliberation must draw on highly personal and unique factors. There are, of course, certain determinate moral norms involved in the deliberation, but their relevance in any particular case is closely linked to the multiple factors "in the context."

Thus, in the Protestant authors, the divine intention associates procreation and sexual love in the covenant of marriage. This is a determinate moral principle. But, the times and circumstances in which a couple determine that their love should issue in a child are not determined by any necessary pattern and must be the object of deliberation. The methods of prevention of conception are also indeterminate and, hence, the object of deliberation.

For the Catholics, both the double purpose of marriage and the inviolability of the physical sexual act are determinate moral principles. When these are respected, the area of indeterminacy consists of the motives which justify the spacing of children and their relevance in the concrete situation of the family. Thus, in both cases, responsibility is best used in reference to an area under human control which, on the basis of one's moral view, can be an object of deliberation in order to determine the right course of action.

In the usage which we have so far examined, responsibility appears to mean something much like the classical virtue of prudence. St. Thomas Aquinas, defining prudence as *recta ratio agibilium*, says that the function of this virtue is to facilitate the application of universal moral principles to action to be done in the concrete. He states that:

actions either concern ends or what contributes to the attainment of ends. Now the ends of human life are determined by nature and thus there is a natural inclination toward these ends . . . but those things which are means to the end in human affairs are not determined, but are diversified in many ways, according to the diversity of persons and business . . . prudence has to do not with ends, but with the means to the end.[14]

However, prudence is not simply calculation of technical means best suited to attain an end. It also requires "rectified appetite," that is, a basic commitment and tendency toward the moral good.

Hence, if my remarks above are correct, the texts and statements which we have examined appear to be speaking, for the most part, about prudence. The authors seem to presuppose the basic intention to respect the divine purposes for marriage. They are directing their attention to the indeterminate and diverse means which can fulfill these purposes. They advise the discriminating application of general and determinate norms to indeterminate possibilities in concrete circumstances. They call for a responsible, that is, a prudential, decision to determine the right course of action. These authors differ principally about which factors are determinate and which are open to deliberation.

CONTEXTUALISTS

We shall take our final examples of the use of "responsibility" in Christian ethical literature from the writings of those authors who are called "Christian contextualists or situationists." This contextualism or situationism is in current vogue. Its advocates seem fond of the term "responsibility." As one recent commentator notes, "the various descriptions [of situation ethics] emphasize that it is an ethic of moral situations in which the individual accepts the responsibility of making free moral decisions."[15]

Contextualists, although they differ considerably among themselves, would all appear to agree that Christian ethics ought to be defined by the three following propositions: 1) it is principally a concern for persons and their good, not a devotion to abstract principles; 2) it is effective through interior, personal freedom rather than through compulsion; 3) it has only one absolute law, the law of love.

Bishop J. A. T. Robinson, perhaps the most renowned of the situationists, uses the word a number of times in quite ordinary dictionary senses, as a synonym for duty, and as the obligation to account to someone for something. However, in an oft-quoted passage in *Christian Morals Today*, he invests the term with weightier significance:

> My concern is that Christians, in love as in war, should have the terrible freedom with which God has endowed us, and should use it responsibly. They must decide *for themselves.* . . . I am concerned that the young, like others, should be genuinely free—to decide responsibly for themselves what love at its deepest level really requires of them.[16]

Bishop Robinson has admitted the existence and relevance of law, the "dyke of love," and of the "moral net" of rules and norms. But he finds on the one hand that these are only guides, being too general to apply to the uniqueness of the existential situation, and on the other hand that the person who merely acquiesces to laws and rules does not summon up the inner resources of personal freedom in the only true moral act, the act of love. Thus, in the last analysis, the moral man is left to himself to discover, guided by love alone, what is the right thing.

Responsibility seems to refer to the attitude of moral seriousness with which the free man passes beyond the clarity and definiteness of the realm of abstract rule and ventures into the imprecision and ambiguity of the concrete situation. There he must do what love demands. Responsibility designates the character of the moral man in a morality of "discovery and involvement," or, in the words of the chapter headings of *Christian Morals Today,* a morality of Freedom, of Love, and of Experience. It seems to serve as a synonym for autonomy, the necessity of self-decision as opposed to the heteronomy of rules and laws.

Joseph Fletcher uses the term frequently: he speaks of the responsible self, responsible decision, responsible estimate. However, he most frequently invokes it in two contexts: first, when discussing the question of the Christian's freedom from the law, second, when requiring deliberation and calculation in moral decision. He writes, "what a difference it makes when love is the only norm (in contrast to a morality of laws and rules). How free and how responsible we are."[17] He then places the legalist's objection to this morality of freedom in the mouth of Dostoevsky's Grand Inquisitor, "Freedom is dangerous. People want law, not responsibility; they want the neurotic comfort of rules, not the spiritual open places of decision making. . . . The Christ must not come back to start again all of that old business about freedom, grace, commitment and responsibility."[18] Fletcher then comments that this sort of legalism:

> enables us to hide behind the letter of the law in order to escape the higher demands of its spirit and to escape the complexities of responsible decision . . . to evade the depth, competence and responsibility of free decision. . . . But if the law cuts down our range of free initiative and responsibility, by doing our thinking for us, we are so much the less for it as persons. Law easily undermines political freedom (democracy) and personal freedom (grace). Situation ethics aims to widen freedom, which is the other face of responsibility.[19]

As in Robinson, responsibility is synonymous with autonomy. This responsibility itself consists in the opportunity and necessity of calculation, deliberation, estimation, guided by love. It calls for critical intelligence, factual information, and commitment to righteousness. "Love must make estimates; it is preferential. That is to say, it is responsible, thoughtful, careful." It "manages all things deliberately, i.e. responsibly . . ."[20]

For Fletcher, then, responsibility refers principally to the manner of choosing and deliberating in moral issues. To choose responsibly means to face up to the real issues, to recognize and respect fully the persons involved in the issues, to elect a course of action dictated by one's own integrity and not by an abstract impersonal rule.

Finally, we turn to an example of the contextualist method in practice, *The Quaker View of Sex*. After criticizing the traditional Christian sexual morality, the Quakers state that, although they are unable to produce "a ready made morality to replace the conventional one," they are convinced that there must be a morality to govern sexual relationships. The attitude which distinguishes the Society of Friends, they suggest, might provide a suitable approach to sexual morality. This involves:

> placing particular emphasis on our individual and personal responsibility. We cannot accept as true a statement that is given us merely because it is given with the authority of tradition or of a Church. We have to make that truth our own, if it is a truth, through diligent search and a rigorous discipline of thought and feeling. Man is intended to be a moral being. That is not to say that he should accept a formal morality, an observance of mores, but that his actions should come under serious scrutiny in the light that comes to us from the Gospels and the working of God in us. . . . This search is a move forward into the unknown; it implies a high standard of responsibility, thinking, and awareness—something harder than simple obedience to a moral code. Further, the responsibility that it implies cannot be accepted alone, it must be responsibility within a group whose members are equally committed to the search for God's will.[21]

This personal responsibility, which appears to mean an attitude of mind, a disposition to search for a moral truth that is not itself evident, serves as a criterion to distinguish the moral from the immoral act. The report condemns, for example, "seduction and even persuasion, and every instance of coitus which by reason of disparity of age, intelligence, or emotional condition, cannot be a matter of mutual responsibility."[22] On the other hand, in judging when it is appropriate for intercourse to take place, they prescribe that "in spirit each should be committed to the other. . . . This would mean a willingness to accept responsibility and some foreknowledge of what responsibility implied."[23] Here "responsibility" seems to mean care, concern about, to the extent of accepting and dealing with the consequences of one's action and with future contingencies. Finally, they write, speaking of triangular sexual relationships, that "not sufficient consideration is given to the fact that a triangular situation can and often does arise in which all three persons behave responsibly, are deeply conscious of the difficulties and especially anxious to avoid injury to the others."[24] Here, responsibility could not mean exactly the attitude of search, nor the careful concern, but rather appears to serve as a synonym for the following phrase—"deeply conscious of the difficulties, anxious to avoid injury."

CONCLUSION

What may we conclude from this potpourri of citations? It should be clear, at least, that in the authors and statements quoted, the term responsibility and its cognates are intended to play an important role in the argument. Precisely *what* role is not at all clear. We must admit that we have not examined any author's attempt to formulate a definition: we reserve that task for chapter four. Thus, in all the texts, the term is used rather than defined. And, as might be expected, a word used so frequently, by so many authors, for such diverse purposes, may lack a certain accuracy of denotation and clarity of definition. This, however, is exactly the point of this chapter: to indicate the variety of usage and the ambiguity of meaning which the term responsibility has in contemporary Christian moral literature.

It is possible, I believe, to discern amid this variety and ambiguity that the use of the word falls into several distinct categories of ethical discourse. First, in some places, responsibility appears to mean a quality or characteristic which people "have" or possess. It is something which describes, qualifies the person, and may be considered as "inherent" in him. This is the way in which we often consider such moral terms as "goodness," "holiness," "virtue," "areté." Responsibility may refer, then, to a general quality, which is intended to describe a person as a whole, much as we use "reliable," "conscientious," "dutiful." It may also mean a more limited quality or accident of the person, namely, an attitude of mind or a disposition of will. It is in this way that we speak of "a sense of responsibility." In general, we might call this use of responsibility the *quality* of responsibility.

Second, certain statements, such as those on responsible parenthood, employ the term to describe a manner of acting. This may, of course, be considered as rooted in and expressive of a quality of the person. For example, the responsible man must have an attitude of reverence for God's law and then deliberate about his situation. To use the antique language, the quality is merely potency and potencies are realized and manifested only in their acts. Thus, a man is known to be responsible only if he is seen to act responsibly. To act responsibly is to act deliberately, thoughtfully, rather than arbitrarily. To act thoughtfully involves understanding the determinate moral norms, the possibilities for choice, and the factual situation, to deliberate about the suitability of the norms, the motives, and the results, in these concrete circumstances. Moral activity is characterized by assessing, reflecting, deliberating, calculating, then deciding on a course of action in the light of these thorough deliberations. Responsibility, in this sense, is a kind of rule because it prescribes or recommends certain

3

Patterns in Moral Philosophy

The purpose of the previous chapter was to put on display some confusion about the term responsibility. The philosophers' task is to dispel confusion. This chapter, then, will be a report on the efforts of moral philosophers to clarify what responsibility means and how it functions within ethics. The preparation of this report involved reading a good deal of moral philosophy, ancient and modern. It soon became obvious that the strategy of this chapter could not be a direct attack, demanding that each moral philosopher yield up a definition, in terms of genus and species, of responsibility. The considerations were too diverse, the viewpoints too different. Our strategy, then, is to surround the subject. There are two "territories" in moral philosophy wherein responsibility is discussed. Each territory comprises a basic question and the cluster of ideas that philosophers have marshaled to define and to answer the question. Our strategy is to enclose these two territories, to identify the question and to line up the ideas that surround it.

If we may change the metaphor, we intend to describe two patterns of ideas. We mean by pattern the questions philosophers have set themselves, the various ideas they have thought relevant for the discussion, clarification and, perhaps, solution of the problem. There are, we think, two patterns of ideas associated with responsibility in moral philosophy.

The first pattern of ideas arises when the question is asked, "how do we know when we may justly praise or blame, punish or reward a man for what he has done?" The moral philosopher here reflects on the "judge's problem": the problem of any man who must pass moral judgment on conduct, whether it be the conduct of others or of himself. He must ask about the evidences, the conditions, the circumstances which must be present in an individual case in order to justify praise or blame for conduct. We shall call this "the pattern of ideas associated with the attribution of responsibility." For the sake of economy, we shall abbreviate this simply to "the pattern of attribution."

The second pattern of ideas arises when the question is asked, "how do we know when behavior and the effects of behavior really belong to me as a human agent?" The moral philosopher here reflects on the "agent's problem": the problem of every man who must pass beyond the infantile illusions of impotence and omnipotence and come into possession of himself as a moral agent. The moral philosopher, taking up this problem, must ask about the actions, efforts, and causes which are involved in conduct being or becoming "my own." We shall call this the pattern of ideas associated with appropriation of responsibility, or in shorthand, "the pattern of appropriation."

Of course, both of these titles are rather artificial. One would not ordinarily say: "attribute" responsibility or "appropriate" responsibility. We would say, "hold responsible" and "take responsibility." We use the terms only for the sake of economical reference. Still, they do have some justification. To attribute means to explain as cause or origin. As we shall see, the pattern of attribution is largely concerned with indicating the moral cause of events, that is, the persons who intentionally, deliberately bring them about. We have also chosen appropriation on the grounds of its etymology, for it means to make one's own (*proprium*). The pattern of appropriation is largely concerned with the problem of self-identity and the identity between one's self and one's actions. True, in English, it suggests taking what doesn't belong to one, but even in this sense the problem of self-identity and the problem of action, philosophically and psychologically, seem to involve the overcoming of alienation, of otherness.

Also, the term "pattern of ideas" might be misleading. We do not mean to imply that when the problem of attribution of responsibility comes up, the judge has a set of necessary and sufficient conditions which he must run through to justify his judgment. The pattern is not a logically coherent system, in which each notion plays a specific role with regard to the others. Rather, these are simply the ideas which many moral philosophers have for the most part thought relevant to the questions about praising and blaming. Not every philosopher considers every idea: some in fact consider only one or two; others combine several into one. Our patterns, then, may look rather kaleidoscopic.

Furthermore, we are not interested in each idea for its own sake. Each one is fascinating and problematic. But we are interested in the notion of responsibility. Thus we will stream-line the consideration of each idea within the pattern: trying to set forth, as clearly and simply as possible, its most prominent features. We shall prescind from, or demote into foot-notes, the problems and complications. We hope in this way to be able to "define" responsibility, not with a proper logical definition, but by setting boundaries around the ideas involved in the various philosophical discussions of responsibility. We hope this will help us to understand what is going on when this word is used in moral discourse.

THE PATTERN OF ATTRIBUTION OF RESPONSIBILITY

Perhaps the most horrifying event which the civilized world has ever witnessed was the genocide of the European Jews during World War II. After the war, when the horror of this crime became apparent, accusations of responsibility were hurled in every direction. Hitler, of course, and the Nazis were responsible. But what of the German people who cooperated both actively and passively? What of those who should have raised voices in protest and did not? Indeed, some have asked, what of the Jews themselves, who could have taken measures to avoid their fate and yet went like sheep to the slaughter?

More particularly, the trial of Adolf Eichmann raised the question of the responsibility of an individual officer: did he initiate and instigate, did he merely execute orders, should he have refused to do so? Here the issue was to establish some grounds for the justification of punishment. Another accusation of responsibility was laid at the feet of Pope Pius XII by Rolf Hochhuth in his play, *The Deputy*: if he who claimed the moral leadership of mankind did not vigorously protest, he was responsible for this monstrous crime. Here the issue is blame rather than punishment.

In these highly complex cases, at least several issues are clear. An event took place which men agree is evil; someone must be blamed and, perhaps, punished. In other cases, an event takes place which men call good or noble. They then ask who ought to be praised and, perhaps, rewarded. In both cases, the events are "moral events." They are not simply facts, like an earthquake or an eclipse. A moral event is one which contributes to or detracts from the human good, however that might be defined, and which comes about through the intervention of a human agent. These human agents evoke the praise and blame of their fellows and, on occasion, elicit punishment and reward. These elements, the goodness and badness of an event, the causality of a human agent, and the subsequent praise and blame accorded his action, are intricately woven together in moral life and in ethical theory. Indeed, a moral act might even be defined as an act worthy of praise or blame.

When a good or evil deed has been done, we ask who is to be praised or blamed. The answer seems simple enough:

praise or blame him who did the deed. We need merely point to the cause: the policeman shot the gun, the child knocked over the vase. Occasionally, a detective must hunt down the agent. To ask "who is responsible for this happening" may simply mean "who did it."

But Uzzah put out his hand to steady the ark of the covenant and the Lord struck him dead. The Lord has been criticized for this ever since, because in the ordinary course of moral reasoning we want to know not only who did the deed, but whether it was "his fault." We are hunting not merely for a cause, but for a culprit. Thus, even after the detective has caught the suspect and the evidence proves that he did the deed, the judge must ask, "was this man responsible for his action?"

True, before we praise a man as a hero, we want to know whether or not his heroism is mere happenstance. But, due perhaps to our sorry human condition, the question of responsibility is usually asked about bad events and evil deeds. The judge's considerations will more often issue in blame and punishment than in praise and reward. Even if the suspect is not blamed, he wins no praise: he is simply dismissed. In general, then, to ask whether a man is responsible is to ask whether the act he performed was his fault. We shall, in these pages, usually speak of it in this fashion, although it is possible to apply most of the considerations to the issue of praise and reward.

The idea of "fault" involves 1) the existence of some standard of action which has not been attained, and 2) the conviction that it could have been attained. A fault, unlike a mistake or an error, is avoidable. It is substandard performance which could have been standard, if the agent had wanted it to be or had taken the trouble, and so on.

In the case of moral fault, the standards are the goods which are deemed worthy of attainment and the rules which direct action to their attainment. When we speak of an event as good or evil, we are usually saying that it is conducive or detrimental to the human good as we conceive it. When we speak of an action as right or wrong, we usually are thinking of the violation of rules which direct action toward the human good. When, however, we call actions praiseworthy or blameworthy, we consider not only the standards, the values and rules, but also the condition of the agent which is relevant to the second feature of fault, namely, whether he could have performed in a standard way instead of acting in a substandard way.

Thus, the question of responsibility does not ask "should I praise him or should I blame him?" It asks "should I render any verdict of praise or blame at all, or should I dismiss the case?" It does not seek the criteria for praise and blame, that is, the standards whereby we denominate an event or person good or bad and an act right or wrong. Rather it is directed to determining whether these criteria can be justly applied to this individual agent. Thus, the judge, legal or moral, must decide, as a precondition to all considerations of innocence or guilt, whether the suspect is responsible: that is, could he have performed the standard action? If he so decides, he "attributes responsibility" to the agent, saying he is, or was, in such a condition that when he acted in this substandard way, he could have done otherwise. It should be noted that to be judged not responsible is not precisely to be judged innocent. A man must be responsible in order to be innocent as well as guilty.

There are at least six important notions which are associated with the attribution of responsibility. There may be many others, but these appear most prominently in the literature. They are intention, motivation, deliberation, voluntariety, excuse, and character.

INTENTION

G. E. M. Anscombe begins her book *Intention* by speaking of the "different senses" of the word. She then remarks, "when we are tempted to speak of the 'different senses' of a word which is clearly not equivocal, we may infer that we are in fact pretty much in the dark about the character of the concept which it represents."[1] The literature bears out Miss Anscombe's opinion, for the discussions of intention are either extremely vague or highly complex. But, with the risk of losing a great deal of precision, we may lift out of the literature the main lines of discussion.

When it is asked about an accused "should he be blamed?" one likely answer is "yes, if it was his fault." It is commonly agreed that it is improper to say that it was "his fault" if he did not know what he was doing. Now, lack of knowledge may mean that the party was not conscious when he acted: he was in a trance, sleepwalking, drugged. It may mean that, although conscious, he was incapable of clear perception: he was hallucinating, drunk, and so on. But it may also mean that, while he was conscious and clear headed, he only *thought* he knew what he was doing: he intended one thing, but actually did something else.

Intention seems to mean the thought of an action being performed or about to be performed, which is present to the agent. Since it is the thought of an action, it is not merely a speculative understanding but includes the thought of the practical engagement of the agent. It is the thought of that which I aim to bring about. "That which" can be activity alone: I intend to study, to exercise; it can also be activity and its consequences: I intend to start a fire and to burn down the barn. Furthermore, the "that which" need not be limited to facts alone, but may also refer to standards: I intend to be brave, to tell a lie. For example, the intention to embezzle is not simply an intention to remove money from a drawer and to alter figures in a ledger. It is the intention to take money fraudulently by breach of trust. The intention, then, bears upon the act in the light of certain standards. Thus, the objects of intention are often stated in words which have distinct moral connotation: lying, embezzlement, adultery.

An intention is often thought of as a sort of foreknowledge of what one is about to do, as a design preformed and then put into practice. This would imply that an act could be called intentional only if it were "thought out ahead of time." But the adequacy of this might be questioned. First, it probably reflects an unhappy mechanical model of the psychology of human action, in which ideas are formed "inside" and then action performed "outside." But it is a deficient conception because it fails to account for the innumerable activities which we would want to call intentional but for which we would be at pains to find the interior performance called "act of intention." A good driver shifts gears habitually, but if he does so to make a grade and is asked, "did you shift intentionally?" he will say, "yes." If asked, "what was your intention?" he will say, "to make the grade." Doubtless he did not *preform* this intention; he simply designed his action to achieve a purpose of which he was "non-thematically" conscious. Intentional action is action designed so that steps are linked to attain a purpose, but the design is more in the doing than in the mind.

Intention, then, is a kind of conceptual design present in the agent, the plan of what he aims to realize. This design or plan includes a conception of action, of results, and of norms. This intention can be present to the agent without always being explicitly so as the theme of his consciousness. Thus, a statesman's actions can all be guided by the intention to uphold the Constitution, although he may seldom explicitly reflect on this. While every intention must at some time be actually thematically present to the agent, intentionality can be, and is for the most part, virtual in the way in which it forms and informs activity.

An action is intentional, then, if the agent has present to himself what the action is, including its relation to norms and at least its natural and expected consequences, and has this present to himself, not simply as an idea, but as "practical knowledge," which he will realize or is realizing. An action is unintentional either if intention is other than that which came about or if the agent had no intention at all.

If we are asking about attributing responsibility for a good deed, we require the presence of a good intention, either actual or virtual. If a man saves the life of a child by leaping into a stream for no other reason than to seize the child, we consider that such was his intention and we praise him. If he saves the life of the child by bumping him quite accidentally out of the way of a truck, we might feel grateful but not inclined to lavish praise.

On the other hand, lack of intention or different intention usually exculpates from blame for a wrong action. In this case, the agent may intend what he thinks is a right action, that is, action in conformity with a norm or law, but be mistaken either about the nature of action or about the norm. Someone intends to liven up a depressive and "quite unintentionally" drives him deeper into his depression; someone, not intending to give offense, fails to comply with a norm of etiquette foreign to him. In both cases he is not blamed.

In cases of negligence, however, lack of intention does not generally exculpate. In such cases it is felt that, due to some duty or obligation incumbent on the party at fault, the intention should have been urging itself, should have been present to him. Thus, a night watchman did not intend to leave open the gate which admitted the burglar; but because he was a night watchman his plan of action should have included closing the gate. The intention here is not something in the mind of the agent, but a design of action associated with a certain office or duty or function, which the bearer of this office is expected to have in mind. His assuming the office is his intention to keep it in mind.

There is considerable discussion about the extent to which consequences must be included in intention. This seems to depend on the extent to which consequences can be foreseen and the extent to which they lie within the control of the agent. Furthermore, it can be asked whether there is a distinction between intending a certain result and permitting it to happen. Finally, the solution to this problem rests largely on the very controverted issue of distinguishing between an act and its consequences.

Ethicians speak very blithely of acts and consequences, although they know in their hearts that it is an extremely sticky distinction. No one questions the fact that acts have consequences. But it is often difficult to draw a clear line between them. Sometimes a specifiable piece of human behavior can be marked off from its consequences with ease: Pope John summoned Vatican Council II; as a result, the *aggiornimento* begins to take place. At other times, it seems pedantic to insist on the distinction. Only in an autopsy would "she killed him by putting arsenic in his coffee" be stated "the result of her act (putting arsenic) was his death." The newspapers would very sensibly say, "she murdered him." Acts and consequences, while sometimes physically and temporally distinct, are bound together in a moral unity which is reflected in our language: murder and treason consist in a string of actions and results, but are a single "moral act." Thus, for the question of responsibility, the "foreseen consequences" depend on how tightly act and results are bound together and also on the agent's obligation, due to his role or situation, to foresee and control the consequences of his actions.

In general, we can say that assignment of responsibility is justified only when the agent's action, which is up for judgment, in some way reflects his intention. This may either be a positive design of action which the agent forms for himself and aims to realize; it may be a plan of action which he should have, in virtue of his status, aimed to realize. What the agent plans to do and how that plan enters into the manner of action and into the results is considered a *sine qua non* for a just attribution of responsibility.

MOTIVE

"Motive" and "intention" are often confused in popular language. One can answer the question, "why did the doctor stop intravenous feedings for this terminal patient?" either by saying, "he intended to alleviate suffering," or "his motive was to alleviate suffering." The answer offers the reason why the doctor acted as he did. As we have seen, however, in more technical discourse, intention usually means the thought of the objective one aims to realize and of the designed action involved in its realization. To intend is to aim at something (*intendere*). Motive, on the other hand, is that which determines the agent to aim at the objective and engage in the designed action. A motive moves, urges, impels (*motum*). Thus, as G. E. M. Anscombe says, the ordinary phrase, "motive of gain" is elliptical: gain is the intention or what is intended; the desire of gain is the motive.[2] A clear and quite common distinction is expressed by John Dewey:

> Intention is what a man means to do; motive is the personal frame of mind which indicates why he means to do it. Intention is the concrete aim or purpose: the results which are foreseen and wanted. Motive is the state of mind which renders these consequences, rather than others, interesting and attractive.[3]

The ambiguity about intention and motivation arises because it is not possible to separate them simply by saying: "intention" answers the question, "what are you doing?"; "motive" answers, "why are you doing it?" Thus, one can answer "why do you visit the old gentleman every day," by saying "in order to cheer him up" or "out of gratitude for his former kindness to me." The former is a statement of intention; the latter is a statement of motive. But it might be that the daily visits are in hope of inheriting the old gentleman's fortune. This has the look of a future objective, which might be intention rather than motivation. However, while it is that which I intend and which contributes to the design of my action, more properly it is that which renders the action attractive to me.

Intentional actions, then, are undertaken for a motive, a reason, in the light of which they are objects worthy of my attention and pursuit. The motive may be either "forward or backward looking." Motives of the first type, which are often expressed in terms much like intentions, refer simply to the worth of an object to be attained; those of the second type refer to occasions in one's past history and interior motions to which they might give rise which render some present or future intention worthwhile. The former are often stated in "in order to . . ." phrases; the latter in "out of . . . gratitude" phrases.

When questions of responsibility are under consideration, an investigation of motives is often in order: *cherchez la femme*. To determine and attribute responsibility one must know not only what a man did or what he intended to do, but why he did it. Indeed, David Hume believed that praise and blame should never be accorded to actions, but only to motives.

Hume's position may seem rather extreme, but it is certainly true with regard to what have been called "indifferent actions." The classical moralists have usually maintained that while some acts are, by their nature, good or bad (for instance, praise of God or blasphemy), there are many actions which, of themselves, are neither. They were denominated good or bad in virtue of the motive of the agent. Thus, to eat a meal is an indifferent act. If it is done out of love for one's fiancée, it is a good act; if it is the first move in a seduction, it is an evil act.

Whatever be the problems involved in the theory of the indifferent act, it is true that we never raise the question of responsibility about many acts which are certainly intentional. We never ask, "is he responsible for driving the car, for reading the paper, for taking a walk." However, if we suspect some fault, we will often seek an explanation in terms of motive. "He reads the paper too much," we say. "Well," someone answers, "he is a political scientist and requires the information for his work." What had appeared as an indifferent act, without any specific moral connotation, can be appraised as a moral or immoral act by learning the motivation behind the practice. Thus, reading the paper can be called a responsible act (in a minor key) not only because it is intentional, but more importantly, because it is done with a specifiable, particular motive.

We have indicated that the question of motivation will usually arise only if a fault is suspected. It certainly does arise when fault is clearly indicated. If the political scientist is obviously neglecting his work and his duties for the newspapers, this is a fault. But he will be less subject to blame if he is motivated by an exaggerated desire for complete and detailed information than by a distaste for writing or teaching. Good, even if misguided, motivation tends to mitigate blame for faults.

On the other hand, it is generally agreed that a good act is vitiated by a bad motive. When it is learned that the solicitude of the young man for the old gentleman was motivated by avarice, admiration turns to disdain. Frequently, however, actions proceed from mixed motives. Such cases can only be dealt with in terms of their individual merits, since judgment will depend on whether the act itself is good, bad or indifferent, and whether the noble or base motives predominate. Often, judgment is stymied: the young man goes to considerable, even sacrificial, lengths, and shows genuine affection for the old man, but he clearly has his eye on the fortune. It might well be said of him, "you've got to give him credit for all he has done, but I don't know about his motives."

Consideration of motives, then, functions prominently in attribution of responsibility. The question of responsibility for indifferent actions usually arises only in connection with motivation. Actual judgments of praise and blame are conditioned by the various ways in which good and bad motives are related to good and bad actions. Some moral philosophers such as Kant have in fact maintained that the only criterion for denominating an act good or bad is the motivation which prompts it.

We noted that an unintentional act, except in cases of negligence, usually is neither praised nor blamed, but is excused. What of the unmotivated act? Some philosophers would say that motive is so intrinsically linked to the concept of action that there can be no "unmotivated acts." However, the phrase is most often applied to acts for which no specifiable reason can be offered—what the newspapers call "senseless crimes." Furthermore, some actions are so casual or so habitual that it is difficult to assign any reason for them. However, the sophisticated observer might say that all of these spring from "unconscious motives."

This phrase, inaccurate though it may be, has the aura of psychology about it. This science has cast doubt on the basis of the classical doctrine of motivation. It had been assumed that the act of free choice consisted of selecting one of several motives which present themselves to the agent. The "doctrine of the unconscious" proposes that the selection itself is motivated by factors unavailable to the consciousness of the agent. On the basis of this position, it has been proposed either that no one is responsible for what he does, or that the definition of responsibility must be radically changed. This matter belongs to the question of freedom and responsibility. We mention it here only to point out that the attribution of responsibility, in the sense of judging that a subject can be justly praised or blamed, seems to presuppose that the agent can offer reasons for his action and that these are the real reasons why he did what he did. To cast doubt upon this would seem to throw the question of praise and blame, punishment and reward into confusion.

DELIBERATION

"The native hue of resolution is sicklied o'er with the pale cast of thought." To be less poetic, Hamlet's resolution involved both an intention (to kill the king) and motivation (out of revenge). But he "thought about it," that is, deliberated about whether it should be done and how it should be done, and thus brought both intention and motivation under criticism. Deliberation, however, usually plays a more positive role. A deliberate moral act is one which is thought about and thought through. To deliberate is to weigh in the balance (*libra*).

When we say that an act is deliberate, we mean that it has been reasoned out, with clear awareness of what one is doing and what will come of it. An act may be intentional without being deliberate: a man quite intentionally jumps into the river to save the boy without considering the steps that go into the action, nor the consequences which might follow. We feel at ease with a good driver, whose individual acts are certainly intentional, designed to propel the vehicle efficiently and carefully to its destination. A deliberate driver, who seems to think out each move, makes us nervous. On the other hand, most people trust a deliberate investment broker, who plans his buying and selling; the plunger might be lucky, but he seldom inspires confidence.

Moral deliberation moves on several planes. One deliberates as to whether one ought or ought not follow a certain path. This is deliberation about motives, the worth of one way over another. This is the classical debate between duty and inclination. But there is also deliberation about the steps which can be taken to accomplish a certain goal. When Aristotle describes deliberation he says,

> we take the end for granted and consider in what manner and by what means it can be realized . . . we continue in this process until we come to the first link in the chain of causality,

which is the last in the order of discovery. For when a man deliberates, he seems to be seeking something and to be analysing his problem as he would a geometrical figure: the last step in the analysis is the first in the construction of the figure.[4]

Deliberation, then, seems to involve both the planning of means to the intended end and the weighing of motives which incline to one or another decision.

When the question of responsibility is raised, it is often appropriate to inquire about the deliberation involved in the act. First degree murder is defined as "intentional murder with deliberation and premeditation . . . as by poison or lying in wait or any other kind of wilful, deliberate and premeditated killing."[5] The extent of planning distinguishes this from second degree murder. While it might be clear that an act was intentional and done with definite motivation, it may be relevant to ask whether the agent had the opportunity to think about, to weigh, his act and its consequences.

As we have said, there are some acts in which deliberation seems to play no part: spontaneous acts, like leaping to the rescue, or habitual responses, like acts of generosity and kindness. Indeed, in such cases deliberation may somewhat tarnish the act. However, in very many of the situations which are called moral, deliberation is required, both to weigh values and to determine means. If it is obvious that neither the possibility nor opportunity for such deliberation was present, responsibility will not be assigned. Such is clearly the case when someone is known, for one reason or another, to be incapable of reasoning, of seeing the connection between principles and acts, between acts and consequences. If such inability is pathological, as it apparently is in psychopaths and sociopaths, we tend to consider such people as dangerous, but not to hold them responsible.

Similarly, if someone is forced to make an important decision very quickly, we recognize that he did not have the opportunity for adequate deliberation and would probably be lenient about blame for failure. Finally, many of the moral situations are highly problematic because no amount of deliberation can reveal preponderance of one value over another or the best procedure. In these cases of "perplexed conscience" it seems unfair to attribute blame for failure. We usually say something like "don't blame him, he did what he thought best in those trying circumstances."

Both common estimation and moral philosophy seem to require evidence of intention, motivation and deliberation in an agent in order to justify the attribution of responsibility to him. With the exception of the cases mentioned, it is considered unjust to praise or blame, reward or punish a man unless he has acted intentionally, deliberately and with motivation. Absence of one or all of these elements will generally excuse from blame and disqualify from praise. The extent, intensity, and quality of these elements will either mitigate or aggravate praise and blame.

The reason for this deeply rooted moral practice would seem to be that a *just* attribution of responsibility is one in which the responsibility is attributed to the *real* cause of the action. This does not merely mean to the right man. More important, it means to the right man as a properly moral cause of his actions. But a man cannot be the moral cause of his actions unless he is acting humanly, that is, in accord with those features which distinguish him from all other causes, inanimate and animal. Western culture has termed these distinguishing features intellect and will. Intention, motivation and deliberation name the coordinated processes of intellect and will in "practical reason." Thus, a man can be considered a moral agent, subject to moral judgments, only to the extent that he gives evidence of acting intentionally, deliberately, and with motivation. He is then performing what the scholastic philosophers called an *actus humanus*, not merely an *actus hominis*.

Intention, motive and deliberation have a positive look about them. They might be thought of as "mental facts" which must be present for just attribution of responsibility, even as physical facts must be present for true predication. However, many contemporary philosophers are prejudiced against "the private world of mental facts." Indeed, closer investigation renders the concept of a "mental fact" rather problematic. It is quite difficult to describe exactly what these words, intention, motive, deliberation, are supposed to refer to.

Further, *evidence* of intention, motivation and deliberation is required for just attribution. If the judge is judging himself, he may find that evidence in introspection. If he is judging another, he must take his word or infer from the facts and circumstances. The patent fact is that a deed is done; the philosophical problem is not so much "who done it," as "how was it done and how do we know how it was done."

The lawyers, who must deal in evidence, have long been aware of this problem. They will not admit a mental fact into court. "Intent, the design, resolve or determination with which a person acts . . . being a state of mind is rarely, if ever, susceptible of direct proof, but must ordinarily be inferred from the facts."[6] Thus, intentions and motivations as such are not admitted in evidence: a lawyer could not argue, "my client ran the deceased down, but he didn't intend to" unless it were possible to show some facts—his brakes failed, he swerved to avoid a truck, etc.

But long ago Aristotle, in the first discussion of attribution of responsibility, recognized that there was a problem involved in identifying precisely what these mental facts were. Again today, several philosophers have followed Aristotle's hints and returned to the problem with fresh insights. We will now briefly discuss Aristotle's notion of "the voluntary," then notice how J. A. Austin and H. L. A. Hart deal with "excuses."

THE VOLUNTARY

In popular speech and in much moral philosophy, "freely" and "voluntarily" are used interchangably. This has led to the "voluntary" being drawn into the controversy over free will. However, Aristotle's treatment, which has been called "the foundation for the juridical theory of culpability which still enjoys general acceptance," was formulated prior to the emergence of an explicit problem of free will in Western thought. Modern commentators on Aristotle warn about reading the metaphysical problematics of freedom into Aristotle's words.

The first and second books of the *Nichomachean Ethics* are devoted to a discussion of the finality of human action and of the nature of virtue. The third book begins with the comment that it will be useful both for the student of virtue and for the lawmaker, who must distribute rewards and punishments, to learn the distinction between the voluntary and involuntary action. It is generally recognized, says Aristotle, "that acts done under constraint or due to ignorance are involuntary."[7] Constraint and ignorance are the two principle rubrics under which he discusses the involuntary.

Constraint is physical or psychological force brought to bear on the agent. "An act done under constraint is one in which the initiative or source of motion comes from without and to which the person compelled contributes nothing." Aristotle himself ventures some distinctions and clarifications of this rudimentary definition, but it has been left to subsequent moral philosophers and to legal theorists to refine, in quite an elaborate way, the notion of constraint. Violence, fear, passion, habit, psychological and social influence, pathological conditions are all forms of constraint which must be considered separately. But they are all, in some sense, factors which prevent or inhibit the agent from taking the "initiative" in the formulation of his decision and execution of his action.

Aristotle limits his second rubric, "ignorance," to a lack of awareness of the details which make up the situation in which the agent is acting. He specifies these details, in a list which will become archetypal in morals and law, as 1) who the agent is, 2) what he is doing, 3) what thing or person is affected, 4) the means he is using, 5) the result intended by his action, 6) the manner in which he acts. Subsequent moralists, such as Aquinas, have added that the agent can also be inculpably ignorant of the moral quality of his action, a point which Aristotle seems to deny. They have also classified the various types of ignorance which have quite distinct bearing on the morality of the act: vincible and invincible, antecedent and consequent, crass and affected, of law and of fact, and others.

Aristotle concludes his remarks with the following definition: "since an action is involuntary when it is performed under constraint or through ignorance, a voluntary action would seem to be one in which the initiative lies with the agent who knows the particular circumstances in which the action is performed."[8] For a more positive characterization of "the initiative" one must read on into his treatment of choice. This he defines as "a deliberative desire for things that are within our power: we arrive at a decision on the basis of deliberation and then let the deliberation guide our desire."[9]

A man is the source or origin of his own actions when he is capable of choice; he is capable of choice when he is able to deliberate, that is, rule his appetitive powers by rational consideration of means to ends; he is able to do this when he is unimpeded by constraint or by ignorance of his situation, that is, when he acts voluntarily. Aristotle sums up: these conclusions are corroborated by the judgment of private individuals and by the practice of lawgivers. They chastise and punish evildoers, except those who have acted under constraint or due to some ignorance for which they are not responsible, but honor those who act nobly.[10]

Thus, Aristotle has clearly stated his conviction that a man is subject to praise and blame only if that man is the source and origin of his acts. He also indicates that man is the source of action due to the intellective and appetitive process called deliberation and choice. But, quite realistically, he recognizes that the evidence for the presence or absence of deliberation and choice is for the most part to be drawn from the circumstances in which a man acts. Thus it is possible, though sometimes difficult and conjectural, to determine by a study of evidence and circumstances whether a man acted under coercion, in fear, in ignorance.

By concentrating on the negative impediments to the voluntary act, Aristotle reflects the common practice, canonized in juridical practice, of admitting "excuses" rather than searching for positive evidence of intention, deliberation and motivation. Quite recently, considerable discussion has centered on excuses and the "ascription of responsibility."

EXCUSES

"Aristotle," wrote J. L. Austin, "has often been chided for talking about excuses and overlooking the 'real problem.' In my own case, it was when I began to see the injustice of the charge that I first became interested in excuses."[11] "The real problem" which, in Austin's opinion, Aristotle saw is that responsibility is not a characteristic of actions but rather "a dimension in which actions are assessed." Obviously, Aristotle did not see the real problem in these terms. But Austin quite rightly recognized that Aristotle, by going at the problem of responsibility negatively through the excuses of coercion and ignorance, realized that "the involuntary" did not describe some special quality of action, but rather referred to the context of circumstantial evidence and customary norms within which judgments of praise and blame are justified. Austin concludes that it is misleading to describe intention, motive and deliberation as qualities of action and then declare that if these qualities are present the agent ought not to be excused. Rather responsibility is precisely action without excuse.

The excuse is a familiar friend to most people, but we are so ready to use it that we seldom understand its nature.

When someone has done something "untoward," a faulty or substandard action, he can be defended in two ways. The action can be justified: trying to prove that the action was, in fact, not wrong but right. The action can be excused: admitting that it is indeed bad, but that due to some special circumstance the agent is not to blame for it. In justification, responsibility is accepted but the wrongfulness of the act is denied; in excuse, the wrongfulness is admitted but responsibility is not accepted. An excuse puts the wrongful act *ex causa*, outside the court of moral verdict. Thus the killing of a man is justified by self defense (it is judged as a right act according to a moral norm), but is excused as accidental (the agent was not entitled to do it, not justified by any moral norm, but could not foresee or provide for it).

Excuses exist in profuse variety. They can only with difficulty be reduced to headings. They refer to various departments of action: execution, decision, deliberation, and so on. Their acceptability depends on diverse and quite concrete factors. There are really no excuses in the abstract.

Excuses loom large in the attribution of responsibility. H. L. A. Hart capitalizes on this to propose that many of the traditional problems of attributing responsibility can be avoided by treating the concept of action as a defeasible (excusable) ascription of responsibility.[12] He contends that philosophers have thought of action statements as descriptions: "he cheats at cards" describes certain physical procedures plus certain inner psychological procedures. Hart suggests that such a statement is not a description, but an ascription of responsibility,—it is in itself a blaming statement. But the statement can be "defeated" by countering with an excuse, a defense of one's actions which is socially and legally accepted. Indeed, every action statement, even the simple "he did it," is best considered an utterance with which we confess or admit liability, make accusations or ascribe responsibility. In this view, responsibility is not a mysterious precondition for praising and blaming, resting on some inner psychological facts. It is rather predicated of the action itself insofar as it is able to be defended or defeated by excuse.

This thesis has been much controverted. Critics have attacked the very notion of ascription, as opposed to description, as well as Hart's abrupt dismissal of psychological causation. The thesis does, however, illuminate the predication of responsibility to faulty or substandard performances. One of the many commentators on Hart's thesis, Joel Feinberg, suggests that blaming for substandard performance is much like entering a notice on a record; the record, in moral matters, being a man's reputation. Thus, the function of an excuse is to show that it would be unfair or unprofitable to mark the faulty performance on a man's moral record, because it was done under such circumstances that it does not, in fact, reveal the kind of person he is. He writes:

> Records and reputations are kept in order to inform interested parties in order that they can assess or appraise as accurately as possible the contribution people can make to success or failure. . . . A person's faulty action is registrable only if it reveals what sort of person he is in some respect about which others have a practical interest in being informed, for example, his predominant tendencies.[13]

L. L. Austin abruptly concludes his tantalizing "Plea for Excuses," with the remark, "here I leave and commend the subject to you." His commendation might well be heeded, for the discussion of excuses is still in its philosophical infancy. Instead of trying to define responsibility in the rather elusive terms of intention, motivation, and deliberation—although these will indeed play a role in understanding excuses themselves—it may prove profitable to attempt an analysis of when and what sort of excuses are generally accepted, and why some exculpate, others attenuate. However, the basic problem with the conception of responsibility as unexcused action, is that at present we suffer from an inadequate concept of action itself.

CHARACTER

"A person's faulty action is registrable to him only if it reveals the kind of person he is." Feinberg's words reflect a long tradition. Aristotle wrote that an act could be called virtuous only if "it springs from a firm and stable character."[14] David Hume stated the case:

> Actions are, by their very nature, temporary and perishing, and where they proceed not from some cause in the character and disposition of the person performing them, they can neither redound to his honor if good, nor infamy if evil. The actions themselves may be blameable; they may be contrary to all the rules of morality and religion. But the person is not answerable for them and as they proceed from nothing in him that is durable and constant and leave nothing of that nature behind them, it is impossible he can, upon their account, become the object of punishment and vengeance.[15]

Educational practice confirms what moral theory affirms: that human likes and dislikes, desires and aversions, tastes—in short, what we call dispositions, tendencies, or inclinations—can be formed into relatively constant "states." Precisely the causes which effect this formation, and the extent to which the formation is determinative of choices, are matters of great dispute. But, with some distinctions and qualifications, the following words of Patrick Nowell-Smith sum up a great deal of moral philosophy:

> Pleasure and pain, reward and punishment are the rudders by which moral conduct is steered, the means by which moral character is moulded; and "moral character" is just that set of dispositions that can be moulded by these means.[16]

The notion of character enters into the pattern of attribution on two counts, both of which are suggested by Hume's words. It is only in terms of something "durable and constant" that it is possible for the judge to assess responsibility for an act; secondly, the practice of praise and blame, reward and punishment is based upon the malleability of character.

When the judge must assess responsibility, he needs to know whether the agent intended to perform the act, what his motivation was, whether he had the possibility and opportunity for deliberation. As we have noted, however, this information is, for the most part, inferential. Even when the judge judges his own action, he is reflecting on what he *has* done: intention, motivation, and deliberation are objects of reflex rather than direct consciousness.

Character is the most important premise for this sort of inference and reflection. Does the act reflect what we know of the person in the light of his habitual conduct? Would he be the kind of person to have intended this sort of act? Would he have been motivated by a base motive? Is he ordinarily reflective and deliberative? For example, recently in New York a girl who carried a "dangerous weapon" to defend herself against attack was not prosecuted: the district attorney said, "she is not a criminal type."

Second, when we praise or blame, punish or reward an act, we usually intend to encourage or discourage the repetition of the act or at least the dispositions which lead to such an act. This presupposes that dispositions can be eradicated or deepened. Aristotle defined virtue as a "praise-worthy state of soul"; Nowell-Smith defines moral character precisely as the set of dispositions which can be moulded by praise and blame. Thus, a man is considered responsible, that is, a fit subject for praise and blame, only if these judgments are considered to promote or discourage praiseworthy or blameworthy dispositions.

This has been a commonplace in moral philosophy. However, since John Stuart Mill wrote "responsibility means punishment," utilitarian moral philosophers have made it the major premise in a determinist doctrine of responsibility.[17] Mill was arguing, against Sir William Hamilton, that attribution of responsibility need not be justified by a metaphysical doctrine of free will. It is not necessary to prove that a man "could have done otherwise" in order to justify punishing him. It is simply necessary to believe, on good grounds, that the punishment will be to the "benefit of the offender himself and for the protection of others." Mill writes:

> The true doctrine of the causation of human actions maintains that not only our conduct but our character is in part amenable to our will; that we can, by employing proper means, improve our character; and that if our character is such that while it remains what it is, it necessitates us to do wrong, it will be just to apply motive which will necessitate us to strive for its improvement, and so to emancipate ourselves from the other necessity. In other words, we are under a moral obligation to seek the improvement of our moral character.[18]

Mill admits that the "feeling of responsibility," namely, guilt, is due to the "expectation of punishment," which results from the causal influence of moral education, exhortation, and other such elements. But he points out that the justification of punishment, or that whereby punishment is moral, lies in the utilitarian reasons, "the benefit of the offender and the protection of others." Thus, his cryptic statement, "responsibility means punishment," means that the practice of holding a man responsible, that is, subjecting him to praise or blame, punishment or reward, is a moral practice insofar as it contributes to the general welfare, not because it is based on a so-called "free act" of the agent. Some authors will insist that responsibility makes sense *only* on the determinist premises, precisely because there must be some assurance that the causes (praise and blame, punishment and reward) will be followed by the proper effects (reform of evil or reenforcement of good dispositions).

APPROPRIATION OF RESPONSIBILITY

We concluded our discussion of the ideas associated with the pattern of attribution with some remarks on character. Character, the total set of morally admirable or reprehensible dispositions or tendencies, comes into being, as modern psychology has demonstrated so convincingly, under the manifold causal influences which touch a human life from its very first moments. Character is, in large part, the product of parental action and affection, of cultural milieu, of educational efforts. However, it has long been felt that the formation of a man's character by these external influences is not enough. This sort of character formation seems to lead to the unreflective, unimaginative morality of custom. Much of Western moral philosophy is inspired by Socrates who urged men to question the customs and traditions which they had received. William Frankena writes,

> Moral philosophy arises when, like Socrates, we pass beyond the stage in which we are directed by traditional rules and even beyond the stage in which these rules are so internalized that we can be said to be inner-directed, to the stage in which we think for ourselves in critical and general terms (as the Greeks were beginning to do in Socrates' day) and achieve a kind of autonomy as moral agents.[19]

This passage, which takes place both in a culture and in the individual, presents to the philosopher a second problem of responsibility, the problem of the moral agent. The moral agent "grows into morality": he is first formed and moulded by the influences of culture and education, given a character, whereby he is directed toward certain patterns of action (intentions), for certain reasons, (motivation) and in terms of certain logic (deliberation). However, he will inevitably be faced with the problem of making these intentions, motivations and deliberations his own, criticizing them, adjusting them, adding to them. The agent who responds typically, as merely one instance of many similar types, is called to respond originally and personally. The agent whose response to action upon him is rather passive is called to become more active. The agent who is only a carrier of his culture is called to become in some manner a creator of the culture.

This process is illustrated by what we call "assuming responsibility." We usually mean by this that a person has sufficient self-possession and moral acumen to move into some area which is not his of necessity. He enters into and takes upon himself the duties and the consequences of the situation. We judge someone unready to "assume responsibilities" if he shows lack of self-possession, self-control, and so on. He is not yet "responsible enough to assume responsibility."

While it is obvious that an agent's acts are his own insofar as he causes them, it is not always obvious that he causes them as a *moral* cause. We saw that the pattern of attribution asked certain questions in order to determine the presence of moral causality as the ground of praise and blame. The present pattern is concerned not with judging agents and actions as guilty or innocent, but with the process of how an agent takes possession of his action, moves from outer-directed to inner-directed, in short, becomes a properly moral agent. We speak of the pattern of appropriation, because to appropriate means to take possession of, to make one's own (*proprium*).

Attribution of responsibility does, of course, depend on the presence of a moral cause. But it is not concerned about precisely how such a cause comes into being. It is concerned principally about judging discrete acts, with the unity of these in character in the background. Appropriation is principally concerned about the unity of acts in the agent as moral person. Furthermore, the pattern of appropriation need not include considerations of the development and the form of moral person since it is concerned principally about the "end product," the decision which produced the act in question. Even "deliberation" is of interest only insofar as it took place and issued in "a deliberate decision, a deliberate act."

Thus, judging a person to be responsible presupposes the existence of responsible agent, although the problems and notions associated with the former can be separated theoretically from the latter. The pattern of ideas associated with attribution of responsibility is that pattern which arises from the judge's question, "How do I justly praise or blame." It comprises the notions of intention, motivation, deliberation, and character. The pattern of ideas associated with appropriation of responsibility is that pattern which arises when the philosopher thinks about the problem which he and every man has when he faces the challenge to become a self-determining being, master of his fate. This pattern comprises the notions of the self and of consideration, conscientiousness, and commitment.

THE SELF

In the first philosophical work to employ the term responsibility prominently, F. H. Bradley objects to John Stuart Mill's contention that "responsibility means punishment." He objects that Mill concentrates wholly on the notion of character as formed by external influences. This determinist position, says Bradley, "altogether ignores the rational self in the form of will; it ignores it in the act of volition, and it ignores it in the abiding personality, which is the same throughout all its acts, and by which alone imputation gets its meaning."[20]

Bradley's objection reflects a long-standing opinion that it is not enough to limit consideration of the nature of the moral agent to character alone. Character explains tendency to act, disposition to act; it does not explain action itself. Furthermore, character denotes a complex of effects, but the moral agent seems in some manner to be one who can or should control, govern, direct, the organization and the actuation of the tendencies and inclinations. Thus, moral philosophers will often insist that the moral agent must be thought of not only as character, but as self, as a center of self-actuation.

The notion of the self is a most difficult one and has been the subject of many philosophical debates, which we do not intend to review here. We simply wish to note that the experience of appropriation, in its various aspects, seems to suggest that the moral agent in some sense does transcend what happens to him. Moreover, he seems to transcend that which has been formed in him, as permanent tendencies and dispositions, since he seems able to dispose of his dispositions. Finally, he even seems to transcend himself, in self-reflection, self-criticism, and self-realization.

In virtue of these various transcendencies, the problem of appropriation appears to be the problem of the self accepting and taking a position toward what happens to it and even toward what it is. The moral agent as self is engaged in accepting and rejecting its own characteristics and, indeed, its very existence. An adequate philosophical consideration of the pattern of appropriation must include an explicit notion of the self as a transcending and reflecting agent.

It could be said that "the self appropriates . . ." But this philosophical phrase is not only a barbarism; it is somewhat inaccurate. The self does not act, *I* act; "appropriation" is not precisely an action at all: it is a way of acting. It is doing all those things we usually call actions: eating, driving, begetting, authoring, campaigning, banking, etc., but doing them in a particular way. The appropriation of action is best expressed by the adverbial phrases, "with consideration," "conscientiously," and "with commitment." The literature which discusses the problem of appropriation often does not distinguish the various features of the process. The vocabulary for the discussion is not settled. Thus, we have selected three terms, consideration, conscientiousness, and commitment, which seem to express the tenor of these discussions.

Before treating each briefly, we should note that we are dealing with what traditional moral philosophy has called "choice." The notion of choice is central to ethics. For Aristotle, it "is intimately related to virtue and a better criterion of character than action." For Aquinas, "all of moral philosophy, advice, exhortation, precept, prohibitions, rewards and punishments," rest on an adequate notion of choice.[21] However, in recent moral philosophy the notion is hardly adequate. Choice is often thought of as the simple selection of one alternative over another. But, to choose is not simply to select; it is to elect. The difference lies in the fact that an election implies the adoption and appropriation of a course of action: one gives oneself over to the course one elects and identifies himself with it. The following remarks describe the manner of choosing which reflects the self as agent capable of appropriation.

CONSIDERATION

The unreflective morality of childhood consists principally in being taught to obey the rules and to do "the right thing." However, it quickly becomes evident both in the life of the individual and of a culture that rules conflict and the "right thing" sometimes seems inappropriate. Alternatives present themselves. The agent who had always done what he was told or what everyone else did now must "choose for himself." In order to take one path rather than another, he must consider the alternatives.

Consideration presupposes awareness that there are alternative rules and courses of action. It proceeds to try to understand what these alternatives are. Understanding alternatives involves more than knowing what the possible courses of action are; it requires some foresight into the possible consequences of one or another choice. Further, the alternatives must be set into the wider context of one's understanding of one's self, and the world. Thus, consideration involves the relatively simple question, what are the alternatives?; the more difficult question, to what will my choice of the alternatives lead?; and the extremely difficult question, what does the choice and its consequences mean for my life, my work, my relation to others?

It is generally thought that a man can truly make his own choice and adopt a course of action as his own only after serious consideration. It will be his own, not merely because he knows what he is doing, but because he has lent himself to the arduous task of divining its meaning for himself. Consideration is an essential part of responsible choice.

Consideration is essentially the same as the deliberation

which was discussed as a part of the pattern of attribution. But it is the same process *from within,* as it were. The judge need only ask for evidence that the agent had the possibility and the opportunity to think through the action and the consequences. This evidence consists in showing that there was some kind of plan of action, in which one move seemed to be related to the next and in which all moves seem to converge toward a purpose. The agent himself engaged in the process of moral choice considers by examining now one, now another alternative, comparing, conjecturing, supposing. The person who has come into possession of himself as a moral agent is esteemed capable of giving counsel to others because he can offer a "considered opinion," that is, one in which all possibilities have been carefully weighed.

CONSCIENTIOUSNESS

While consideration plays a vital role in moral choice, it is essentially an intellectual process, employed in every area of human endeavor. It can be simply a technical calculation, made in any situation in which there are alternatives. However, it seems that for situations commonly called moral something more is asked of the agent than technical skill in thinking through and interpreting his action. He is required to adopt certain rules of judgment, criteria of right and wrong conduct, and to stick by these rules with consistency. He is required to be serious about his considerations, not allowing himself to be diverted by extraneous and distracting factors. He is required to stay with his considerations even though they seem to be leading him to an unpleasant conclusion. These requirements make up what is often called conscientiousness. Richard Brandt defines a conscientious person as

> . . . one who is strongly motivated to avoid doing anything wrong, and who is willing to make considerable sacrifice to do what he thinks right. He is one who is scrupulously careful to be sure that his conduct is right; he is constantly on the alert

about the moral justifiability of what he does or plans to do. By implication, then, he is a person who stands ready to behave in ways obviously required by moral principle.[22]

While conscientiousness is not a currently popular word, it does express something we look for in the morally mature person: seriousness, constancy and consistency in both his considerations and his conduct. It is conscientiousness rather than consideration that is commonly thought to require "will power," and it is often thought of in contrast to impulsiveness.

Conscientiousness is perhaps a more profound expression of appropriation of responsibility than consideration because the moral self seems more deeply involved. He must continually make the effort to "stick with" the principles he has chosen and, with constancy, try to make his conduct conform with them. Austin Farrar says that the moral self-judgment involved in responsibility "is not essentially a habit of blaming past actions, but a habit of imposing on one's conduct the law of one's mind. . . . The ultimate responsibility acknowledged and enforced by conscience is that of acting in accordance with our serious valuations."[23]

COMMITMENT

Consideration is a process of thought; conscientiousness is an attitude or disposition of the person. But in the moral life something must close off consideration and something must exemplify the disposition in act. This is usually called decision or choice. However, the currently popular word, commitment, is expressive. While decision and choice connote the closing off of deliberation and the selection of one possibility among many, commitment suggests the active engagement of the person to a course of action, to a cause, or to a way of life. The self hands itself over to its chosen course. Commitment seems to express the act of choice insofar as it expresses the willingness of a person to be identified with and by a certain course and the willingness to bear the burdens of being so identified.

To commit oneself is a most profound move toward self-appropriation. It is a commonplace in moral philosophy that a man makes himself a certain kind of person by his choices. "It is by action," says Aristotle, "that some men become just and others unjust, and it is by acting in the face of danger and developing fear or confidence that some become brave and others cowards."[24] But the existentialists have gone further: one not only becomes a certain kind of being, one actually makes oneself to exist by commitment. "Man being condemned to be free," writes Sartre, "carries the weight of the whole world on his shoulders: he is responsible for himself and for the world as a way of being."[25] By "way of being," Sartre means human existence as such. Existence is that part of the real which comes into being through "negation," which is the act of freedom. Man, alone capable of negation, creates his own existence and thus is totally and inescapably responsible. If it is only by choice, by commitment in absolute freedom, that the self and the world come into existence, then the self is totally responsible, totally and incontestably the author of being.

Without having to go quite as far as Sartre, it is possible to recognize that the moral quality of a man depends upon and grows out of his choices. He is, in great part, identified by his commitments. He forms his life into a unique entity and becomes "his own man." Thus, the responsible man is one who commits himself and is known to be committed.

We have described very broadly the problem of appropriation as it appears in very diverse literature. We have suggested our own names for the various aspects of the problem as they appear in that literature. In conclusion, it should be noted that appropriation is seldom viewed as a series of acts. It is rather a process of growth toward mature moral capability and judgment. The end product of this growth, if it is successful, is "the responsible man": one who can be counted upon to act with consideration, conscientiously, and who will commit himself to pursue what he considers right. Responsibility, then, appears as a quality of the person as a moral agent. It is a habit, or virtue, which inclines a person to considered, conscientious, committed conduct. This is what John Dewey had in mind when he wrote:

> The commonest mistake in connection with the idea of responsibility consists in supposing that approval and reprobation have a retrospective bearing instead of a prospective bearing. The possibility of a desirable modification of character and selection of the course of action which will make that possibility a reality in the future is the central fact in responsibility.[26]

Dewey thus associates the idea of attribution and the idea of appropriation by noting that "one is held responsible that he might *become* responsible, that is, responsive to the needs and claims of others, to the obligations implicit in his position."[27]

One is responsible when he deliberates carefully about his deeds and their consequences and honestly acknowledges that they are his own. Responsible attribution of responsibility, responsible praise and blame, is intended to so modify character that an agent "takes into account bearings and consequences which he has failed to consider in what he has done." As one of Dewey's disciples put it, "when our eyes are turned toward the future, responsibility becomes a possibility, a habit of meeting life in such a way that growth takes place and there is an acceptance of responsibilities."[28]

This "habit of responsibility" does not, like courage or temperance, incline one to a particular sort of activity, but to a general manner of proceeding in all actions: the general manner characterized by consideration, conscientiousness and commitment. The phrases, "accept or assume responsibility," or "the responsibilities of this office," reflect this. They imply that the job or task is not a simple and clearly-defined function which can be accomplished by following directions. Rather, it involves areas of discretion: a program is provided and the ways and means of fulfilling it are left up to the responsible party. Austin Farrar characterizes the responsible man in these terms:

The rule which the responsible man imposes upon himself . . . is not so much a rule prohibiting or commanding certain definable actions . . . as it is a rule of keeping one's eyes open for certain sorts of demands in certain types of situations. What we must do in response to them is not laid down by the rule, it has to be extemporized on the occasion.[29]

To say that the responsible man can "extemporize on the occasion" does not mean that he is a moral superman who goes beyond the rules. Rather, it implies that he is in a sense a moral virtuoso, who is in firm possession of himself and of the rules. He is aware that moral rules are not recipes which detail every ingredient that goes into a moral action, but that they outline programs which must be worked out in concrete situations. He has so incarnated the spirit of rules and the values that he can confidently judge how they are relevant in this present occasion. If "conscientious man" suggests rather unbending devotion to principle, "responsible man" implies mastery and discreet use of principle. There are not, alas, many such men, but such is the ideal at which the work of appropriation aims.

CONCLUSION

We have attempted to display the two patterns of ideas associated with responsibility in moral philosophy. As patterns they are but outlines, often lacking in detail. Indeed, some parts may be missing: perhaps sense of guilt and remorse should be treated in the pattern of appropriation and the question of the relation of responsibility to freedom has not been made explicit.[30] Furthermore, we do not have a formal definition to show for our effort. Instead we have a definition in the sense of a restriction and a bounding of questions and concepts. As we look over these two patterns, we can see that responsibility is an analogous notion: it is used in two distinct ways which have a common center of reference.

In the pattern of attribution, the judge's question about the propriety of praise and blame takes him into the issues of intention, motivation, deliberation, and character. In the pattern of appropriation, the agent's question about the development of self-possession takes him into the issues of consideration, conscientiousness and commitment. But it is clear that the question and notions of attribution rest in some manner on the question and notions of appropriation. While the judge's question looks principally for external evidence of moral causality and need not strike so deeply into the interior of moral agency, the moral agent must exist for the judge's question to have ultimate meaning: praising and blaming must somehow reflect and contribute to the existence of truly moral persons. Thus, while it is possible to separate out the considerations which are more suited to answer the judge's question from those more suited to the agent's, both questions finally meet.

It may be possible to elucidate the relation between attribution and appropriation by using more conventional terms. A fault (or responsibility) is justly imputed to someone only if that person is liable. His liability is evidenced by the fact that he intentionally, deliberately and with certain motivation performed the faulty act. This is, strictly speaking, sufficient answer to the judge's question. However, it is possible to pursue the issue further. It might be said, "while he is clearly responsible for this deed, why does he do such things?" One possible response is, "because he is not really very responsible; he has not yet developed the moral maturity and self-possession to handle himself in that situation." This does not necessarily excuse him, because he has indeed intentionally, deliberately and with motivation done something which deserves blame. But it may stimulate some thought about how to bring him to a greater personal responsibility.

We may employ here the more conventional term, accountability, to refer to the ability of a person to account to himself and to others, not simply by stating intention and motive, but by a rational exposition of the moral principles which he has considered and is conscientiously committed to. Thus, it can be said that imputation supposes liability and liability refers to accountability, either as a presupposition or as a desideratum. Responsibility expresses all these relationships. It may be said, in a slight paraphrasing of John Dewey's words quoted above, that men are held responsible (imputation) because they have acted as responsible causes (liability) and so that they may become responsible persons (accountable).

In the second place, it should be noted that both patterns prescind from properly normative questions, that is, from consideration of the nature of the rules and values which serve as standards. This is clearly the case in the pattern of attribution, which considers only the agent's subjective condition enabling him to or preventing him from fulfilling the standards, and does not consider the standards themselves. It is also generally true of the pattern of appropriation, although it must be remembered that conditions and dispositions of the agent, which play such an important role in this pattern, can be considered "values." Furthermore, in the extreme case of the existentialists there are no norms other than the self-committing act of the agent. However, for the most part the pattern of appropriation deals with the problem of appropriation of rules and values which are discovered elsewhere. Thus, neither attribution nor appropriation are properly normative. Nowell-Smith's remark about conscientiousness is applicable to responsibility in general:

> Conscientiousness is not the disposition to do certain sorts of things that are in fact valuable, but the disposition to obey certain rules; and its value therefore depends on the value of the rules, . . .[31]

Finally, it is important to note that attribution of responsibility concerns discrete acts, while appropriation of responsibility has to do with the unity and unification of acts in the agent. The judge's question is asked to determine whether this or that act, or at least, this or that series of acts, should be praised or blamed. The questions are asked about the intention, motivation and deliberation relevant to this act in particular. Only the question of character broadens the scope to inquire about the habitual intentions, motives and deliberative powers of the agent. On the other hand, the agent's question is asked to determine how this act can be integrated into the continuing reality of the agent. Consideration involves the interpretation of particular acts or courses as part of the whole life of the agent. Conscientiousness is an abiding characteristic of the agent. Commitment is an essential element in the process of self-identity and self-realization. Thus, the overall concern of the pattern of appropriation is the unity and unification of action and courses of action in the self, the abiding reality of the moral agent.

With these patterns of ideas in mind, we will now turn to some important theological literature about responsibility. We shall try to discern the similarities and the differences in the use of the term and, more importantly, try to identify the reasons for the differences.

4

Responsibility in
Modern Religious Ethics

*Because each man is in a sense responsible for his moral disposi-
tions, he will also be responsible for his conception of the good;
otherwise no man would be responsible for his own evil deeds.*

NICHOMACHEAN ETHICS III, V

*Now we know that whatever the law says it speaks to those who
are under the law, so that every mouth may be stopped and the
whole world may be held accountable to God. For no human being
will be justified in his sight by works of the law, since through
the law comes knowledge of sin.*

EPISTLE TO THE ROMANS, 3, 19-20

These two quotations sum up most strikingly the difference
between the religious and the philosophical doctrines on
human responsibility as they have developed in the western
world. Aristotle's words express one of the fundamental conceptions of his ethical system. The word here translated as
"responsible" is in the original *aitios*. This word is derived from
aitia, "cause" or "source." Thus Aristotle teaches that a man
is the cause of both what he is and what he does. He makes
himself the kind of man he is and in this sense is responsible
for what he is. Only because he is responsible can he be fittingly
praised and blamed for both his character and his behavior.

The mainstream of the western philosophical tradition has continued to view responsibility within the context of considerations set by this thesis. To speak of the responsible man is to speak of the man who is a moral cause: who deliberates and chooses intentionally and voluntarily to do good or evil and on this account can be judged, rewarded or punished by his fellows.

Similarly, the passage from St. Paul states one of the basic convictions of his theology. The word which the Revised Standard Version translates "accountable" is, in the original Greek, *hypodikos*. This word, a relative of *dike,* judgment and justice, properly means "subject to trial." Paul is saying that the whole world, all men, Jew and Gentile alike, stand accused before God and await his judgment. All men are under the power of sin; all have sinned, both those under the law and those without the law. No man has any excuse. Thus, "the whole world is laid open to God's judgment," as the *Bible of Jerusalem* translates.

But God's judgment has already been rendered. While Jew and Greek are equally guilty, both are equally justified. "There is no distinction; since all have sinned and fall short of the glory of God, all are justified by his grace as a gift, through the redemption which is in Christ Jesus." (Rom 3, 23) Thus, this text affirms the most fundamental of all Christian doctrines: all men are both judged and justified in Christ Jesus. "Accountability" or "responsibility" before God means that man is subject to God's condemning judgment and is recipient of his saving justification.

Everyone who is familiar with the history of Christian theology is aware that this doctrine has stimulated the most acrimonious debates and posed the most difficult problems for the proper understanding of the Christian faith. It clearly implies that both the condemnation and the justification of man are sovereign acts of God which are based neither upon man's previous deliberate sin (the doctrine of original sin) nor upon man's previous merit (the doctrine of grace). While "accountability and responsibility" in the juridical sense and in the tradition of moral philosophy require some deliberate transgression and some meritorious act in order to justify blame and praise, this Christian doctrine teaches that God's blame and praise do not depend on these preconditions. Christian theologians have been plagued with the most difficult problem of the relationship between the freedom of man and the omnipotent judgment and justification of God.

This Pauline doctrine of the universal accountability of all men, condemned without their deliberate fault and justified without their own merit, stands in sharp contrast (as Pelagius realized) to the Aristotelian assertion of praise and blame based on merit and demerit. However, alongside the Pauline theology of judgment and justification, another doctrine of responsibility develops, more in accord with philosophical and juridical requirements. It also has its roots in Scripture (see Mt 25, 31-46, on the Last Judgment; or II Cor 3, 10-15; 5, 10). The Lord God is supreme lawgiver, the supreme and final judge. He will scrutinize each man's life as a whole and each action in particular. He reads the hearts of men, their intentions and their motives. No man can escape his gaze; no man can offer excuse. Out of his mercy or his justice, God will gather a man to himself or condemn him to eternal punishment.

According to this teaching, God calls all men to account for their free and deliberate actions. He distinguishes the sheep from the goats: some are guilty, some innocent, not merely because he has declared them so, but in some sense because of what they themselves have chosen and done. In this way the whole of human morality, consisting both of observance of laws and sincerity of motives, is attached to the ultimate destiny of man. The religious power of this doctrine lay in its declaration that men are not ultimately answerable merely to themselves or to their rulers and peers, but to God himself, Lord of living and dead.

The first, the Pauline doctrine of accountability has remained the property of the dogmatic theologians. Augustine vindicated free will against the Manicheans, then the grace of God against the Pelagians. Then follow the interminable debates: Infra-lapsarian Calvinists against supra-lapsarian Calvinists, Jansenists against Jesuits, Jesuits against Dominicans, and on and on. The second, more properly ethical doctrine of accountability has fallen into the hands of the Christian ethicians and moral theologians. These were often concerned less with the sinful condition of man than with the particular sins of particular men. Thus they invoked all of the apparatus of "Aristotelian" accountability in order to prepare a man for the final confrontation with his judge. Accountability or responsibility in this tradition is identical with what we have called the pattern of attribution.

We do not intend to pursue the extremely difficult theological problems associated with the Pauline doctrine. We mention it here simply because the problem which we will deal with in this chapter, namely, the notion of responsibility in contemporary Christian ethics, seems to be a mélange of the theological doctrine of total accountability and of the moral doctrine of specific accountability. Any understanding of responsibility in contemporary theological literature presupposes, I believe, the intertwining of these two related but rather distinct positions. In this literature, responsibility is intended to convey both the total, inescapable relation of man to the judgment and grace of his Creator and Redeemer as well as his involvement in the discrete activities required of the moral man.

I begin this chapter with an illustration of what I mean by the intertwining of theological and ethical accountability. This illustration is taken from the brief section of Karl Barth's *Church Dogmatics* II/2, entitled "The Sovereignty of the Divine Decision." Barth's remarks on responsibility simply set up the questions which we intend to pursue through other authors. These questions will be taken in turn to Bernhard Haering, Dietrich Bonhoeffer, H. Richard Niebuhr, and Robert Johann. Each of these authors has proclaimed the centrality of the notion of responsibility for Christian ethics. While Barth states this, he does not explicate it to any great extent. Haering states it and attempts to use the notion of responsibility as a conception in which theology of the supernatural and human moral experience can be made relevant to each other. Bonhoeffer states it and deals with it principally as a question of the theological foundation of ethics. Niebuhr states it and discusses it as a matter of theory of norms. Johann affirms it and treats it as a basic description of the moral self or agent.

We will read all these authors with the hope of seeing more clearly the kinds of questions and issues with which the notion of responsibility is associated in the development of religious ethics. Against the background of moral philosophy which we have sketched and in association with certain theological issues which we will note, we may be able to discern, at least dimly, certain criteria for a responsible use of responsibility in Christian ethics.

KARL BARTH

God cannot draw man to Himself without involving him in responsibility. . . . What we have to establish is that the being and essence and activity of God as Lord of the covenant between himself and man include a relationship to the being and essence and activity of man. It is as he makes himself responsible for man that God makes man, too, responsible.[1]

Often Karl Barth condenses into one succinct statement the sum and substance of one of his important teachings. This is such a statement. It appears in the first pages of Chapter VIII of the volume entitled *The Doctrine of God*. This chapter, "The Command of God," initiates Barth's theological ethics. The command of God is God's claim upon man, God's decision concerning man, God's judgment about man. When he discusses the sovereignty of the divine decision, Barth writes, "It is the idea of responsibility which gives us the most exact definition of the human situation in the face of the absolute transcendence of the divine judgment."[2] We will locate this idea within the context of his theological ethics and outline the problematic to which it, like much of the theological writing on responsibility, gives rise.

Barth asserts that theological ethics, and in fact all ethics worthy of the name, must be done as a part of the doctrine of God, because all of our true knowledge about man's works and ways must derive from our knowledge of God's works and ways toward us. But God's sole manifestation of himself is that which he makes in Jesus Christ: the eternal manifestation of his gracious will to covenant with man, to draw man into covenant partnership with himself. Thus, what we are and do and what we are to be are determined by this gracious and eternal decision of God.

This divine will toward us, manifested as the gospel of God's grace, also lays a claim upon man: it is then law, requiring us to correspond to this grace, to be obedient to it, to bear witness to it by our lives and our activity. We are called upon to accept God's action toward us as right and to accept that, in fact, he is our righteousness. But at the same time this command is a permission, for it frees us from our selves, from our ethos, to respond and accept God's righteousness as ours.

Yet the divine command does not simply claim our being and our obedience and grant us the freedom to obey. It is also a sovereign decision about what will count as obedient behavior, a decision about what human activity can be called good or bad. God does not merely call for man to obey; he determines precisely what that obedience will consist in.

> The claim of the divine command is concerned with [our] decisions both as a whole and in detail. It is in these decisions that we give our witness to the fact that we belong to God. If they are subject to God's claim, this includes the further and greater fact that they are measured by the will and act of God, that the will and act of God is in some sense the prior decision

by which they are all asked whether or not they attest and praise his great love. Because the will of God expressed in his Law is the good which as such requires our active recognition, it is also the criterion of the good and evil nature of our conduct. . . . As he is our Lord by reason of his command, he is also the Law by which we stand or fall.[3]

God, then, has made himself responsible for man by his gracious decision to draw man into covenant, a decision reached and realized in Jesus Christ. He has made himself responsible for man's conduct by commanding man to witness to this gracious decision; a command that claims obedience and that determines what obedience must be. What of the being and action of the man who is thus treated by God?

Barth tells us that "the idea of responsibility gives us the most exact definition of the human situation in face of the absolute transcendence of the divine judgment. We live in responsibility, which means that our being and willing, what we do and what we do not do, is a continuous answer to the Word of God spoken to us as a command." Man is linked to God and confronted by him. He is called to fulfill the true purpose of his existence as a covenant partner with God. He is tested and questioned as to how he fulfills this purpose. "This is the essence of his responsibility. And with what he is and wills, does and does not do, he is ineluctably caught up in one continuing responsibility, in the constant need to render an account."[4]

This responsibility arises from the "true and proper confrontation" between God and man, which only the Christian knows, but which is objectively true for all men. God confronts man with his decision and his command, the only command which generates an absolute and inescapable obligation. When so confronted, man knows that he is not alone, that he is in a situation in which he must answer to someone other than himself.

This responsibility requires of us moral reflection, that is, the examination of what we are and what we will in this mutual relationship between the command of God and human existence. We must diligently examine our attitude to the divine decision, we must prepare our answer to it, declare our readiness to accept it. We must continually ask ourselves the question demanded by our responsibility: what ought we to do?

This question, which Barth explores at some length, has nothing to do with the practical questions about ends and means, possible consequences, objective obligations or even moral values which we saw in the philosophical patterns. At each point in the question, we are to ask ourselves whether, in whatever we are about to do, we reject all ultimate reliance upon human considerations and prepare ourselves to accept the divine decision and to witness to that alone in all we choose and do.

This admittedly inadequate summary of Barth's remarks on responsibility provides the occasion to perform two important tasks. In the first place, we classify Barth's statement as a theological affirmation. This provides the opportunity to define what we mean by "theological affirmation," a term of considerable importance for the further analysis of the religious ethic of responsibility. Second, Barth's theological statement is a rather striking exemplification of the differences between "responsibility" in a typical Christian context and "responsibility" in moral philosophy. This allows us to set up clearly the problematic that we will bring to our four principal authors.

Barth's remarks on responsibility constitute a theological affirmation. Theology is human reflection, carried on in faith, upon the source of faith, the word of God revealed in the Scriptures and the continuing life of the Christian Church. This reflection takes as its premises the propositions presented to faith by the revealed word. It seeks to understand them in themselves and in their inter-relation. In so doing, it will employ concepts and terms which are not themselves contained in the propositions presented to faith, but which are drawn from human experience and philosophical reflection on this experience. This is not done with the intention of translating the propositions of faith into philosophical propositions, but simply with the intention of elucidating and explaining the word of God. Thus, for our purposes we will define a theological affirmation as a statement offered as the conclusion of thoughtful consideration in faith upon the revealed word of God in the light of reflective human experience.

When Barth writes, "responsibility is the most exact definition of man's situation in face of the absolute transcendence of the divine judgment," he states the conclusion of reflection upon several theological premises. These premises are, first, that God elects man to covenant with himself and commands man to be faithful and to witness to his election. Second, the whole life of man is caught up in this election and is thus subject to the divine mercy and justice. These are propositions found in the revealed word of scripture and presented to the faith of the Church. They would not otherwise be known, or would be at best only opinions. As the revealed word, however, they are the certain objects of Christian faith and the initial premises for Christian theological reflection.

In the course of this reflection a concept is introduced which is not present in the theological premises. The theologian has learned of "responsibility" in other contexts, the experience of human life and the reflection thereon which is called philosophy. The content of the term is elucidated in moral philosophy, as we have shown before. It refers to the experience of moral approbation or disapprobation and to the experience of appropriation of action. The philosophical elaborations are attempts to state the grounds for the just attribution of the former and the necessary conditions for the latter.

When the theologian employs such a term within his own discipline, it does not remain unchanged. By adoption into theological discourse its boundaries are stretched. Its connotation shifts in the light of the new purpose to which it is put. We notice this in the case of "responsibility," and it is our contention that failure to recognize this stretching and shifting has led to some uncertainty and loss of clarity in its use.

Two principal differences distinguish the theological affirmation of responsibility, as we find it in Christian tradition and in this statement by Barth, from the affirmations of moral philosophy. The first refers to the attribution of responsibility; the theological affirmation asserts that man is made responsible and that his total life is responsible. Barth writes, "I am invited and made responsible and enabled to fulfill my responsibility . . . as this particular man, this one beloved by God and therefore a responsible partner in the divine covenant."[5] Again, he writes, "that God is gracious to us in Jesus Christ means a total divine claim to our obedience and a total decision concerning good and evil in the choice of our decisions. It means our total responsibility."[6]

In the pattern of attribution in moral philosophy, man is not *made* responsible, but *held* responsible. When a man is "held up" for praise or blame, the justice of so doing depends on the presence of the grounds that we have mentioned. A man must have done something and he must have done it voluntarily and intentionally. The attribution of responsibility rests upon the previous occurrence of a human action done in a certain way. What, then, can it mean to say that a man is *made* responsible, *enabled* to fulfill responsibility?

We do of course say "make responsible" in ordinary and in legal language, as (for example) "the court made him responsible for the welfare of the child." This phrase, however, refers more to the appropriation of responsibility than to attribution. We "make responsible" only for duties; we "hold responsible" for actions that fulfill or fail to fulfill these duties. Thus, to "make responsible" is to tell a man he must appropriate a certain course of action, for discharge of which he will be held responsible. Likewise, the phrase "enable to fulfill responsibilities" is perfectly intelligible if we are referring to acts which remove obstacles, set up possibilities, and even form character. However, in both cases the theologians intend something deeper. God does not simply assign duties, remove obstacles and strengthen character. He establishes, in his very creation, a responsible being: man. Only because man is *made* responsible by God's acts of creation and redemption, can he be given duties and enabled to fulfill them. It is in this sense that Christian ethics has recognized that an indicative precedes its imperative: you are made God's beloved children: therefore act as such!

Further, the contention that man's life is involved in "total responsibility" is somewhat problematic, from the viewpoint of the pattern of attribution. The philosophical discussions about attribution of responsibility are intended to clarify when and under what conditions a man should be held responsible. Responsibility is discrete: a man can be praised or blamed if certain conditions are fulfilled; but if they are not, both praise and blame are inappropriate. In such a case he is not responsible; he is excused. Thus we say that if a man is acting intentionally or voluntarily, he is responsible; if he lacks one or another of these conditions, he is not responsible for what he does.

The discussion of responsibility in Barth omits any reference to the conditions for attribution of responsibility. He says nothing about "the voluntary," about intention, deliberation, motivation, and so on. He does demand self-examination, but it bears only on one issue, namely, whether we are witnessing to God's grace in all of our decisions and actions. Once again, it is worthwhile to notice the peculiarity of "total responsibility" from the point of view of the pattern of attribution.

The second major difference between theological responsibility and philosophical responsibility concerns the pattern of appropriation. Barth, in accord with long Christian tradition, declares, "I am not my own; my action is not my own: I and my action belong to God." Now the purpose of the pattern of appropriation is to elucidate the conditions under which a person performs an action that is truly his own. The conditions are those which, when fulfilled by the agent, make it possible for him to say, "this is my action, it expresses me." Unlike the pattern of attribution, which implies the presence of a judge, appropriation concerns the agent, in his own freedom and personal transcendence. Theological responsibility affirms that God lays claim to our actions, controls them, governs them. His sovereign decision not only judges whether we are doing good but also determines what the good is that we must do. Hence it is possible to ask what it means to speak of a responsible action which is not in some sense my own action.

As we turn to our four major authors we put these questions: what is the responsibility with which I am endowed by God—made responsible—in relation to the responsibility in which I am held responsible for my own actions? How do I responsibly judge the human good and appropriate it in relation to the good which God has judged appropriate for me? In asking such questions we are requesting our theologians to clarify the fundamental relationship that exists between God and man, the nature of human life as it exists within this relationship, and the place which the perception of human values and human norms has in relation to the perception of the divine will for man.

BERNHARD HAERING

The concepts of personal salvation, of commandment and of law certainly retain their full meaning. However, they are not the central concepts of Catholic moral teaching. This is much better expressed, in our opinion, by the word "responsibility," understood in its religious sense.

THE LAW OF CHRIST[1]

Bernhard Haering is one of the foremost theologians in this "age of renewal" of the Roman Catholic Church. While the other important figures, Rahner, Congar, Schillebeeckx, have devoted their attention to the questions of dogmatic theology,

Haering has been the inspirer and leader in the long-desired renewal of moral theology. The words quoted above from his major work, *The Law of Christ*, state the theme of his program of renewal. He wishes to place the concept of responsibility, "understood in its religious sense," at the center of Catholic moral teaching. The traditional concepts of salvation, commandment and law, long the principal subject matter of moral theology, must then be understood in the light of "responsibility."

The importance and the impact of Haering's work can only be understood in relation to the traditional moral theology which he set out to "renew." Catholic moral theology of the nineteenth and early twentieth centuries represented no mean intellectual effort. It was a careful, comprehensive, and systematic attempt to state the duties of the Catholic Christian toward God, toward his Church, and toward his fellow man in the various institutions in which he lived. It was concerned both about the general principles of morality, found in the Decalogue and in the natural law, and about the problems of conflicts of principle, with which it dealt in its casuistry.

However, it had lost contact with dogmatic theology. Unlike much of the Protestant "theological ethics," which was absorbed into dogmatics, it had attained an independent status. Consequently, the great theses of dogmatic theology, the redemption, the sanctification of man by the grace of the Holy Spirit, incorporation into the following of Christ, exerted less and less influence in its pages. Instead of the supernatural life of grace, it treated man's nature and the natural law; instead of the following of Christ in love, it centered on the salvation or perfection of man by obedience. The counsels of perfection, the extraordinary effects of grace, were relegated to a secondary discipline, ascetico-mystical theology. The actual, if quite unintended, result was the sundering of religion from morality, of love from law, of grace from nature.

Haering's concern, since the publication of his first book, *Das Heilige und Das Gute*, a study of the "mutual relationship of religion and morality," has been the creation of a moral theology in which man's religious life and his moral life are again seen in profound unity and interpenetration.

> Our moral life must be nourished entirely and utterly on the religious relation to God. Religion must not be looked upon as a mere external aid and sanction to morality but as its very spirit. Only if it is imbued with religion, centered in the religious, can morality be correctly judged.[2]

Haering's first task is to state the theological basis for the Christian moral life. He does so in terms of the intimately linked doctrines of the *imago Dei*, man's likeness to God, and the *Nachfolge Christi*, the imitation of Christ. "Man's likeness to God is the significant key word of moral theology . . . a moral teaching based on the imitation of Christ."[3] Haering's second task is to expose the moral constitution and the moral life of man in a manner congruent with the theological doctrines. He does so in terms of a personalist value theory. He finds in the notion of responsibility the link between the theology and the ethics, between religion and morality. ". . . The term responsibility is best suited to express the interpenetration of the moral through the religious and the distinction of the two."[4]

THEOLOGICAL FOUNDATIONS

Haering asks how "morality can conform to the basic laws of the religious . . . be animated by its essential spirit." The basic law of the religious is the conception of the Holy advancing toward man and of man turning toward the Holy. This much the phenomenology of religions has stated. However, only Christian revelation manifests the true nature of this Holy and the manner of its advance toward man. This revelation proclaims, "The Word was made flesh and dwelt among us." God's eternal Word, the inner expression of his own nature as Love, is spoken and becomes part of human history in Jesus Christ. This Word made flesh expresses and realizes God's will to enter into fellowship with man. He declares this fellowship, establishes it in his flesh and invites man to enter it. In this revelation, the heart of religion is manifested: it is dialogue between the living God and man, "the encounter between the Word of God and the response of man."[5]

Religion is dialogue between God and man. But this dialogue is "in Christ." It is nothing so superficial as a conversation; it is an intimate union. For in Christ the divine and the human are hypostatically united. Christ is the message of the eternal love of God. But he is also, in virtue of his humanity, the response to that love. Further, in virtue of his humanity all mankind is caught up in him. All men are created in Christ and re-created through Christ. It is principally in this sense that men can be said to be created "in the image and likeness of God." This is the creation in grace, the re-creation by the Holy Spirit. Thus, there can be true community and fellowship in the dialogue between God and man because man is created in and bears the image of God. Haering writes:

> *Deus et Anima,* God and the soul, the awesome and beatifying mystery of the I-Thou communion between God and the soul is the mystery of the Word of God. In the Word, the Logos, through the Word and in the image of the Word are we created. In Christ, the Word made man, God comes to us and we to him. Man's likeness to God is the significant key word of moral theology.[6]

By creation in God's image we are drawn into fellowship with him. The *imago Dei* in man refers to man's original created nature as open to God's communication and as capable of response, and also to the re-creation in grace, whereby man receives the Holy Spirit, is formed into the brother of Jesus Christ, and responds to the Father, through the Son, in love, faith and hope. The image, then, is both constitutive of man's nature and of his re-created nature. But it is also a reality which can be deepened by growth in the response of love through the following of Christ, for the fellowship in which we exist is not only a state of being but a way of being, a form of activity. We are called to follow him in whose image we are created. By love and obedience, we imitate him who makes the perfect response to God's call. Thus, by his grace, Christ binds us to himself and by our love we bind ourselves to Christ. We listen to his words, we attend to his example, we seek his will for our lives. Imitation of Christ follows upon the establishment of fellowship and follows upon that fellowship itself.

Haering draws together the basic themes of incorporation in Christ, the law of Christ, and the following of Christ. He describes the Christian as one who lives in the law of Christ. But this law is within him, in virtue of his incorporation into Christ through the Holy Spirit. This law *is* Christ. The imitation and the following of Christ do not consist in a mere external conformity, but rather in a life which flows from a most intimate and real union with Christ.

In drawing together these various expressions of the Christian life, Haering makes the most of the German word *Nachfolge*, which means both "imitation" and "following." This gathers into one term the various biblical notions of "following," "example," "imitation," "union," and "discipleship." All these scriptural themes refer to the essential features of Christian reality: the person, word and act of Jesus Christ lays claim on the decision, deeds, and manner of life of men in order to exemplify and carry on in them his work. However, in the history of Christian spirituality, various nuances have been stressed: external imitation of the life of Jesus by poverty and suffering, internal conformity by loving obedience, sacramental and mystical union with the risen Lord. Haering stresses the second and third notions, indicating that the response of loving obedience grows out of and deepens the mystical and sacramental union. The moral life does not simply effect fellowship with God; it springs from fellowship with him.

The establishment of the fellowship is the work of God alone. He initiates it by speaking his Word of Love and drawing man into that Love, incorporating him into Christ, through the gift of the Holy Spirit. This incorporation enables man to respond in the dialogue which God has initiated. Haering points out that the response has two facets. There is a direct response to God, which is religion properly so called. Man listens reverently to the Word of God addressed to him in scripture, in preaching, in his personal experience. He responds to it with gratitude and joy. He harkens to God's word of truth, of promise, and of love, and responds in acts of faith, hope and charity. This is the response of worship. Its object is God himself.

But there is a second form of response. The word of God is directed to man in the created order of persons and things. All creation has come into being in and through the Word. It also, in all of its temporal and material aspects, speaks to man of God's love. It mediates his message. "The believer," says Haering, "detects in the order of creation the message of the Lord and Creator; the child of God hears in all things the word of his Father."[7] Thus the Christian, faced with the created world, is summoned to work in this world, to fulfill himself and its potentialities, in accord with the word of God which is spoken in its values.

This second form of word and response constitutes the moral life, properly speaking. "The moral order is concerned with the fulfillment of the order of creation. It is response to God, a correct response precisely to the extent that man takes his terrestrial tasks seriously and earnestly accepts created values."[8]

Religion, then, is man's worshipping response to God himself, who speaks his Word of love. Religious morality is man's response to God's word mediated through the created world, which is a message of God because it is itself created and re-created in the Word of God, Jesus Christ. This response can be appropriately called by the properly moral term "responsibility."

Haering now proposes a definition of responsibility within his theological context:

> We could say that the religious attitude is response to God's word and love. It is directly faced with God himself. The moral life is a response—responsibility in view of one's fellowmen, the community of men and all earthly goods and tasks in order to give God a full and living response. . . . Moral responsibility makes the moral attitudes and decisions a real response to God precisely to the extent that man takes his terrestrial tasks seriously and earnestly accepts the order of created value. . . . Hence, we understand Christian morality as responsibility in the sense that the Christian in his relationships to himself, to his human co-world, to the world of creatures, perceives a word and message which ultimately comes from God. This responsibility further requires that in his thinking, speaking and acting, in his personal relationships, and in his shaping the world he give a fitting reply, that he act responsibly and so much so that everything in the last analysis becomes a reply, a response that is worthy to be offered to God, the Father of all men.[9]

PERSON AND VALUE

If man's morality is to be responsibility, that is, a response to God's word spoken through creation, it may be asked how man discerns that word. Haering answers this question in terms of what might be called "a Personalistic-Value doctrine." This constitutes the center of his fundamental or general ethics. It marks a considerable shift from the traditional "Nature-Finality" doctrine of scholastic moral theology.

"Person," writes Haering, "is a spiritual substance in unique and concrete existence, whose essential task is to move through self possession toward openness to the Other. Personality means the fulfillment of this task: the vital interiority in openness to the World and to the Thou."[10] In Haering's view, "person" designates a being constituted essentially by the capacity for and the actuality of communication with another person. The person lives, with a necessity arising from its very existence, in a community of word and response. The interpersonal community of word and response establishes the "spatial" dimension of society, in which common goals and institutions represent and promote the communion of persons. The interpersonal community also takes place in a "temporal" dimension, history. History is not simply the passage of time but man's present life as it has come out of his past and is to be shaped in anticipation of the future. In sum, the person is a unique spiritual-corporeal being, created by and creative of word and response, living in and through interpersonal communion, within a time which bears the marks of his response.

Person and personality, community and history are all "in Christ." Thus man's response to another person will ultimately be a response to God, since it is taken up in Christ's own loving response to the Father. Community is the mystical body of Christ. It is so either actually, in the Church, vivified by the Holy Spirit and the sacraments; or it is so virtually, in the whole human race as it struggles toward community. Man's history in Christ is the "Kairos," the history in which God is working out man's salvation and in which each man's moral decision is a providential moment granted by God to further that work. Thus, Haering sees the appeal of I to Thou, which constitutes the essential structure of human personhood, the appeal of human persons to form societies and the appeal of man's own future, as all mediating the message which God speaks to man.

In the light of this understanding of the human person, Haering explains how man can perceive the message of God. The person's fundamental reality is his potential to be open, to open himself, to the other. This potentiality is centered in his active powers. But these powers are not merely "intellect and will," as traditional scholastic philosophy has proposed. Rather, it is man's "value experience" (*Werterlebnis*) in which potentiality for personal communion is centered.

Haering lays great stress upon "values" and "value experience." His teaching in this respect is deeply colored by the German value-philosophers, in particular, Max Scheler. These authors, among whom Dietrich von Hildebrand is best known to English readers, maintain that value is known as the object of an original emotional intuition, or more properly, a spiritual intentional affectivity, which they call *Gesinnung*. It is a spiritual affectivity because it is a unity of concrete apprehension and sensitivity; it is intentional insofar as its content is determined by its object, value. For some of the value philosophers, such as von Hildebrand and Nicolai Hartmann, value is an ideal essence, existing in itself but capable of being intuited by value-experience and realized in activity. However, Haering prefers the position of Scheler for whom value is Person offering and accepting love. As we shall see, Haering maintains that the basic value which is intuited is the communion of persons and, ultimately, the Person of God offering himself and summoning unto himself.

Haering argues that value experience is a spiritual affectivity in which the spiritual and the sensitive powers of the person recognize and respond to the presence of value. While it involves both sensitivity and rationality, it cannot be reduced to either. It arises from an intuitive comprehension of the most fundamental tendency of the person. It is the cognitive grasp of the inner ordination of personal being. Now, this tendency or ordination is precisely the tendency to open the self and to enter into communication with another self. It is the tendency toward the fulfillment of the self, not as an isolated entity but in becoming a person in dialogue with another person. The relationship of communication, or the terms of the relation, the self and the other as persons, are the object of this tendency.

Because this value-experience is a spiritual affectivity, it may be called *Gesinnung,* but its real identity is Love. It is the dynamism of the person which urges him out toward others. Value experience is fundamentally love of value. However, it is necessary to distinguish the initial response to value, in which value is recognized, from the acceptance of the value, in which the person takes a position with respect to that value. The first response is in a sense love, because the spiritual affectivity does not simply know value as a thing or a fact, but as something to be appreciated, respected and, perhaps, possessed. But the second is love properly speaking, because man's freedom accepts, cherishes, makes his own, the value presented.

Haering has described man's fundamental active power as capacity for value experience. He has also intimated therein what he means by "value." If value experience is the spiritual affectivity which comprehends the person's basic orientation, and if the basic orientation is toward communion with a Thou, then that communion itself, or more properly the term of the communion, the person, is value. The person as such, existing in concrete uniqueness and as potentiality for communion, is basic value. The center of value is "the Value-Person" (*die Wertperson*).

The person is basic value; the center of value. He is also the bearer of value. There are attributes, qualities and dispositions which pertain to the person and which realize in the person the openness and unity which constitute his personality. These are sometimes called virtues, which in Haering's view are the qualities required for the enduring response to the other and to objective values. These attributes and dispositions are properly "moral" values. They are not "things in themselves," but flow into, are manifested in acts. The value of acts depends upon and is sustained by the decision of will and interior dispositions which animate it. Thus, moral values are those qualities of persons which realize their personhood and which inspire action.

The person, with various qualities and dispositions, is surrounded by a world of realities which can contribute to the development of the personality. Things, institutions, practices, physical and cultural conditions may effect the person positively or adversely. Insofar as they do so positively and can be appropriated by the person in his movement toward personality and communion in love, they might be called "objective values." Such values must be coordinated with the moral values of intention and disposition for the full moral determination of an act. A man must not only intend the actualization of personal value; he must also adopt those objective realities which can in fact contribute to it. This, however, can be determined only in terms of the actual situation in which a man is at a specific time.

Haering, then, seems to distinguish value into *basic value*, which is the person in communion of love; *moral values*, which are the qualities and dispositions of persons that enable them to communicate in love; and *objective values*, which are the external factors that can be assumed by the person and contribute to the openness and unity of personal existence. These values are capable of being ranked in terms of their elevation and their importance in the promotion of personality.

VALUE AND NORM

Haering has given primacy to a personalistic value doctrine in his ethics of responsibility. But he has entitled his major work *The Law of Christ*. He refers, of course, to the *ennomos Xristou* (I Cor 9, 20), to the "law of the spirit of life in Christ" (Rom 8, 2). But we must relate this law, the new law of life, to the value doctrine which he has proposed.

Value is predicated principally of the person: the existence of persons in the fullness of their reality, that is, in the communion of love, is the basic value. Dispositions are values insofar as they express and promote personal value; factual realities are values insofar as they promote personal values. However, value is apprehended in *Gesinnung* as concrete and immediate. It is possible and necessary for human thought to generalize the experience of value and to formulate universal statements which express and direct values. These statements, arising from the dynamism of value experience, do more than express value: they direct action to realize, foster, protect or appreciate some area of value. These statements are called norms or laws. A norm is called law insofar as it is the expression of an authoritative legislator.

All norms and laws are based upon value and value relations. Haering writes:

> Value dictates norm . . . a norm of morals is not an arbitrary restraint interfering with liberty, but the summons and invitation to the exercise of liberty, arising from the value in the object, an invitation to man to preserve and nurture value in freedom. A norm which is not founded in value and which does not present a duty through relation to value has no moral force binding the will.[11]

Since the value and the relations arising from value are diverse, there are several sorts of norms. The will of God is the ultimate norm of morality. God is highest value, not only as man's ultimate end but as the Person opening himself and entering into communion with man. The will of God is the expression of this value and creates the value which is the encounter between God and man.

Christ is the norm of morality insofar as he is the expression of the relationship between himself and the Father and the expression of the relationship in which men exist with God. He is the norm insofar as his life, word and example manifest the values of fellowship and communion with God. This is more than external manifestation. It reveals that the Father's will to fellowship is expressed not only in the life, words and example of Jesus Christ, but also in all the personal and objective values of the creation recapitulated in him. Thus, the created order itself expresses the divine will for fellowship.

This created order, the order of being, is then the order of values. An order of norms can be discerned in this order of values. These norms state the hierarchy of values and command them to be protected. They are directed to the freedom of persons, calling them to realize the values in the light of their proper rank and importance for human life ordained for communion of love. While these moral norms have been expressed in many different ways, including the classical formulations of "natural law," Haering formulates his basic norm for an ethic of responsibility as "in spirit and action, man must attain full correctness of being."[12]

The full correctness of being is not simply an order manifested in the "natures of things," but is the order of value revealed to man in his existence as person and as person in Christ. As man comes to understand the dimensions of existence as person, as one called to love and to the communion of persons, as he realizes the dimensions of his existence "in Christ," called to open and to give himself, even sacrificially, he will discern the order of being.

The order of being is reflected within the person by the order of love. Love is, as we have seen, involved in the very perception of value; more importantly, it is the actual acceptance of value. Insofar as love rightly perceives value, it will perceive not single values in isolation but the order of value: things subservient to and for the service of persons, dispositions as expressions of persons, persons in their uniqueness and inviolability yet ordained to communion. Love recognizes and realizes the order of values. It might be said that "love is the only norm of Christian morality," but only if "love" means "order of love," in which the range and hierarchy of values is perceived and realized in action.

The love which discerns the right order of value is not merely human. It is "the love of God which is poured forth in our hearts by the Holy Spirit" (Rom 5, 5). The grace of the Holy Spirit renews the disposition (*Gesinnung*), imparting to man's spirit "a new life . . . of inner impulse and ever-expanding urgency."[13] It is inner guidance, summons, invitation to love. In virtue of this new and interior law the Christian is urged far beyond the negative proscriptions and minimum requirements: he is directed toward lofty ideals and goals. Furthermore, because this new law imparts to the heart of man the love of the Holy Spirit, making him love God in all things, it is a law of freedom. The Christian does all things, even the commanded, lovingly and therefore freely. This then is the Law of Christ, the love of God imparted to man in the Holy Spirit, whereby man is conformed interiorly to Christ's own love for his Father and for men. The central thesis of *The Law of Christ* is expressed in these words:

> The New Law, the law of grace, does not allow us to put in place of prominence the ethical "ought," and to relegate to second place grace as mere help to fulfill the law. The order of precedence is not "Law and Grace," but "Grace and Law." Conformity to Christ through the grace of the Holy Spirit is first; then comes the guidance of grace to corresponding acts. The ethical "ought" and the cooperation of man comes only third. Grace is more than Law, and more than summons. But for the Christian, the law is the summons and the expression of grace. Those "in Christ" see the commanding will of God, both in external law and in inner impulses, as the intention of God's Love. In the task, they see always the Gift.[14]

ETHIC OF RESPONSIBILITY

The words just quoted seem to align Haering with the form of ethics which has been called "*Gesinnungs-ethik*,": an ethic which stresses right disposition and purity of intention as the essence of morality. Indeed, Haering quite readily accepts the title. However, he wishes to make it very clear that his *Gesinnungs-ethik* is also and essentially *Verantwortungs-ethik*, ethic of responsibility engaged in "terrestrial tasks." In fact, it is an ethic of responsibility precisely because the "fundamental disposition, love and loving obedience to the intention of God, demands that we take seriously the ordering of creation, the power of sin and the victory of Christ which must be rendered visible in the history of man."

It is now possible to see what "responsibility" means for Haering. He opens his moral theology with a theological affirmation about the relationship between God and man. This is the divinely-initiated dialogue: God speaks his loving word in Jesus Christ and in the world created and redeemed in and through him. This word invites man's response: the response of religion in the words of prayer and worship; the response of morality in recognition, acceptance and promotion of created value. The essential relation between God and man is thus one of word and response.

Haering then proceeds to explicate the response of morality. He proposes an anthropology in which man is conceived as person, that is, a being essentially constituted by communion. The person's most radical power is *Gesinnung* whereby he knows himself as ordered to value: the value of the other as loving and beloved. This *Gesinnung* is, both in its root and in its perfection, love. Thus, the essential structure of the moral life is the appeal and response of love.

But the response of love to value must be made in freedom and this freedom is blocked in many ways, by value blindness, by distortion of the right order of value. The grace of God, imparted through the Word, moves, enlightens, inspires the *Gesinnung* and rectifies love. Man must then respond to the love which works within him and to the values which this love reveals. He must respond freely; he must respond fittingly, that is, in accord with the right order of values. This is responsibility: the free acceptance of the right order of values, in which the word of God is discerned.

Haering has made it clear that the order of values is to be interpreted personalistically. The person in his existence as beloved of God and potential partner for human love is basic value. The order of values thus begins with respect for the uniqueness and freedom of the person, both one's self and others. There must be concern for the formation of genuine and profound personhood. Further, all of the qualities which render possible community of love between persons must be protected and fostered. The virtues and the personal gifts must be promoted. Finally, the institutions and the psychological and physical environment within which persons must live and grow should be the object of deep concern. Man must work for the development of economic, cultural, social and political life in such a way that these institutions become atmospheres in which liberty, justice, truth and love can thrive.

In all this the historicity of man must be kept in view, for orders which once suited man may no longer do so: the human person grows in self-understanding and deepens in recognition of his needs and potentialities. His moral decisions must be taken in the light of and with a view to this growth. Man's history as well as his nature is the call and summons of God. However, Haering writes, "This principle of structural responsibility does not allow an individual situational ethics or an unprincipled love ethics. Love must always seek for that order of love which is the best possible at the time."[15]

For Haering, then, the ethic of responsibility is the moral side of the response to God's word. It is a response, made in loving and free obedience, to the values which are revealed to man's natural and graced insight. It is directed immediately to fellow men, as persons, for their good and growth in good. It is directed ultimately to God, whose intentions for man are manifested in the values which appear in every historical situation. In short, "Responsibility means the effort to make a choice which can be offered to God as a response to his love as Creator and Redeemer, a choice which builds up the brotherhood of free persons to the glory of God."[16]

CONCLUSION

Haering's work of renewal of moral theology aimed, as we have remarked, to restore the unity of religion and morality which has somewhat disappeared from that discipline in recent centuries. He proposed that an ethic of responsibility might restore "the interpenetration of and distinction of the religious and the moral," so that man's whole life might become "a reply, a response worthy to be offered to God." He has chosen to develop this ethic of responsibility in terms of a personalistic value doctrine which, as we have also noted, shifts away significantly from the nature-finality doctrine of the traditional moral theology.

This attempt at unification of the religious and the moral in the light of the personal-value theory is concentrated in Haering's remarks on the nature of conscience. He describes the moral phenomenon of conscience as the experience of a profound and painful sundering of the inner unity and harmony of the human spirit. This occurs when the spirit freely and deliberately rejects value. It is rent asunder because its very being is orientation toward value. The person in his spiritual affectivity is an ordination to the value of communion in love. Rejection of value, then, is in a very real sense the rejection of its very being.

This experience (and its contrary, conversion to value) centers on the unity and harmony of the person, the I. But because that unity and harmony are correlative to value, and value is the person of the Thou, the experience of conscience reveals the Other who summons and calls the self. Furthermore, the inexorably imperative nature of this summons of value, of the Other, suggests that the metaphor of conscience as the "voice of God" contains a profound truth. Haering writes:

> The greater the dimension of moral depth within conscience, the more significant its religious foundation appears. Inevitably the religious must reveal itself as the ethical deepens and develops, for conscience is in the very roots of its being a religious phenomenon with its ultimate origin in man's likeness to God. The profound depth of conscience is revealed to man only if he

transcends value and its challenge, only if he harkens to that which is beyond, to the Person, holy, insistent, source of all value, only if he discerns in the loud cry of his own soul the echo of a genuine summons from the person who calls.[17]

Conscience binds together the spirit of man, whose likeness to God consists in its profound unity, with the values of the moral life, and the values of the moral life with the insistent, imperative summons of God, the "Value-Person." Man's very religious life, in the broadest sense, will consist in his ordering activity in his own life, his interpersonal relations, his society and his world. In each of these ordering activities his perception of value, made possible by his human faculties, is enhanced by the grace of the Spirit. In virtue of that same grace the ordering activity becomes a fitting reply to God's summon, a form of worship. In this way, Haering's ethics reflect Paul's words to the Corinthians, "your service of almsgiving not only supplies the wants of the saints but overflows into thanksgiving to God" (II Cor 9, 12).

The theology of word and response, upon which Haering bases his theological ethics, draws into one unified theological conception nature and supernature. The ethical doctrine of person and value, central to his fundamental ethics, draws into unity the person as ethical subject and the realm of value. This doctrine of conscience is meant to draw into a unity in the moral consciousness of the believer his religious relation to the living God and his moral efforts to live as a human person in community and history.

The unification of the religious and the moral in theological and ethical conceptions and in the conscience of the believer is Haering's attempt to counter what he and many of his contemporaries consider the drastic split between the supernatural and the natural in Roman Catholic theology. This is, of course, a problem for dogmatics; in the decade preceding Vatican II it was the most hotly-debated theological issue.

But Haering is concerned with the effects of that dogmatic separation in the concepts of moral theology and in the ethical conscience of the believer.

Briefly, that effect has been the practical irrelevance of the supernatural for the Christian's moral life. The doctrine of the supernatural proposes that man has been elevated, in virtue of the redemption of Jesus Christ, to the supernatural plane, that is, into a state of participation by grace in the inner trinitation life of God. He is enabled by grace to perform supernatural acts, namely, the acts of the theological virtues of faith, hope and charity, the object of which is God himself. All the rest of man's activities are raised to this supernatural state; that is, by grace they are directed toward the attainment of his supernatural end, the vision of God, rather than simply to their possible natural end, man's natural happiness.

In the classical formulation of this doctrine, however, the reality of this supernatural life is not considered to impinge in any way on the experiential life of human knowing, willing and acting. Karl Rahner describes the classical doctrine as having taught that: "Supernatural grace is a reality which we know about from the teaching of the Faith, but which is completely outside our experience and can never make its presence felt in our conscious personal life. . . . Thus, in this most widespread view of it grace is a superstructure above man's conscious spiritual and moral life . . . the relationship between nature and grace is thought of as two layers laid very carefully one on top of the other."[18]

The moral theologians who accepted this interpretation of the supernatural tended to reduce to a minimum any reference to the experiential effects of grace in the moral life, to consider man's natural life and the natural law, which he can know by his reason, as the sole field for their considerations. While this natural life was indeed elevated to supernature, this had no immediate empirical effect either on its form or on its content. The ancient dictum *gratia perficit, non destruit naturam* was taken to mean that grace left untouched the structure, form and content of the moral life. The moral life has to be described in terms of obedience to moral laws, either the positive divine law, promulgated in scripture or by the church, or the natural law.

In recent years many theologians have criticized moral theology for these failings. But thirty years ago the famous dogmatic theologian, Yves Congar, pointed to precisely these defects in his review of a widely used manual of moral theology. He praised it for its clarity and judiciousness; then he went on to say:

> One can only be disappointed to see these qualities put at the service of a legalistic, juridical conception of moral theology. The author, if one judges by his book, is a complete stranger to the notion of the supernatural reality of grace, which is conferred upon our souls and develops organically through the theological and infused moral virtues, and whose vital response and natural tendencies constitute and command the life of the Christian. The author does not even mention sanctifying grace among the principles of our moral action.[19]

This is the divorce between dogma and moral, between nature and grace, which Haering faces. However, in *The Law of Christ* he does not undertake a study of the dogmatic problems which contributed to the divorce. He simply sets out, on the basis of his word-response theology and his personal-value ethic, to reshape the moral conceptions of this type of theology. The presence of Christ and our incorporation into him do have experiential effects. Our understanding of what we are doing when we live morally is changed: we are responding to God in our human responsibility. Our perception of values is deepened and sharpened: we see the importance of persons and what contributes to their good. Our motivation is enlivened and redirected: we are moved by God's own love to seek him in all things through the activity of ordering the world in accord with his intention. At each point in his special moral the Imitation of Christ, the presence of enabling, guiding grace, and the primacy of love is emphasized. Thus, we can say that Haering's moral theology employs the notion of responsibility, that is, of response to God, in and through the response given to personal and objective value, in order to make relevant to man's experienced moral life the theology of the supernatural.

The term "responsibility" is given theological employment. Haering uses it to link together his dogmatic affirmations about the word and response and his ethical affirmations about response to value: the human life of responsibility (response to value) is in fact the graced life of responsibility (response to God speaking in value). Within this framework, responsibility can be thought of as an attitude or disposition of the Christian who recognizes the interpenetration of his response to God and his response to men.

This theological use seems far from the philosophical patterns; however, it has some interesting affinities. Haering's theological responsibility says much more than that God judges human action, its intention and motivation, in the manner described in the pattern of attribution and in the theological form of that pattern mentioned in the introduction of this chapter. Still, human action is thought of as taking place in the presence of another, who transcends all human life, who can judge motivation, intention. But this other is not simply judge: he is the creator and inspirer of new life and motivation. He is the one who summons in values and through the voice of conscience. The theological responsibility and the philosophical pattern of attribution are alike in that both involve the presence of another.

Theological responsibility, as Haering uses it, aims at the unification of religious conceptions and motivations and ethical conceptions and motivations. It aims ultimately at the unification of the moral understanding and action of the person, a unification which comes only through correct response to value. The philosophical pattern of appropriation also aims at unification. It is concerned with drawing into a unified self

—the responsible person—the extrinsic and diverse demands on the moral life. It promotes moral decision which arises from unifying consideration, conscientiousness and commitment.

There is a most interesting distinction, however, between the theological term and the philosophical patterns. For Haering, responsibility is the whole of the moral life: it describes not only the subjective condition of the agent or the objective judgment of the observer on that condition. It also is itself directly normative: responsibility *is* response to value, the value of persons; responsibility *is* the ordering activity which this response implies; responsibility *is* answering to the imperative summons of God.

In conclusion, we might say that Haering's use of the term responsibility has a directly theological purpose: to make relevant the theology of the supernatural to the moral life. It expresses something of the pattern of attribution insofar as the moral life takes place in the presence of another—that is, God. It has affinities with the pattern of appropriation in that it expresses the need for unification of moral action in the person. But it does not abstract from the normative; it is itself intended to be a normative conception. Man's responsibility is ultimately "his loving obedience in the imitation of Christ, the echo, the image, the participation in the triune, eternal life of God, in the Word and the response of love."[20]

DIETRICH BONHOEFFER

From God alone there proceeds human action which is not worn away and wasted in conflicts of principle but which springs from the accomplishment of the reconciliation of the world with God, an action which soberly and simply performs what is in accordance with reality, an action of responsibility in deputyship. It is now no longer established in advance what is "Christian" and what is "secular"; both of these are recognized, with their special qualities and with their unity, only in the concrete responsibility of action which springs from the reconciliation which has been effected in Jesus Christ.

ETHICS[1]

When we pass from Bernhard Haering to Dietrich Bonhoeffer, we move from one theological world into another. Each works within the methods and presuppositions of a different theological tradition; each confronts distinct theological and practical problems. Both, however, affirm with equal insistence the centrality of the concept of responsibility in Christian ethics. We will find that this word bears a meaning which is conditioned by its presence within the theological method, presuppositions and problems of each author.

Haering is interested in the renewal of moral theology. He begins this work by positing the theological doctrines which he considers the necessary theological ground for ethics. He then quickly moves into the properly ethical areas of anthropology and values. Bonhoeffer is interested in theological ethics. While in no sense unconcerned about the properly ethical, either in theory or practice, his *Ethics*, as we have them, are almost totally directed to stating the theological grounds for ethics.

Haering's renewal aims to restore to moral theology and to Christian life the relevance of the Catholic doctrine of the supernatural. Responsibility links his theological position with a personalist-value doctrine, designed to impress on the Christian conscience the presence and influence of grace and the example of Christ. Bonhoeffer's restoration of theological ethics is directed toward a unification of the dualities endemic to Lutheran ethics. In the words of the quotation that opens this section, he wishes to erase from ethics the "conflicts of principle which wear away" human action; he intends to deny that one can distinguish in advance between "the Christian and the secular."

Haering posits a theological ground for his value theory: God summons man through created values, recreated in Jesus Christ. Bonhoeffer strives to formulate a theological ground for the radical unity of Law and Gospel, for the work of God's right and left hand; he finds it, again in the words quoted, "in the accomplishment of the reconciliation of the world with God . . . the reconciliation accomplished in Jesus Christ."

Neither Haering nor Bonhoeffer draw upon the two philosophical patterns to any extent. There is some hint of the basic idea of the pattern of attribution—imputability—insofar as both authors reflect the general Christian concept of all human life standing before God's judgment. There is considerably more allusion to the pattern of appropriation—accountability—since both authors are motivated by a similar purpose: to express the Christian's "responsibility" to the world. In order to fulfill this responsibility, he must commit himself to work in and for the world and he must engage in discriminating, deliberate judgments about moral action. Still, neither author enters extensively into a discussion of appropriation. We find in both an attempt to use the word "responsibility" in what Haering calls "its religious sense," that is, a sense which is intimately related to certain theological affirmations. As we have seen, for Haering this is a theology of the relation between God and man in personalist-value terms. We now intend to show that Bonhoeffer elaborates his ethic of responsibility within the context of a theological problem, Lutheran dualism, and within his theological answer to that problem, the reconciliation of all things through the Incarnation of Jesus Christ.

THE THEOLOGICAL PROBLEM

The most fundamental problem for all ethics is the problem of good and evil. It is precisely this problem which initiates theological ethics. For man knows good and evil only because he is severed from his origin in God. Bonhoeffer writes:

Instead of knowing himself solely in the reality of being loved and chosen by God, he must now know himself in the possibility of choosing and of being the origin of good and evil. . . . Man knows good and evil, but because he is not the origin, because he acquires this knowledge only at the price of estrangement from the origin, the good and evil that he knows are not the good and evil of God but the good and evil against God. . . . Man knows good and evil, against God, against his own origin, godlessly and of his own choice, understanding himself according to his own contrary possibilities; and he is cut off from the unifying, reconciling life in God. . . . Man's life is now disunion with God, with men, with things and with himself.[2]

When man falls away from his origin, from life in God where he would know reality and the good, he turns to himself for knowledge. He begins to relate all things to himself in his self-knowledge, and thus he draws all things into the dis-unity which exists between himself and God. "For the man who is in disunion with God, all things are in disunion, what is and what should be, life and law, knowledge and action, idea and reality, reason and instinct, duty and inclination. . . ."[3]

As a consequence of this radical disunity, all ethics, all determination of good and evil, appear hopelessly abstract. This abstractness consists in formulating principles about an isolated man, detached from his historical influences and situation, as well as from his origin and reality in God. Ethics relies on the formulation of rules, on definitions of the good, on concepts of duty, which are severed from reality, the source of good and the real foundation of obligation. Its principles and definitions, then, have no grip on true human life. Ethical man is divided in himself, from his own life, from reality as such. He exists in "irreconcilable cleavage."[4]

Christian theologians have always meditated upon *Genesis* 1-2 and upon *Romans* 7. They have always recognized the "irreconcilable cleavage" in which man, fallen away from God, exists. They have usually portrayed this cleavage in terms of the violent conflict or constant ambivalence of moral life and decision itself. Bonhoeffer, who is well aware of this, wishes to protray its effect for ethics, the understanding of the moral life.

Christian ethics, he claims, has often tended to view the moral life of man in terms of two spheres. It has spoken of the divine, the holy, the supernatural, the Christian, as opposed to the worldly, the profane, the natural, the pagan. Bonhoeffer's own Lutheran theological tradition has done this with insistence and tenacity. The doctrine of Law and Gospel is fundamental to Luther's doctrine of justification; the doctrine of the two kingdoms is fundamental to his ethical thought. But it is not so much Luther as the "pseudo-Lutherans" who harden this dialectic tension into two autonomous spheres of reality.

Formulated in innumerable ways, this doctrine in essence proposes that man's life is lived within a religious sphere which has its own structure and form and within a secular sphere which has quite different laws and imposes quite different demands. Both, of course, are from God; but God is working differently in each and hence makes different demands within each. In one, he calls for faith which justifies; in the other, works which manifest justification. In one, he pours forth love; in the other, he administers justice. In one, he encounters the soul of the individual; in the other, he confronts the orders of society.

In a brief essay entitled, " 'Personal' or 'Real' Ethos," Bonhoeffer objects vigorously to one form of this duality which had achieved some popularity. The Lutheran theologian, Otto Dilschneider, had proposed that "Protestant ethics is concerned with man's personality and with this personality alone. All the other things of this world remain untouched by this Protestant ethos. The things of this world do not enter ethically into the zone of the demands of the ethical imperative."[5] The Christian ethic is directed solely to the creation of Christian dispositions of charity and patience, so that Christian individuals who work within the institutions of society might inspire others, encourage them, try to form new outlooks. But Christian ethics has nothing to say to these institutions themselves. Bonhoeffer responds, "the isolation of the person from the world of things is idealistic and not Christian. Christ does not detach the person from the world of things but from the world of sin; there is a great difference."[6]

Thinking about ethics in terms of these dualities raises crucial theological and ethical problems. Theologically, it casts doubt on the universality of Christ's redemption and undermines the total claim which he asserts over all mankind. It stirs up the tortuous question of the relation of justifying faith to works. Ethically, it tends to establish two autonomous realities, regardless of how strenuously the theologians strive to link them. Each reality has a structure, a purpose, norms and rules quite independent of the other. Man is expected to live in two worlds. The result is either that he lives in one and not the other or that he tries to live in both. If he takes the first option, he will live either a "spiritual existence which has no part in secular existence, or a secular existence which can claim autonomy for itself and can exercise this right of autonomy in its dealings with the spiritual sphere."[7] If he opts for the the second, he "becomes the man of eternal conflict." In both cases the unity of life is destroyed. It falls apart into abstractions—secular vs. Christian, vitality vs. self-denial, the Commandments vs. the Sermon on the Mount, intention vs. consequences. "In consequence of false abstractions, one is now held fast in conflicts which must eternally remain unsolved; practical action cannot pass beyond these conflicts and is wasted and worn away by them."[8] Ethics becomes a barren "knowing of good and evil"; a knowing which has no grip upon life and decision and actions.

Bonhoeffer knew this as more than a speculative theological issue. He felt it as an agonizing personal experience. He had seen his Church paralyzed before the monstrous Nazi evil. He had heard this justified in the name of the solid theological doctrines of Law and Gospel, of two realms, of orders, estates, and callings. He eventually suffered and died because he refused to take a position of evangelical non-involvement. While in prison, he jotted down the practical reflections which correspond to the theological considerations we have just quoted:

> . . . he [the German] could not see that in certain circumstances free and responsible action might have to take precedence over duty and calling. As a compensation he developed in one direction an irresponsible unscrupulousness, and in another an agonizing scrupulosity which invariably frustrated action. Civil courage however can only grow out of the free responsibility of free men. Only now are we Germans beginning to discover the meaning of free responsibility. It depends on a God who demands bold action as the free response of faith, and who promises forgiveness and consolation to the man who becomes a sinner in the process. . . . The responsible man seeks to make his whole life a response to the question and call of God.[9]

This is the problem which dominates Bonhoeffer's ethical thought: how are we to think about ethics so as to overcome the disastrous duality which leads to futile abstractions in our understanding of ethics and to frustration and disintegration of decision and action? Can these dualities be so reconciled that man's *whole* life can be understood as a totality and man's decision and action unified and brought to bear upon his real problems? Bonhoeffer is appalled by an ethic which is neither able nor interested in meeting the real problems. The Christian ethics which he knew, trapped in its abstractions, could speak no significant word to these concrete problems.

It was this that led him to write the shocking words which would probably have opened his completed *Ethics*, "The knowledge of good and evil seems to be the aim of all ethical reflection. The first task of Christian ethics is to invalidate this knowledge."[10]

THEOLOGICAL THESIS

Bonhoeffer's problem is a theological problem. The history of ethics, it is true, contains innumerable statements about the cleavage within man. Christian theology takes this as a datum of revelation and finds its cause in man's disunion from his Creator. The various formulations which perpetuate this cleavage under the guise of ethics are based in theological doctrines: Law and Gospel, faith and works, flesh and spirit, creation and redemption, and so on. While all these formulations are based upon theological doctrine, Bonhoeffer finds it remarkable that they do not seem to square with the prime source of theology, the New Testament:

> Now anyone who reads the New Testament even superficially cannot but notice the complete absence of this world of disunion, conflict and ethical problems. Not man's falling apart from God, from men, from things and from himself, but rather the rediscovered unity, reconcilation, is now the basis of the discussion and the point of decision of the specifically ethical experience. The life and activity of men is not at all problematic or tormented or dark: it is self-evident, joyful, sure and clear.[11]

The most radical problem is therefore to find how these dualistic formulations, which do indeed have some basis in Christian revelation, especially insofar as they reflect the deepest cause of human disunity, can be squared with the more dominant proclamation of the reconciliation of all things in Christ. Does a Christian ethic take as its starting point the disunity or the unity, man in sin or man in grace, Adam or Christ? And wherever it starts, is it doomed to remain in a conflict of opposition? This problem requires a consideration of the starting point of theological ethics and of the consequences of that starting point.

Bonhoeffer addresses himself without trepidation to his question: "The point of departure for Christian ethics," he writes, "is not the reality of one's own self, or the reality of the world; nor is it the reality of standards and values. It is the reality of God as he reveals himself in Jesus Christ."[12] If the problem of ethics is the reconciliation of duality, that problem must be met by turning to the one place where God and man, man and the world, and man within himself are reconciled. This place is "Jesus Christ, the Reconciler of the World."[13]

It is not in the least surprising that Bonhoeffer should choose this as the starting point for his ethics. Commentators have often noted that throughout all of his writing Bonhoeffer expresses a consistent concern for "the concreteness of the message." From the very beginning of his theological career he had been repelled by the abstract, theoretical nature of theology. He sought the "concrete message" and he found it in the doctrine of the incarnation. Eberhard Bethge has said: "Incarnation is at the heart of Bonhoeffer's theology. There cannot be any speculation about God before or outside of this concreteness."[14] If he seeks to reconcile ethical dualities which he sees as futile abstractions, he quite naturally turns to the place where God's message and command becomes concrete: Jesus Christ.

The central message of the New Testament, says Bonhoeffer, is that God loved the world and reconciled it to himself in Christ. This reconciliation is accomplished because the beloved Son became flesh, took upon himself true and total humanity, its suffering and its joy, even its sin. This man Jesus is rejected by his own and is crucified; but God raises him up and glorifies him. Thus, God condemns sin in the flesh of Jesus and accepts man in him. In accepting him, who is our brother in the flesh, he accepts all man and all of human life.

> The man whom God has taken to himself, sentenced and awakened to a new life, this is Jesus Christ. In him it is all mankind. It is ourselves. Only the form of Jesus Christ confronts the world and defeats it. And it is from this form alone that there comes the formation of a new world, a world which is reconciled with God.[15]

Bonhoeffer is careful to state that his theology of incarnation is not simply a *Konscendenztheologie;* it is incarnation in the fullest sense: Jesus Christ as incarnate, crucified and risen God. "In the incarnation we learn of the love of God for creation; in the crucifixion we learn of the judgment of God upon all flesh; and in the resurrection we learn of God's will for a new world."[16] To separate these moments in the life of Jesus Christ into a theology of the cross and a theology of glory is to perpetuate the dualities. It is in the unity of Jesus Christ suffering and risen that God enters into worldly reality: thus the whole of human reality is accepted by God. In the words of a text which occurs frequently to him, Bonhoeffer writes, "Jesus Christ . . . is the 'Yes' which God addresses to the real man. . . . The name of Jesus contains within itself the whole of humanity and the whole of God."[17]

This reconciliation of all things, of all the dualities of human life, is so complete that Jesus can say, "I am the Life." In the unity of his person all human life is contained; he is its origin, its essence, its purpose. Because he is the Life, he is our life; we are not our own. As God has addressed his Yes and No to the man Jesus, so it is addressed to us, to our life. But this does not dissolve our life into two, but gathers it up into the one unity of his life. All human defection, pain, suffering is condemned in him; all human joy, beauty, growth is affirmed in him. Thus God's word is addressed to all creation as it is summed up in the one life of his beloved Son.

Bonhoeffer can now assert, on the basis of this theological affirmation, that "there are not two realities, but only one reality, and that is the reality of God, which becomes manifest in Christ in the reality of the world . . . not two spheres but one sphere of the realization of Christ, in which the reality of God and the World are united."[18] God is ultimate reality. This reality is manifested in the reality of Jesus Christ, who is "real man." But because of the incarnation, all things are taken up in him and thus constitute one reality. The real world is manifested in the reality of Jesus Christ, who reveals the ultimate reality of God.

Jesus is real man: not simply in the anti-Docetist sense, but because he is the man affirmed and accepted by God. Reality is that which is as it ought to be, namely, existing as the object of God's affirmation. The real is that which is accepted by God, that to which God says Yes. Jesus Christ first receives this Yes; then all that is taken up in him is affirmed. Thus, all God's creation, in all of its aspects and its diversity, is apprehended as reality, because it is apprehended in Jesus Christ, with whom the Father is well pleased.

All men, then, being equally the object of the Father's approbation in Jesus Christ, participate in the reality of God and the world. "In Christ we are offered the possibility of partaking in the reality of God and in the reality of the world, but not in the one without the other. . . . Participation in the indivisible whole of the divine reality—this is the sense and purpose of the Christian enquiry concerning good."[19]

It must be admitted that, while Bonhoeffer explicitly treats "the concept of reality" several times in the *Ethics* and deals with it at length in his early work, *Act and Being* (a study of the epistemological presuppositions for theology rather than an ontology), nowhere is the meaning of "reality" made quite clear. He seems to use the term most frequently as the contrary of "abstractness"; for example, "to attempt to understand reality without the real man, Jesus Christ, is to live in an abstraction." In this sense, it seems to be synonymous with "the concrete." Thus, it most often seems to refer to the actual, experienced life of man. But it does not, on that account, mean mere experience, mere facticity.

Bonhoeffer insists that "reality" involves certain relationships. The real is real only in the reality of God, or in the real man, Jesus. Here it is implied that the reality of things is what they are revealed to be in relation to God's revelation.

Hence, Jesus Christ is "real man" because in him both sin and justice are revealed by God's condemnation and justification. The world is real insofar as its fallenness and redemption are revealed in God's judgment and acceptance of it. In virtue of this revelation of its reality, man can live and work in it and judge and accept it for what it is, broken and healed. Even the reality of God is "revelation, the self-witness of the living God."[20] But when all is said, Bonhoeffer never produces any explicit definition of "reality." It might be ventured, however, that his inclination to speak of "reality" in terms of God's action and his preference for "act-ontology" are congenial with the classical Lutheran doctrine of forensic justification.

Man does in fact participate in the reality of the world and in the reality of God through the real man, Jesus Christ. However, his being in Christ is more than a static participation. It is also a becoming, which is called in Scripture "being conformed to Christ." The world must be formed in his likeness and this formation comes only by being drawn into the unique form of him who was made man, crucified, and rose again. This means that man must live as one who is sentenced by God—thus bearing all sufferings—and as one raised up by God, a new man in Christ. But to be conformed to Jesus Christ means to be oneself a "real man," that is, to be before God precisely what he really is, a man. This involves the freedom to be a whole man living a real life in the world.

The formation of Christ in men and in the world is not an abstraction but a concrete action which takes place here and now among us. It takes place in *our own* here and now, that is, in the concrete situation in which we must take decisions and for which we bear responsibilities:

> . . . by our history we are set objectively in a definite nexus of experiences, responsibilities, and decisions from which we cannot free ourselves. . . . In our historical identity, we stand already in the midst of Christ's taking form in a section of human history which he himself has chosen. . . . Ethics as formation, then, means the bold endeavor to speak about the way in which

the form of Jesus Christ takes form in our world . . . concrete judgments and decisions will have to be ventured. . . . Here there are concrete commandments and instructions for which obedience is demanded.[21]

In this last quotation we come upon the word "responsibility." This is the proper place for it to appear in the logic of Bonhoeffer's thought. He has attacked the problem of ethical duality from the standpoint of the doctrine of the incarnation. This doctrine tells him that God becomes real man in Jesus Christ and that all men and all creation are summed up in him. We can then speak of reality as the world and as humanity which is the object of God's approbation in Jesus Christ. We can affirm that all men participate in the unity of God and creation in Christ. We can proclaim that this participation can be furthered by conformation of the world to Christ.

This conformation is concrete, taking place in actual decision in real historical situations: this is the "realization, the making real, among God's creatures of the revelational reality of God in Christ."[22] In fact, "After Christ has appeared, ethics can have but one purpose, the achievement of participation in the reality of the fulfilled will of God."[23] We are made participants in this reality through Christ's fulfillment of the will of God, whereby we are reconciled. We ourselves participate in this reality through our realization of the will of God, which is our responsibility.

In all of this, we are still plagued by the word "reality." Ethics is concerned with "the realization of the revelational reality of God." The revelational-reality of God is his judgment and justification of the world. To "realize" this in human action would seem to mean that the Christian's judgments and conduct must attempt to expose the sinfulness of the world and yet accept it insofar as he must, in order to work toward the ordering of life in accord with the essential characteristics of those worldly institutions which are re-established in Christ (the mandates) and the forms of the preserved life (the natural). It is acting in such a way that the world, in its god-lessness, can be reconciled to God.

"Responsibility" is the word which describes the kind of life which these theological affirmations imply.

> We give the name "responsibility" to the life in all its aspects as a response to the life of Jesus Christ as the "yes" and "no" to our life. This concept of responsibility refers to the concentrated totality and unity of the response to the reality which is given in Jesus Christ. . . . Responsibility means, therefore, that the totality of life is pledged and that our life becomes a matter of life and death.[24]

Bonhoeffer says that responsibility means that we respond with our entire life to the word of God addressed to our entire life. In the light of the theological problem which he has posed—the problem of duality—and of the theological solution he has offered—the Incarnation—it is possible to understand the meaning of "respond with entire life." The word of God is the word of reconciliation. This not only reconciles man to God, but reconciles all things and all men before God. The word is not addressed to portions of life, one word being spoken in one sphere and another in another sphere. God speaks one word which encounters the whole of human life. Thus, our hearing of that word and our obedience to it is made with our "entire life." That is, we do not have a divided allegiance, or two standards of obedience, or two ethics. We are not at this moment Christian and at another moment secular. Responsibility means, first of all, that our ethics, our response to God's word, engages our whole being in one world and in one field of action.

This affirmation of responsibility is intended to counter speculative and practical dualism. In the first place, it denies that there are two commands of God to man. God does not confront man in Jesus and in the Gospel, ordering him to live a life of private selflessness, and then confront him again in the order of the world and in the Law to command public dutifulness. He meets him only once, in Jesus Christ, in the concrete command, which demands responsible action and decision in the concrete world of the mandates and of his vocation, and of the "here and now." Secondly, Bonhoeffer's position counters the effect of this "double command" ethics, the division of the field of man's action into two realms that grow into autonomous realms, with laws and exigencies that are quite unrelated. This autonomy leads to the paralysis of decision, lack of seriousness, frustration of action, and refusal to criticize or condemn.

On the other hand responsible action, while it recognizes that there are ambiguities and contradictions within the field of its action, moves resolutely into the problems posed to man's real life. It may contract guilt in so doing, but it is irrevocably committed to the one world of man's real life. Finally, Bonhoeffer attacks that moral purity and self-justification which carefully skirts all taint of "guilt" by taking refuge in one or another of the realms behind a law or in an office or a vocation. Such moral isolationism allows the growth of autonomous institutions which have monstrously evil effects on human life while the isolationist stands aside, assured of his own purity.

It appears, then, that the idea of responsibility is introduced for polemical purposes. It is invoked as a refutation of ethical dualism and as a remedy for its consequences. The stress is upon response with the *"totality* of one's life." It is, first and foremost, an incitement to "get involved." It does not at this point say *how* one is to get involved or *what* one is to do. In this, it differs greatly from Haering's conception. Haering intends to replace a human nature-finality approach with a person-value approach to ethics. The person is called to action by values, which are specific goods to be realized in action. Thus, Haering's responsibility involves a response to definite value in definite acts. Bonhoeffer's stress at this point in his argument reminds us of the existentialist emphasis on engagement that we saw in the pattern of appropriation: responsibility means free commitment of oneself to act, regardless of what the act might be.

However, Bonhoeffer cannot say "regardless of what the act might be." The Christian knows clear limits and definitions of responsible action.

> God and our neighbor, as they confront us, in Jesus Christ, are the limits . . . and the origin of responsible action. Irresponsible action may be defined precisely by saying that it disregards this limit, God and our neighbor. Responsible action derives its unity and ultimately its certainty from the fact that it is limited in this way by God and our neighbor.[25]

Bonhoeffer must now set forth the limits of responsible action, the positive and normative determinations of what one must do to act as real man in the real world. He does this by elucidating a doctrine of the command of God.

"We live by responding to the word of God which is addressed to us in Jesus Christ. Since this word is addressed to our entire life, the response, too, can only be an entire one."[26] This word of God is not merely a justifying word; it is also a commanding word. It is the command of God: "the total and concrete claim laid to man by the merciful and holy God in Jesus Christ." This command embraces the totality of life; it forbids, but also permits; it binds but also sets free. It comes to us in concrete form, addressed to us in concrete historical moments.

Bonhoeffer's words recall Barth's doctrine of the command of God. However, Bonhoeffer adds some considerations which make a striking difference in this doctrine. He says that God's command is a permission, as does Barth. But it is permission for man to live in the world as a man. "The purpose of the commandment lies not in the avoidance of transgression and not in the torment of ethical conflict and decision, but in the freely accepted, self-evident life in the Church, in marriage, in the family, in work and in the state."[27] The word of God addressed to man in Jesus Christ was the "Yes" which accepts all creation, which initiates the "really real." That same word is a commandment which frees man to act in that real world, but it frees him to act responsibly.

The emphasis in Barth's well-known conversion of the Divine Command to permission is on God's granting to man the freedom to correspond and attest joyfully to the grace which has been granted him in his election to Covenant-partnership in Jesus Christ. God's permission freeing man is identical with his justifying of man; man's own freedom is identical with his justification. Bonhoeffer, however, stresses the validation of the penultimate which comes from the claim that God lays on the whole life of man, a claim manifested in the mandates. If for Barth God's permission frees man to live before him as a beloved son, for Bonhoeffer it frees man to live in the world and engage in the fulness of life. It is, as he says, "the warrant for ethical discourse," that is, the authorization which permits man to enter into the full relationships of human society.

All of these relationships form the unity which is human life in Christ. But in this unity of the one life in Christ, God's command confronts man in four distinct forms: the mandates which concern man's life in the church, in marriage, in work and in the state.

A mandate is:

> a concrete divine commission which has its foundation in the revelation of Christ and which is evidenced in scripture; it is the legitimation and warrant for the execution of a definite divine commandment, the conferring of divine authority upon an earthly agent . . . it implies the claiming, the seizure and the formation of a definite earthly domain by the divine commandment.[28]

Bonhoeffer has chosen his word well. By avoiding the classical terms—"orders," "estates"—and substituting "mandate," he has rejected the concept of a given, static institution from which ethical rules can be deduced, a structure which can become an autonomous sphere. He has introduced the concept of a commission, given to man to do a particular work, to undertake a certain duty. In other words, a mandate confers responsibilities. The mandates concern life in the church, in marriage, in work and in the state.

The mandates indicate the sectors of responsibility, or the "loci" in which responsibility is executed. But while these are sectors or portions of life, they are united, not only by the one command of God but by being in the "one world." "The world is the sphere of concrete responsibility which is given to us in and through Jesus Christ."[29] Although Bonhoeffer does not actually develop the idea until the *Letters and Papers,* we can glimpse here the meaning of his famous "worldliness." The command of God directs and permits man to act in the real world, the one world of things and institutions. He does not dwell in this world as a stranger, or make occasional forays into it to "sanctify" it, or merely suffer it as penance for his sinfulness. This real world is the sphere where he is to be a man and a Christian. This is the world which is to be conformed to Jesus Christ. Thus all of its conditions and exigencies affect Christian ethical concerns; there are no true Christian ethical concerns which do not meet these exigencies and demands.

The structure of the responsible life, then, consists in a life bound both to God and to man (because God himself has bound these up in Jesus Christ) and a life which is free (because God has freed man to live in the world). Life bound to God and man is called deputyship. Our life, Jesus Christ, was deputy for God in the world and deputy for man, in taking upon himself their sinfulness. Thus, the Christian lives in deputyship, representing God before men and selflessly taking their needs upon himself. He is thus concretely inserted into the real world of concrete relationships. He acts in conformity with reality in that world. That is, aware that this world is itself in Christ, he meets all its demands and exigencies. He acts with full accounting of the limits of his own creatureliness and of God's grace. He commits the deed, done with full seriousness, to the ultimate judgment of God's grace.

The Christian is not only inserted into the world of human relationships but also into a world of things and institutions. These also have been caught up and reconciled in the real man, Jesus Christ. The Christian now licensed to work with things in the real world must do so responsibly. This responsibility implies, first, that things, institutions, causes, sciences, and so forth, must be seen in their "essential, original, and purposive relation to God and man."[30] They are all meant to serve the person and not to dominate him. Second, responsible action with regard to things requires searching out the law of being which is "inherent in each thing, whether it is a natural object or a product of the human mind."[31] Each thing has its proper laws of growth, structure and process, which cannot be ignored without detriment to the thing itself and to the person who uses it.

This perspective makes it possible to re-introduce into Protestant ethics the concept of "the natural." Bonhoeffer defines the natural as "the form of life preserved by God for the fallen world and directed towards justification, redemption and renewal through Christ."[32] In its formal aspect it is known through Christ and validated in Christ; in its content it has its own relative independence and structure and is known by reason, the consciousness of the natural. The natural is the form of life and conditions for life which are not established by the will of any individual, but which preexist human determination. It consists in the inner laws of each being that indicate the sort of activities whereby that being shall be preserved and interdict activities which will both destroy that being and the agent himself. Bonhoeffer discusses the application of the "natural" to the ethical questions of preservation of life, of suicide, of reproduction.

Man acts in freedom. He is freed to act in the world, but

he must do so "with due consideration for the given human and general conditions and for the relevant questions of principle. . . . he must examine the motives, the prospects, the value and purpose of his action."[33] In all this he is aware that the decision he takes and the deed he does is truly his own. He is not protected by any law; he cannot take refuge in any principles, which might justify his inaction or his failure. But, because he is acting under God's command, he acts also under God's grace. Thus he can accept guilt for his failure and for the ambiguities of the results and motivations of his action because he commits his action to God.

Finally, just as the world and the mandates designate the total field and the sectors of responsibility, the final responsible decision and deed is done in the most concrete circumstances. Each man lives surrounded by a "limited field of accomplishments." He finds himself involved in concrete relationships of work, interests, social and cultural contacts, and so forth. It is precisely in the place where he is that God's call in Jesus Christ meets him and summons him to responsible action. Bonhoeffer rescues the classical notion of vocation from the sanctioning of the *status quo* which it has in Lutheranism and from the flight from the world it connotes in Catholicism. He considers that vocation means the summons to act responsibly in the concrete place where one is. This may require leaving that place or criticizing it when one discovers that responsible action is impossible. This is recognized when one sees, after serious consideration, that one is unable to meet the demands of true responsibility, namely, the total response of the whole man to the whole of reality. Thus a sphere of accomplishments which distorts or segments one's total responsibility to Christ must be rejected.

CONCLUSION

By responsibility Bonhoeffer means, then, that a Christian may and must work in the world and take account of its needs, its nature and its possibilities. This is justified and commanded on the basis of the theological doctrines of incarnation, reconciliation, and justification, as Bonhoeffer has interpreted them. Responsibility implies that if the Christian may and must work in the world, he will appropriate and, if necessary, critically re-examine the principles and standards for action of the real world. Thus he must look to "the natural" for the inner laws of being which can guide his decision and action. He will then be acting "in accord with reality." But it is clear that he does so because that reality is "in Christ." To act in accord with reality is to act in accord with Christ.

Finally, responsibility refers not only to a permission to engage in the world and to use its principles and take account of its exigencies. It also has the force of an imperative. Man is responsible because the word of God which accepts the real world in Jesus Christ is also a command to "realize" Christ in the world. Christ, or the revelational reality of God in Christ, is realized by acting and judging in accord with reality. These decisions and judgments, because they are limited by creatureliness and sinfulness will be beset with ambiguity and failures. However, they are taken in Christ and undertaken under God's command, and so may be committed to his merciful judgment.

Thus the one command of God accepts the world as a totality and commands man's action within it as a totality. There is one set of laws for the guidance of action, the laws of reality assumed in Christ, expressed in the natural, diversified in the mandates and concentrated in a personal vocation. There is the risk of guilt and uncertainty, but the ventures of decision are made within assurance of the ultimate justification of God.

In this scheme, we have a set of definite theological doctrines: incarnation, reconciliation, participation and conformation, justification. They are interpreted and brought into focus in a "secular" ethical conception, responsibility. Although it is risky to trace the genealogy of ideas, it seems likely that

Max Weber's use of the term had impressed Bonhoeffer. Weber was a personal friend of Bonhoeffer's family; Bonhoeffer's work, especially his *Sanctorum Communis,* shows considerable familiarity with Weber's writings. While he does not explicitly attribute his use of responsibility to Weber's influence, the Weberian connotations can easily be discerned.

Weber contrasts the idea of an "ethic of responsibility" with "an ethic of ultimate ends." The ethic of ultimate ends contains absolute injunctions and interdicts any use of means which would compromise those absolutes. Its principal concern is with the moral purity of intention and it almost necessarily requires a withdrawal from the ambiguities and contaminations of worldly affairs. An ethic of responsibility, on the other hand, engages in a search for the best available means within a highly deficient world. It is principally concerned with the consequences of action, knowing that it is sometimes necessary to use violence to effect peace. It is aware that action must be a perpetual manipulation and balancing of the evil and the good in every decision. The vocation of politics, concerned with real men in the real world, can be followed successfully only by responsible men, men with "the trained relentlessness in viewing the realities of life and the ability to face such realities and to measure up to them inwardly."[34]

Bonhoeffer is looking for an ethical conception that will tell Christians that they must work in the real world. They must take account of its needs, its exigencies and enter into its ambiguities. The doctrine of the incarnation provides a theological justification. It rejects the dualities of "Christian" vs. "world," "sacred" vs. "secular" and converts into relative and polemical contraries such distinctions as law and gospel. Given this theological stance, it is necessary to find an ethical notion which expresses the importance and value of involvement in the world. Weber's notion was ready-made. It does for the world of political life what Bonhoeffer wishes to do for religious life: it insists that the ethic relevant to these lives must have a sense of reality and immediacy. It urges engagement rather than withdrawal, consideration of contingencies rather than a priori absolutes; it allows for uncertainties and guilt instead of demanding an absolutely untainted conscience. As Weber wrote, "No ethics in the world can dodge the fact that in numerous instances the attainment of 'good' ends is bound to the fact that one must be willing to pay the price of using morally dubious means or at least dangerous ones— and facing the possibility or even the probability of evil ramifications."[35]

But it is precisely here, in the Weberian conception of the necessary contraction of guilt in responsible action, that Bonhoeffer anticipates a serious objection. Is it not true, he asks, "that the high authority of conscience . . . is unwilling to sacrifice its integrity to any other value, and therefore refuses to incur guilt for the sake of another man."[36] His answer to this provides an interesting contrast with Haering and reveals forcefully the import of his doctrine of responsibility.

Bonhoeffer and Haering define conscience in almost identical terms. Haering writes, "conscience [is] the spiritual instinct for self preservation arising from the urge for complete unity and harmony."[37] Bonhoeffer says, "Conscience . . . makes itself heard as the call of human existence to unity with itself . . . it protests against a doing which imperils the unity of this being with itself."[38]

For Haering, as we have seen, conscience calls the self to the harmony of its own existence by recognizing the call of value, and ultimately of the Highest Value-Person. Conscience is the center of responsibility, because it is the source of response to value. Bonhoeffer, on the contrary, contrasts conscience and responsibility. While conscience calls to unity, it is to unity with *self* that it calls: "the call of conscience has its origin and its goal in the autonomy of a man's own ego."[39] Thus it warns man against the surrender of the self for the sake of the other; against all that might imply, as does the summons of Christ, loss of one's self.

Yet Christ, who was without sin, became guilty and shared in the fellowship of human guilt. The Christian, then, must follow Christ into this fellowship, taking upon himself the guilt which is inevitable consequence of involvement with the realities of human life and institutions. The Christian conscience is liberated from laws of its own finding, freed to act in the responsible actions which require entry into the solidarity of human guilt.

Bonhoeffer clearly denies that he advocates acting against one's conscience. In fact, even the liberated conscience must respect the natural conscience, which "contains the fundamental features of the law of life." He simply wishes to stress that acceptance of responsibility involves acceptance of the guilt of failure and of evil consequences. He notes that responsible action must often decide not simply between right and wrong but between right and right, wrong and wrong.

Conscience and responsibility are in conflict. But Bonhoeffer does not at all mean that man can now "sin freely." He means that the "self-righteousness of high-principled action," that is, the integrity and purity of one's own conscience, is no longer ultimate. Christ, Lord of conscience, is ultimate. He himself undertook, and summons his disciples to undertake, the burden of guilt. "It is precisely in the responsible acceptance of guilt that a conscience which is bound solely to Christ will best prove its innocence . . . the responsible man becomes guilty without sin."[40] These are the words of a man who entered the conspiracy against Hitler's life, which one who held strictly to the ethical dualism of law and gospel could never do "in good conscience." Before he died, he wrote, "The meaning of free responsibility . . . depends on a God who demands bold action as the free response of faith, and who promises forgiveness and consolation to the man who becomes a sinner in the process."[41]

Bonhoeffer, like Haering, gives responsibility theological employment. The doctrine of the incarnation and reconciliation abolishes the "dual morality" of law and gospel. Man's life of faith and his life of action are drawn into a totality. To say that man is responsible is to say that he has been freed to enter into the world and to work for the realization of Christ therein; it also means that he is bound, obliged to do so. Thus, while Haering wished to link the human value and value response to the Source of value by the language of responsibility, Bonhoeffer wishes to link the command of God to the real world. The command of God demands "true worldliness . . . taking life in one's stride, with all its duties and problems, its successes and failures, experiences and helplessness."[42]

This theological responsibility has affinities with the philosophical patterns. Like the pattern of attribution, it suggest action performed in the presence of another who judges and estimates that action. This judge reads the heart and scrutinizes the motives. But he judges not the discrete act but the whole life: the question is not whether this act was done intentionally, deliberately, but whether this total life was lived fully in responsibility, that is, engaged in the realities of life. Like the pattern of appropriation it suggests the need to unify action into a responsible self. Bonhoeffer several times stresses the importance of intelligence, discernment, due consideration of the given human conditions, of questions of principle, examination of motives, value and purpose of action. But this care for considered, conscientious action is not designed merely for the integration of the autonomous self; it is all committed to God: I am not my own, but my Savior's.

> In self-examination, the Christian's gaze is not directed away from Jesus Christ and towards his own self; it remains entirely on Jesus Christ since Jesus Christ is already present and active within us; since he belongs to us, the question can and must certainly now arise, whether and how in our daily lives we belong to him, believe in him and obey him.[43]

Thus we find in Bonhoeffer, as we did in Haering, that responsibility, employed for a theological purpose, goes considerably beyond the philosophical patterns. The theological use has distinctly normative overtones. Responsibility is not simply a prolegomenon to normative ethics, but suggests weighty obligations. Responsible life *is* life bound to God and to man; responsible action *is* correspondence with reality; responsibility *is* deputyship: standing for men before Christ and standing for Christ before men.

H. RICHARD NIEBUHR

When my world is divided into two domains, the natural and the supernatural, or the physical and the spiritual, or the secular and the religious, in which different powers are at work, and different meanings and patterns of action are evident, then I have two selves. But insofar as in [faith] trust I acknowledge that whatever acts upon me, in whatever domain of being, is part of, or participates in, one ultimate action, then though I understand nothing else about the ultimate action, yet I am now one. . . . To respond to the ultimate action in all responses to finite actions means to seek one integrity of self amidst all the integrities of scientific, political, economic, educational, and other cultural activities; it means to be one responding self amidst all the responses of the roles being played, because there is present to the self the One other beyond all the finite systems of nature and society.

THE RESPONSIBLE SELF[1]

We remarked that the passage from Haering to Bonhoeffer might seem a trip into another theological world. But we discovered that the Catholic moralist, who had read Scheler, and the Lutheran theologian, who had read Weber, were united by a common concern. Both Haering's attack on the naturalism of scholastic moral theology and Bonhoeffer's attack on the dualism of Lutheran theological ethics were intended to call the living Christian person into confrontation with his real world. Now we pass again into what seems a very different theological world: that of an American who acknowledged that he was more indebted "philosophically to G. H. Mead than to Aristotle; theologically to Jonathan Edwards than to Thomas Aquinas."[2] However, as is fitting for one who appreciated dialogue, H. Richard Niebuhr's discussion of responsibility makes a perfect response in the conversation with Haering and Bonhoeffer.

Haering proposes his "ethic of responsibility" as an emendation of the nature-teleology of scholastic moral theology. Bonhoeffer's "responsible life" is a revision of the deontology of Lutheran law-gospel ethics. Niebuhr offers his "responsible self" as an alternative to both teleology and deontology. He forces us to ask whether the teleology and deontology, from which Haering and Bonhoeffer only partially extricate themselves, can bear the weight of an ethic of responsibility.

Furthermore, in his *Christ and Culture* Niebuhr had sketched the ethical approaches of "the Church of the middle." The "synthetic approach," represented by Aquinas, draws Christ and human culture together into a great synthesis by means of a universal teleology, whereby God, creator and redeemer, directs all life to himself as final end. The "dualist approach," represented by Martin Luther, contrasts the world of sin under law to the life of faith under grace: man lives in obedience to law and in the obedience of faith. The "conversionist approach" sees the Lord of history transforming all things into the praise of his glory by seeking and empowering human response. Niebuhr, it has been said, "tended (despite his explicit disavowal) . . . toward conversionism as the most adequate Christian answer . . . and expression of the meaning of God in Christ in relation to culture and morals."[3]

Niebuhr's description of a "conversionist ethic" is written in terms that have become familiar to us in Haering and Bonhoeffer.

> Man the creature, working in a created world, lives, as the conversionist sees it, under the rule of Christ and by the creative power and ordering of the divine Word . . . He finds room

for affirmative and ordered response on the part of created man to the creative and ordering work of God . . . for the conversionist, history is the story of God's mighty deeds and of man's response to them.[4]

It appears to us that Haering and Bonhoeffer, as they renew and revise their own ethical traditions, move gradually toward the positions which Niebuhr calls "conversionism."

Thus, H. Richard Niebuhr enters our study at a most opportune moment, as a third voice in the conversation about responsibility. His remarks respond quite directly to the Catholic theologian who is dealing with a nature-finality ethic and to the Lutheran theologian who is contending with law-gospel dualism.

RESPONSIBILITY AS NORMATIVE

The last work of H. Richard Niebuhr's long career was *The Responsible Self*. In it he examined explicitly a theme which had been consistently developing in his thought. It has been said that "in all problems of natural religion and Christian faith Niebuhr's primary convictions are those of the primacy of God and man's absolute dependence upon him . . . in and through all other relations man is fundamentally related to an ultimate 'Other' who confronts him at once as the haunting enemy of his natural religion and as the bestower of grace."[5] This is the theme of *Radical Monotheism:* "for radical monotheism the value-center is neither the closed society nor the principle of such a society but the principle of being itself; its reference is to no one reality among the many but to One beyond all the many, whence all the many derive their being, and by participation in which they exist."[6] It is the theme of the paragraph from *Responsible Self* with which we began this section "to respond to the ultimate action in all responses to finite actions . . ."

When he finally seizes upon the term and the concept of responsibility as a fitting expression of this problem, he explains, "Responsibility affirms: 'God is acting in all actions upon you. So respond to all actions upon you as to respond to his action'."[7] Here is the familiar "indicative- imperative" pattern of the Christian message. How does Niebuhr conceive of their relationship? What is the ethical import of "so respond . . ."?

We will take up the second question first. Christian theology has sometimes interpreted the "response" in a purely religious way: man's response to God is his worship, his faith. At other times the ethical response has been stressed: man's response is his obedience, his sacrifice. However, the Scripture uses a phrase which joins the religious and the ethical: man's response is his "obedience of faith" (Rom 1, 5). Likewise, Niebuhr never separated the religious from the ethical in his account of faith. "Faith is the attitude and action of confidence in, and fidelity to, certain realities as the sources of value and the objects of loyalty."[8] Faith is elicited by the revelation of God. This revelation is in Jesus Christ. "When Christians refer to Jesus Christ as the revelation of God they do not or ought not have less than the three notes of faith in mind, the note that the valuing, saving power in the world is the principle of being itself; that the ultimate principle of being gives and maintains worth; that they have been called upon to make the cause of that God their cause."[9] The revelation of God in Jesus Christ is the demonstration of God as faithful, steadfast, true.

It would not be enough for man to respond to this revelation by simply saying, "Yes, that is true." The revelation is "an event which elicits the confidence of selves in their ultimate environment and calls upon them as free selves to decide for the universal cause . . . the human response to such revelation is the development of integrated selfhood."[10] Thus, faith is not simply an acceptance of the truth of God's revelation, nor an act or attitude which leaps beyond the world of a man's experience. It is not even an understanding of one's self before God.

Integration of the self in the presence of the First Person is not only an affair of the practical understanding of all events that happen to the self or its community. The elicited trust and loyalty of radical monotheism express themselves in the positive response to such events. The radical faith becomes incarnate insofar as every reaction to every event becomes a response in loyalty and confidence to the One who is present in all such events.[11]

The response, then, must be an ethical one. "Responsibility" suggests the ethical connotations of the response of faith. Thus, in the *Responsible Self* Niebuhr investigates the meaning of responsibility, first as a general human phenomenon, then as interpreted by Christian faith.

"All life has the characteristic of responsiveness."[12] The "life sciences," physiology, biology, psychology, sociology, have found in action-response patterns a most fruitful instrument for the understanding of their proper phenomena. In man's personal life he is constantly engaged in "the conversation of life," in which he forms his response in accord with the questions which are put to him. Is it not possible to analyze man's ethical life in terms of this model?

Ethics, says Niebuhr, seeks a twofold end: knowledge of self and, consequently, guidance in the activities of decision, choice, commitment. Two great models have dominated the ethical understanding of man's life: man as maker and man as citizen. The former conceives of human life as material before the creative mind and hand of the artist, who shapes it in the light of an ideal form, his ultimate purpose; the latter considers life as surrounded by systems of inexorable laws, of nature and society, to which the agent must obediently bow. Niebuhr suggests that a third image is emerging today: man as engaged in a dialogue, a conversation in which nature, society, and his fellows pose questions to which he must respond fittingly. "The word [responsibility] gives us a new symbol with which to understand not a really well-known phenomenon or an old idea, but the actuality of that human existence of which other aspects came into view when we employed the older symbols . . ."[13]

Man the maker, man the citizen, and man the responder are "root metaphors," that is, symbolic expressions based upon "synecdochic analogies": one particular aspect of human experience is employed to elucidate and interpret the whole of experience. These symbolic forms are the means whereby men distinguish, organize and relate experience. They make it possible for us to apprehend and understand ourselves. As "root metaphors" they serve as the ground for "world hypotheses," constructions of insights and understandings through which we seek to understand the meaning of human life.

This is metaphysics in the grand style, or perhaps premetaphysics. However, each of these symbolic forms has a more precise counterpart in moral philosophy. The image of man the maker gives rise to the teleological theory of norms; that of man the citizen to the deontological theory of norms; and that of man the responder to what Niebuhr once (and only once) called a *cathekontic* ("fitting") theory of norms.

Theory or doctrine of norms plays a very specific role within ethics. Niebuhr, as we have seen, refers to the "double purpose of ethics: to obey the ancient and perennial commandment, 'know thyself'; and to seek guidance for our activity as we decide, choose, commit ourselves and otherwise bear the burden of our necessary human freedom." This double purpose is pursued by three sorts of inquiries. "Know thyself" requires an investigation of the subject on whom moral demands are laid and who can accept or reject them: a doctrine of the moral subject. "Guidance for activity" requires investigation of that which activity aims to accomplish: a doctrine of value or the good; and an investigation of the norms which direct action to its good: a doctrine of norms. Norms are, to use the ancient language, *mensura et regula*, the measures and standards whereby actions are tailored so as to be called morally right actions. They are expressions or statements, sometimes quite precise (rules), sometimes very general (principles), which all say essentially: in this sphere, act in this or that way if you wish your action to be right and yourself and your accomplishment good.

The title, *The Responsible Self,* suggests that Niebuhr is undertaking an inquiry of the first type, a description of the characteristics of the moral subject. The book has been described as "a phenomenological analysis of man's moral existence . . . the basic pattern, the morphology of the life and action of the Christian community in the moral sphere— the way of thinking and acting that is true to its character as a community of men before God."[14] Certainly this book is not a handbook of rules; it is rather the critical analysis which must precede any discussion of prescription and regulation.

However, the phenomenological and descriptive intent does not preclude a statement of norms. For the doctrine of norms deals with the standards and measures whereby action can be called morally right. If one wishes to describe right action, one must present the standards whereby they are right. Niebuhr will say that right action is "fitting action" and he will say that "fitting action is action that fits into a total interaction as response and anticipation of further response . . ."[15] He will then indicate how—that is, in accord with what principles—action can be made to fit into the total interaction. Indeed, Niebuhr compares his "fitting response" to Aristotle's mean, which is certainly the norm and measure of action. We claim to find, then, in Niebuhr's *Responsible Self* a doctrine of norms for responsible action. Admittedly, they are not specific rules and regulations of a moral code; they are rather the "first principles" of morality: the most general standards to which human action must conform in order to be right and good.

THE DEFINITION OF RESPONSIBILITY

Niebuhr writes, "the idea or pattern of responsibilty may summarily and abstractly be defined as the idea of an agent's action as response to an action upon him in accordance with his interpretation of the latter action and with his expectation of response to his response; and all of this in a continuing community of agents."[16]

This definition contains four elements: response, interpretation, anticipation of response (accountability) and continuing community of agents (social solidarity). Response is, presumably, a descriptive category: all human action, including moral action, is by its very nature response to stimulus. This means at the very least that it is impossible to explain a human action without reference to some antecedent action or event to which it is in some way related. However, it is not called a "moral action or the action of a moral self" unless it is response to interpreted action. Moral response is not merely reaction. It is mediated through intelligence, which compares, contrasts, defines, and so on. Again, the moral action is not only a response to a previous action which it interprets: it is also formed in anticipation of a future action which will be stimulated by our own response. It is made "in anticipation of answers to our answers." Finally, the response issues out of a consistent scheme of interpretations in the agent and in the community of agents in which action and response take place. Otherwise it would be impossible either to interpret the action or to anticipate the reply.

Before we examine these elements of responsibility we must note the context in which response is made. Man responds within society and within a history. He responds within a society because he comes into being and comes to know himself within a community of others.

> To say that the self is social is not to say that it finds itself in need of fellow men in order to achieve its purposes, but that it is born in the womb of society as a sentient, thinking, needful being with certain definitions of its needs and with the possibility of experience of a common world. It is born in society as mind and as moral being, but above all it is born in society as self.[17]

The moral self responds within a history because it is "time-ful": a being whose present does not stand alone, but contains its past and its future. The past is inscribed deeply in this self; but the self lives toward the future by its purposiveness, expectations, anticipations, hopes. "The self existing always in a now is one that knows itself as having been and as going into existence and into encounter."[18] These two dimensions of the moral self, community and history, are not accidental features from which the moral self can be abstracted; they are essential constituents of its moral selfhood.

These reflections upon man's sociability and historicity are not original. They are, as Niebuhr admits, variations on a theme often played in Western moral philosophy. However, he does transpose it into a new key when he insists that the moral response must be a response to the *universal* community, in a *total* history. He writes,

> In the ethics of the fitting we find ourselves led to the notion of universal responsibility, that is, of a life of responses to actions which is always qualified by our interpretations of these actions as taking place in a universe, and by the further understanding that there will be a response to our actions by representatives of the universal community. . . .[19]

Niebuhr notes that when we seek to make a fitting response we not only respond to that which acts upon us, but also to a third. This third, which may be a cause to which we give our loyalty, an understanding of inanimate nature, or a particular reference group within our society, defines and makes possible our interaction.

There is in each dialogue of action and response this transcending reference to the third. Every particular response points beyond itself and its immediate object. Niebuhr insists that "there seem to be indications in the whole of the responsive, accountable life of man of a movement of self-judgment and self-guidance which cannot come to rest until it makes its reference to a universal other, and a universal community, which that other both represents and makes his cause."[20]

As man lives in community and in history, he not only responds so as to sustain that community and continue that history. He is also called upon to enlarge the community and the history in which he lives until it is universal. His actions are to be "fitting," not only insofar as they fit into a single process of interaction, but insofar "as they fit into the total movement, the whole conversation. We seek to have them fit into the whole as a sentence fits into a paragraph in a book."[21]

It should be obvious, however, that our responses do not in fact have this universal character. We are puzzled when we are told to "respond to the ultimate other, in the universal community, in the totality of history." While the very process of action and response may be triadic—of its nature involving a reference to a third—while this continual self-transcending reference may drive man's responses out beyond the immediate dialogue, still it is only through "self-judgment and self-guidance" that the actual process takes place. Put more simply, this movement does not simply happen: we must *make* it happen.

RESPONSIBILITY AND REINTERPRETATION

The movement toward universal community can, it seems, be blocked and closed off. The reason is clear: Man's moral life appears to be an "ethics of defense." He finds himself constantly threatened by physical, psychological, social and cultural destruction. Every action which bears upon him can be seen as a threat to his existence and he tends to respond to every action in terms of self-defense.

> Our actions are those of men who try to do what they think is fitting, in order that they may maintain status in a society which they believe threatens them with isolated existence, with a kind of social death; or who must gather wealth, prestige or righteousness in order that they may be remembered, be not relegated to the realm of those who might as well not have been or otherwise end in nothingness.[22]

This "ethics of defense" results in the phenomenon of polytheism or henotheism, which Niebuhr has described so brilliantly in *Radical Monotheism*. Man is led in his effort to survive to center his life in certain "values" which he feels can protect him or over which he feels that he can exercise control. Thus he has either many centers of value, which are "gods," the objects of human trust; or one such center in which, although it is only finite, he seeks to locate all his devotion. The continuing process of transcendence, which is natural to the dialogue of action and response, is choked off and divided into finite centers of value.

The transcendence of dialogue, while "natural" to it, can be stifled. On the other hand, the concentration in finite centers of value, also in some sense "natural," can be countered. Man, naturally responsive and naturally defensive, is also free. His freedom consists precisely in his ability to interpret. He can reinterpret his past and the possibilities of his future. He can understand that his responses are taking place in a context quite different than he had suspected. Our recollections of the past are not simply brute facts, but interpretable events; likewise our predictions of the future grow out of the possibilities which our interpretation places before us. This freedom of interpretation is found "at the point where the agent commits himself to inquiry into the further, longer series of interactions and into the responses taking place in a larger society, or at the point where he commits himself to resolute questioning of the adequacy of his stereotyped, established interpretations."[23]

It is now clear that the "elements" of the idea of responsibility—response, interpretation, accountability, and social solidarity—can be considered not merely as descriptive of moral action, but also as normative for moral action. The response which is demanded from man is a "universal response." It is not, in fact, universal, but rather a defensive, limiting response. Thus, man must "commit himself to inquiry . . ." Man not only responds, but he must respond adequately; he not only interprets, but must interpret rightly. He is not only inextricably woven into a society, but must broaden the limits of that society. He is not only caught up in a continuous interaction, but must strive to keep the interaction moving and expanding. These are norms: formulations directive of action. They are not, it is true, "rules," since they do not describe any particular acts which must be done. But they can be called "principles" in the sense of normative formulations which in a general way inform every particular rule. Like the "First Principles" of the scholastics and the Categorical Imperative, they are incumbent "always and everywhere."

"Act in accord with reason" has been one of the most frequently urged normative principles of western moral philosophy. Niebuhr modifies this by writing, "act in accord with interpretation." Both words refer to the intellectual process of organizing and distinguishing experience so as to grasp its meaning. But interpretation goes beyond the rationality which designs a plan of action or the rationality which apprehends and applies a law. It is rather the taking of an intellectual stance, from which a whole perspective is opened. It is not an abstract understanding, but a "view of life" which involves both the apprehension of meaning and, in intimate connection with this, the appreciation of value.

The manner in which we interpret the action upon us is crucial. Every ethical system proposes in some sense that a man must interpret his life and his action as taking place in community and in history. The view of what this community is, how it is constituted and where its limits are, will determine his conception of ethical action. Duties, obligations, interests, tasks, will all be defined in terms of this conception. This is also the case with man's view of his place in history. Niebuhr is not satisfied to point to any finite community or any finite age. He tells us that we must "redefine . . . what is fitting response in a lifetime and a history surrounded by eternal life, as well as by the universal society of being."[24]

RESPONSIBILITY AND REVELATION

All interpretations of human life and moral action which come to less than this universal scope are, in Niebuhr's view, inadequate. They must be challenged, questioned, broken open. But the task of reinterpretation must have a starting point; the challenge to the sufficiency of lesser interpretations must arise from somewhere. Niebuhr seems to believe that there is in man a suspicion that his limited interpretations are not enough and an innate tendency to transcend them. But his fear of destruction is too great; he constantly draws back into the closed centers where he feels secure. But into this security and fear breaks the revelation of God. This revelation, made concrete in Jesus Christ who has entered our worldly and personal history, is the starting point for an interpretation which can convert the ethics of defense into the ethic of responsibility.

The heart of this reinterpretation is man's feeling of absolute dependence. Each man inescapably and radically experiences his absolute dependence. At the center of all of the natural and social factors which maintain his existence, there is a radical action whereby he is this *I*. "The radical action by which I am and by which I am present with this body, this mind, this emotional equipment, this religion, is not identifiable with any of the finite actions that constitute the particular elements in physical, mental, personal existence."[25] Every man, in reflection, becomes aware that he is "flung into existence and held there" by a power not his own.

Man responds to this realization of absolute dependence either in distrust or trust. Either he distrusts the power which has flung him into existence and seeks to forget it or to defend himself against it by "ethics of defense"; or he is given the confidence in the creative power whereby all things exist. This interpretation in trust or distrust qualifies all particular interpretations of action and response. In distrust every action is a threat from which I must defend myself; in trust every action is an expression of the creative source of being and thereby good. Response in distrust leads to a diversity of responses, made disparately toward the variety of action which touches us. The self reacts not to the one source of its being, but to the manifold actions whereby body, mind, society, emotions are sustained. Niebuhr says this is the "situation of response to all others except that otherness by which the self is self, of responses by forces in the body and the mind, but not of the self as self."[26]

The crucial question can now be stated: "How is it possible to be *one* self in the multiplicity of events and of one's interpretations of them? How does the self as such become responsible instead of remaining a concatenation of responsive systems, fitting their actions now into this, now that series of events?"[27] The answer at this point should be obvious.

One becomes a responsible self by responding in all responses to the One who is the source of one's being. And one is enabled to so respond only because one is purged of the distrust of being and its source and can interpret all actions and all being as good and trustworthy. This reinterpretation is possible only because God has manifested himself in Jesus Christ as good creator, redeemer and sustainer. In Jesus Christ men are given an image of trusting response to the source of being; men are empowered to make this response. In Jesus, the Source of being has revealed his loving providence for men. Jesus is, in Niebuhr's words, the Paradigm of Responsibility. He is the one whom we see interpreting all action upon him as the sign of God, his Father. Niebuhr also names Jesus the Redeemer to responsible being, for he also empowers by his action and presence in men their trust in ultimate reality as benevolent Father.

This conversion from distrust to trust at the radical center of our existence, the feeling of absolute dependence, issues in a reinterpretation of all contexts and situations and actions in which we are involved. It is the solution to the most basic ethical problem, the problem of the one in the many. This is not a speculative problem: it is felt as the tension between the one self and the multiplicity of powers and actions with which that self is engaged. But more important for Niebuhr, this is the problem which men seek to solve by recourse to polytheism or henotheism. Man gives in to multiplicity by the establishment of multiple centers of loyalty or he seeks to unite all loyalties in one finite, and hence ultimately dissatisfying, center of value. Niebuhr has been seeking an ethic for monotheism and he finds it in the ethic of responsibility.

The norms of responsibility, then, do not direct a man toward some sort of romantic universalism in which all particular realities are erased. They do not command attention to ultimates at the expense of concrete immediate problems (as seems to be the case with Barth). Rather, the "principles" of a monotheistic ethic command that no limited context, no finite value, be ever considered as final. They forbid the deification of a present community or a present age. They command the continual critique of existing centers of value. More positively, the principles of a monotheistic ethic make it possible to accept and work in the whole of creation, for the one who is known as creator is also known as good, trustworthy. He is good creator, sustainer of what he has made and redeemer. As sustainer and redeemer he works in his creation with one intention and draws all diversity, even the diversity of good and evil, into one final context.

Thus Niebuhr can write, "Responsibility affirms: God is acting in all actions upon you. So respond to all action upon you as to respond to his action."[28] Here again we see the indicative-imperative of Christian ethics. The indicative states the situation in which man has been given the ability to reinterpret his being in trust, through the revelation of God in Jesus Christ. The imperative, which follows from this, summons him to an observance of the principles of interpretation, accountability, and solidarity, as each action is responded to in faith. Within the scope of this indicative and imperative, it is possible to delineate in some detail the particular ways in which a man can respond to the particularities of his existence so as to be responding to God creator, redeemer, sustainer.

RESPONSIBILITY AS A PRINCIPLE

Earlier in this investigation we asked two questions. First, what is the ethical import of "so respond to all actions upon you as to respond to the action of God"? Second, what is the relationship between this imperative and the indicative which precedes it, "God is acting in all things upon you"? We have attempted to answer the first question in terms of the doctrine of norms. "So respond . . ." is an imperative which directs an agent to conform his action to the three principles of responsibility: interpretation, accountability, solidarity. These are the formal principles for the molding of "fitting action." I call them "formal principles" because they are not in themselves guides for choice and action. They are rather the rules for ethical reasoning. The actual determination of what the "fitting action" should be requires also "material principles," that is, a knowledge of the actual facts of the situation.

The second question is exceedingly difficult to answer. How is the theological affirmation that God is acting in all things related to the ethical imperative, "so respond . . ."? Quite clearly, the theological affirmation makes a difference for the ethical imperative, for the breadth and extent of the response are affected by theological interpretation. But even more, it seems that the very meaning of the imperative depends on the theological interpretation implied in the indicative.

We have seen Bonhoeffer working to unify the duality of the two-sphere ethic. He did so on the theological plane exclusively. The two spheres are reconciled in Jesus Christ.

Henceforth man does not live in two worlds and under two commandments, but in one world, created and redeemed and under one concrete command. His ethical action is to be measured by the needs and the nature of that world. We now see H. Richard Niebuhr working to unite, not a duality in the theological perspective, but the almost infinite multiplicity of actions which call for man's response. He sets about this task quite differently than Bonhoeffer. He begins the unification by noting that there are certain unifying principles in the very nature of human response itself. One cannot respond humanly without interpreting, anticipating future response, maintaining consistency in community and time. Furthermore, the contexts of community and history themselves exhibit certain constancies, for example, the triadic structure of response in community, or the compresence of others in personal history. Moral response takes account of these constancies and operates in accord with the principles inherent in human response itself.

However, just as moral experience exhibits the principles of response and the structure and constancies of human community and history, it also reveals the vitiation of the possibilities of full response and the distortion of the process of transcendence into ethics of defense. Man, who in his creation is enabled to respond to all being, limits and restricts his responsiveness, out of fear and desire for self-preservation.

Now God reveals himself as trustworthy in Jesus Christ. Man is given trusting faith in him who is faithful. There is no longer any need for defensive ethics because the last word is life, not death. In virtue of this the principles of responsibility can direct response to ever-widening communities and toward an ever-extending history.

This is the reinterpretation of man's situation which makes possible the transformation of his ethics. The reinterpretation is contingent upon the revelation in which God discloses himself as faithful. I come to know God differently: He who was feared and distrusted as Enemy, as inimical force behind all the inimical forces of our existence, is now known as trusted and trustworthy Friend, as benevolent Father.

This radical conversion qualifies all action: trust in the source of being overflows into trust toward all being, which is ultimately derived from the trustworthy source. In virtue of this we are able to respond in and with faith, hope and love to the One and to the many.

A man can now look upon the principles of responsibility from the viewpoint of one who knows and feels that his every action answers the action of the ultimate Person, who is faithful, who is the source of all being. Thus he can read these principles as saying, "Interpret your action and response in such a way that your response does not absolutize a finite value; anticipate that beyond your immediate response there will be an ultimate response from one who accepts; move to establish a community in which all men can respond to the action of the One." Responsibility means: meet in all your intentions the one intention of him who draws all things to himself.

So far we have an analysis, both descriptive and normative, of responsive action and its principles. This is properly ethical. We also have a theological statement about God's revelation in Jesus Christ, which empowers man to live in accordance with the principles of responsibility, to interpret all action upon him as actions of God, creator, sustainer and redeemer. This is properly theological. However, we are still lacking a link between these two. We can still ask: given the fact that man is responsive being and that he responds to action upon him with interpretation, and given the fact that he is also redeemed to responsible being by the revelation of God in Jesus Christ, why ought he so respond? Why ought he expand his response to the universal community?

Niebuhr offers an answer in his brief philosophical essay, "Center of Value." There he exposes a "relational value theory" whose fundamental observation is, "value is present wherever one existent being with capacities and potentialities confronts another existence that limits or completes or complements it."[29] Value exists only in the relations of beings one to the other. It is "the good-for-ness of being for being in their reciprocity, their animosity, and their mutual aid. . . . 'Right' means that relation between beings, good-for-each-other, in which their potentiality of being good for each other is realized. . . . The 'ought' in which the sense of right comes to expression is a statement of what is owed to another being."[30]

Niebuhr states that such a value theory must concern itself with the "multi-dimensionality of value," that is, "the multi-dimensionality of beings in relations to each other." This multi-dimensionality requires a center, a starting point, namely, "some being or beings in relation to which good is judged to be good and evil, evil, in relation to which also the rightness or wrongness of its relations to other beings is examined."[31]

The total determination of an ethical system hinges on the center of value which is chosen. The meaning of particular values, of the ought, of the right, derive from this value center. It is, then, in the fullest sense normative for the ethical system. It is apparent, of course, that there are many ethical systems, because there are many potential centers of value. These are all in a certain sense "religious," since any value is accepted through faith, as we mentioned above. But all of these "polytheistic theologies of value, usually called philosophical," suffer from a major defect. By giving privileged position to one finite reality they cut off inquiry into great realms of value and confine the definition of the good to an arbitrarily chosen field.

However, as we have seen, man is prone to the ethics of self-defense, to the polytheism or henotheism which he feels will protect him. Into this breaks the revelation of the one God. With this revelation comes the power to move out of the ethics of defense into the larger realms, into the ethic of responsibility, which can accept all finite values and yet never forget that they must be set relatively within the total inter-relation of all being to the transcendent Source of being and value.

This is precisely *cathekontic* ethics, the ethics of the fitting, in which we have "a notion of universal responsibility, that is, of a life of responses to actions which is always qualified by our interpretation of these actions as taking place in a *universe*" and under the eyes of "one who regards our actions from a universal point of view, whose impartiality is that of loyalty to the universal cause."[32]

We should not be surprised to find that Niebuhr, like Haering and Bonhoeffer, intends responsibility in a much broader sense than the philosophical patterns. As in our former authors, hints of both patterns are present: action takes place before the judgment of another and action must be integrated into the self. However, the other is not merely judge but source of all being and value; the self is integrated not only by development of the habits of considered, conscientious action, but by his awareness that in every response he responds to the One who acts upon him.

Once again, as in Haering and Bonhoeffer, we see the concept of responsibility shifted from the peripheral position which it has in philosophical ethics to a central position. In the religious ethics of these three authors responsibility does not refer to conditions prerequisite for praise or blame nor to conditions for self-integration. Rather it states the most basic and central conception of the ethical system: the manner in which the human ethical life is related to God.

We noted that in Haering and Bonhoeffer responsibility carried normative connotations which are not present in the philosophical patterns. It is possible to see this even more clearly in Niebuhr. We have already proposed that the three characteristics of responsibility—interpretation, accountability, and solidarity—could be interpreted as normative principles for the design of fitting action. We wish to go further and propose that the concept of responsibility is the first normative principle of Niebuhr's religious ethic.

We mean that the concept of responsibility serves as the basic concept, in the light of which all other principles are understood and interpreted, all actions are denominated right, and all persons called good. This is the case because it is only by responsible action, that is, action which (in accepting and responding to each particular value) looks beyond this to the universal community and to the universal Other, that value can be realized at all, since value consists in the interrelatedness of all being. The meaning of the moral life and the force and coherence of an ethical system which seeks to direct it rest upon the concept of responsibility. It is the first rule and measure, the principle, of the ethical life of the monotheistic believer and in some mysterious way of all men.

Finally, the shift of responsibility from the periphery of ethics to its center and from a descriptive to a normative principle takes place in Niebuhr, as in Haering and Bonhoeffer, under the pressure of a similar concern. All are at pains to unify what seems to them disparate and disjointed. Haering links nature and supernature; Bonhoeffer links law and gospel. Niebuhr seeks to draw into unity the multitude of responses to particular actions and values and the response to the One, who reveals himself as sole Lord. In each case this attempt to integrate the ethical and the religious arises from a definite conception of God and how he deals with men. It is this conception of God and his ways which seems to promote responsibility into its central place as first normative principle.

> So far as [the self] acknowledges in positive and negative faith, in trust or in distrust, the One in the many, it accepts the presence only of One action in all actions upon it. . . . I am one in my many-ness and so responsible as self, as I face the One action in the many actions upon me. Monotheistic idealism says: "Remember God's plan for your life." Monistic deontology commands: "Obey God's law in all your obedience to the finite rules." Responsibility affirms: "God is acting in all actions upon you. So respond to all action as to respond to his action.[33]

ROBERT O. JOHANN

The image of responsibility involves a certain metaphysical under-standing as it is disclosed in human experience. It is precisely a metaphysics of selfhood. It sees the real as made up of individual centers or powers of action, involved existentially in a field of inter-action, but not systematically related to each other. . . . The whole-ness of reality is rather that precisely of an ongoing encounter in which the other continually comes to the self to become part of its history.

"AUTHORITY AND RESPONSIBILITY"[1]

Robert Johann, Professor of Philosophy at Fordham Univer-sity, enters this conversation about responsibility as something of a stranger. Unlike Haering, Bonhoeffer and Niebuhr, he has yet to win international renown. He is of a younger gen-eration, his thought is still developing and he has not written extensively. He also enters the conversation as a philosopher rather than a theologian. Haering and Bonhoeffer are unques-tionably theologians; H. Richard Niebuhr was as well, although on occasion, as in *The Responsible Self*, he would call himself a Christian philosopher. Johann, however, is a professional philosopher—although he also calls himself a *Christian* phi-losopher—whose reflection upon the structure of human ex-perience does not abstract from his personal commitment to God in Christian faith. Thus we are not returning to the moral philosophy which we left in the second chapter.

While some philosophers do go beyond the moral issues properly speaking into a metaphysical analysis of responsibil-ity, we have not yet seen anyone attempt to extend this philosophical analysis to a study of the metaphysical relation-ship between the responsible man and the Transcendent. This is the problem with which our present study is occupied and so Johann, who treats this point quite explicitly, seems a most appropriate philosopher to invite into the conversation. While he makes no direct reference to divine revelation and to faith, he is clearly a religious philosopher and is working toward the development of a theistic moral philosophy, one which (as H. Richard Niebuhr has said) takes as its starting point man's existence as lived in relation to God. Johann's ethic, or his proposals for an ethic, are quite clearly religious, involving an explicit reference to God.

As the opening quote makes clear, Johann sees the image of responsibility as grounded in human experience. He sets out to elucidate that experience philosophically and to present a metaphysical basis for responsibility. This procedure is in marked contrast to our former authors. Haering works as a theologian, developing his concept of responsibility out of reflection upon the revealed word: God's word, Christ, spoken in creation and redemption, calls and man's graced nature responds. While he utilizes philosophical conceptions of person and value, he does not analyze them closely in themselves; he draws them quickly into his theological perspectives. Bon-hoeffer is perhaps the least philosophical of our authors. He works almost exclusively within a theology of the incarnation and, as we remarked, makes little effort to explicate his use of "reality" and "nature." Niebuhr does write as a philosopher in "Center of Value." He also insists that the object of his inquiry in *The Responsible Self* is not simply the Christian life but human moral life in general. However, the full meaning of responsibility depends upon a "reinterpretation of existence" in the light of God's revelation.

Johann, on the other hand, claims to find in experience itself and in the metaphysics implicit within experience the meaning of the concept of responsibility. There is not, nor need there be, any explicit reference to the revealed word in order to elucidate the essential structure of human responsibility.

We have seen the notion of responsibility move into central position—in fact, into the position of a "first normative principle"—in the three examples of religious ethics which we have examined. We suspected that this might be due to the theological premises of these ethics. But in order to see the issue more clearly we will follow Johann's metaphysical analysis of responsibility. If we find that he can offer a coherent account of human responsibility on the basis of an analysis of experience, we can then ask whether it is necessary to turn to theology or, if one turns to theology, what it contributes to the understanding of responsibility found in reflective human experience.

Johann has written: "The ontology of the person implicit in the notion of responsibility leads us immediately into the realm of morality."[2] This provides a program for our study. We shall first state his notion of responsibility, then his ontology of the person, and finally examine the ethical considerations consequent upon that ontology.

THE NOTION OF RESPONSIBILITY

"The idea of responsibility," writes Johann, "is one which not only speaks to people today, corresponding as it does to the growing sense of the creative role of the person and of the person's transcendence over determinate institutional structures, it is also one which goes to the very heart of human freedom and moral behavior."[3] In this Johann agrees with Niebuhr, to whose *Responsible Self* he often refers. He also accepts Niebuhr's typology, ethics of man the maker, man the citizen, and man the responder. He also analyzes the notion of responsibility in terms of response, although, as we shall see, in a more metaphysical manner than Niebuhr.

Johann distinguishes several senses of the word responsibility. It often means being the origin of one's acts, being able to give an account of them and being held accountable for them. It also means, especially in Existentialist writers, the achievement of personal identity by free and decisive action. These two meanings refer to what we have called in chapter 3 the patterns of attribution and appropriation. Johann points out, as we have done, that in both these cases there is an abstraction from normative questions. In the first, responsibility is the condition for both moral and immoral behavior and does not distinguish between them. In the second, the commitment is more important than that to which one is committed.

But a third meaning of responsibility emphasizes the note of responsiveness. "Presupposing that our actions are ours, and that we must accept accountability for them and stay with them if we are going to achieve identity as persons, it lays stress on the fact that our actions are precisely responses. They are answers to a world that is acting upon us."[4] This world exists independent of us and makes demands upon us. Our actions must fit into dimensions and structures of the reality which surrounds and acts upon us. "The responsible man is not the one who is merely concerned with the personal character of his action, but much more importantly, with its adequacy to the demands and exigencies of the occasion."[5]

If man is to respond to the demands and exigencies of the occasion, and if these demands and exigencies arise from reality, it is vitally important to specify the dimensions and structure of reality. In the first place, Johann insists that in the moral order this reality presents itself as personal. "Morality is less a matter of conformity than responsiveness . . . a man is a moral being only in an interpersonal context . . . to be moral is to be steadfastly heedful of the personal other and genuinely responsive to the exigencies of communion in each situation."[6]

We must seek the demands and exigencies of our moral life in this world of interpersonal relations. But this is not a static world: it is one of on-going encounter, continual meeting, engaging, rejecting. As Johann seeks to show in his metaphysical analysis, this world of interpersonal experience is precisely "the real." When it is seen comprehensively, it includes not only the community of human persons, but an absolute Person. This absolute Person, who is absolute being and absolute love, is the ultimate source of all the exigencies of the real and it is in communion with him that all the potentialities of the real are fulfilled.

Thus the response of responsibility is first the response to persons: a response to the call to interpersonal communion. But beyond the response to the communion of finite persons, there is response to the appeal of One beyond all immediate situations. In this continuing, expanding and transcending response man participates in and in a fashion forms and creates the real. Johann writes:

> What is the ultimate context and the unifying ground of man's responsibility? The answer is Being itself. . . . It is the correlativity and openness to Being itself that gives man his identity as a personal subject, as "I," and it is by being responsive to the exigencies of this Value in all that he does, in all his encounters, that man achieves integrity as a personal subject. . . . Any human response is implicitly an affirmation of Being itself. Man is by vocation Being's agent, the attendant of Being, called to promote its full presence in each situation in which he finds himself. . . . Our vocation is to be responsive to Being . . . [and its] abiding claims on our responsibility.[7]

THE ONTOLOGY OF RESPONSIBILITY

Johann has taken the notion of responsibility out of the relatively clear discourse about "response to value, to others, to action," and plunged it into the opaque realms of being. He defines "creative responsibility" as "devotion to Being itself. It is the service of the Infinite in and through the finite, man's part in God's own work of promoting and expanding his presence among men."[8] But lest such language appear mere mysticism, Johann proposes an ontology, an explication of the notion of Being, within which he locates the notion of responsibility.

Ontology begins as a reflective analysis of human and personal experience. Experience does not mean for Johann what it did to the classical empiricists, merely sense data. Experience is the total life of the self, that is, of that being which is present to itself and knows itself as original source and center of activity. The self knows itself in its activities, as source of those activities. But its activities are always references to the non-self, the other. Johann writes: ". . . experience as the life of the self includes not only the self but also the whole range of the Other with which it deals as well as the whole range and variety of its dealings."9 Experience is an all-inclusive whole, whose elements—the self, the other, and activity—are not isolated but integrated into one life. Furthermore, experience is dynamic, since the active nature of the self and the continually changing other make for the continual emergence of new patterns.

Johann moves a step further. Experience, as "concrete integration of the self and the other in a dynamically open and all inclusive synthesis," is in fact "the real." "The real" is not something outside and over against thought. It is not something on the other side of appearance. It is the experienced synthesis of self and other in their manifold interrelationships. Further, it is not finished plentitude, but continual growth and development. "Reality has the structure of an on-going, free encounter. It is a continually-to-be-achieved relationship between myself and all the rest."10

Reality is *my* experience. But it is not *only* my experience, and thus is not totally subjective and incommunicable. The other, both person and object, are within my experience. The self draws into itself the other with its own proper structure and relationships. Each self's experience is inclusive of and is included by the other. Thus, Johann writes: ". . . the whole of the real and the whole of any person's life are one and the same, single and absolute. If this one absolute which embraces all selves is lived by each from his own point of view so that it becomes identically his experience, his life, it does not thereby cease to be the one real in which all communicate and by which all are encompassed."11

Radical and incommunicable subjectivism is thus rejected. Still, while the whole of reality is present in each life, the concrete synthesis of reality is historically contingent: the real presents itself to each man only in terms of his own life. Each man encounters the common universe of being, but in terms of his own contingent situation. It is precisely in virtue of this community and singularity of experience that the reflective understanding of reality is always perfectible.

It is of crucial importance to note that the real as synthesis of self and other is not simply *there*: it is continually being made. Experience, and consequently reality, is not given but achieved. It involves the self, aware of itself, but going out of itself to encounter and integrate in thought and action the other into itself. "The real is precisely that synthesis of the self and the truly other which each man must achieve for himself and which, born of his free response to that which never ceases to come to him, is always fresh and always new . . . reality can be achieved not by thought alone, but by thoughtful action."[12]

"Free response," in the lines above, is our clue to responsibility. But we cannot follow this clue until we have clarified the notion of the person. We must begin, here as everywhere in philosophy, with experience. The person, both self and other, is encountered in everyday experience. As we have seen, experience is the total life of the self in synthesis with the other. Thus, experience is immediately articulated: one experience includes self and other. The other, the non-self, can be either another self, a person, or an object. An object is that which is encountered as a thing. It is that which "is unable to take me into account."[13] It can be dealt with in many ways and known under many aspects. But everyone can deal with it and know it in the same way. It is accessible to all knowers and can be conceptually defined in terms of its formal structure. Being-as-object is always being "experienced from the outside, presenting its surface to the knower."

Being-as-subject, however, is being "known from the inside." For the knower knows himself, affirms himself. He exists in an interiority, the immanent spiritual activities of knowing and willing. Thus, being as subject is known not simply in terms of its formal determinations as *this kind* of being, but in its uniqueness as *this* being, because it knows itself as an original source of its activities. The self is aware of self as "unique responsible origin."

 Being-as-subject is not only the knower knowing himself, but every other encountered as "unique responsible source." Among the beings which the "I" encounters, some are able to take him into account and respond to him with an act of free initiative. As distinct from the world of being-as-object the world of persons, of being-as-subject, is a world where each being takes account of the other, takes positions with regard to the other and is involved in an interchange of activities of willing and knowing which flow from each as center and source of free initiative. "This inclusiveness of me in another's world, whether it be actual or only grasped as possible, is the touchstone of the personal and immediately and irrevocably separates the person from the mere thing."[14]

The person, then, is a being who knows himself as subject. But to know oneself as subject is not to encounter an isolated, closed interiority. The interiority of the subject, while intimately his own, is an interiority of activity which is evoked by the activities of other selves. The person both knows himself and is himself as person in communication with other persons.

Persons are "co-sources of the dialogue in which they are concretely engaged."[15] This dialogue is initiated when any being encounters another being who is able, in any way to invite, summon, solicit or demand the taking of a position toward it. This is fundamentally a dialogue of freedom, for in it the "I," invited by the other, accepts or rejects the invitation, follows or ignores the summons. In this free engagement each self transcends itself, for the act of the "I" is not simply his; it is an act in which the "Thou" intrinsically and necessarily participates. The meaning of the act is bound up with both, "it is mine as given, yours as solicited."[16]

In intersubjectivity, then, the self transcends self because his act exists not simply as his, but as "ours." "As *ours*, it is born of being, precisely as transcending each of us in our isolation as finite selves, precisely as embracing us both."[17] However, the intersubjectivity of two persons is not isolated and self-sufficient. There are other persons whose presence is insistent: who threaten or support, repel or demand entrance into the intersubjectivity established between two. Furthermore, the intersubjectivity established in an immediate, present situation must perdure through future and quite different situations.

The transcendence of self moves beyond the intersubjectivity of two persons toward the establishment of a community of persons in which this intersubjectivity can exist. It moves from an immediate engagement in interpersonal activities toward a comprehensive engagement which will be adequate to future and further situations. In the last analysis, the person not only transcends himself in intersubjectivity, but each intersubjectivity is transcended in a movement toward universal community and comprehensive reality.

Universal community can exist only where every participant responds not only to every other participant (which is impossible) but to the radical intention to form community. This intention does not issue from each separately nor from the "general will," but from Another to whom each participant is responding. Likewise, the movement toward comprehensive reality passes beyond every immediate situation and the totality of all situations to the source of all situations, that is, to the source of being.

In the very structure of personal being there is thus intimated the full set of relationships which constitute existence. The self is being in self-awareness as source and origin of activity. The activities of the self are engaged by and participate in the activities of other selves, and each self knows itself in the transcendence of intersubjectivity. But this transcendence is not limited to single instances of intersubjectivity. It is called beyond each single instance and each single situation toward the universal and the comprehensive, ultimately to the source of being, who is absolute Subject and absolute Being.

All of this, Johann claims, is located in experience, as he has explained it. However, he notes, ". . . the fact that reality is located in experience does not mean that we will automatically find it there."[18] The lines or vectors of all these relationships are intimated in experience, but they are there only inchoatively, imperfectly, incompletely. Thus the self is aware of the pull of other selves on his activities, but he can fail to respond, can attempt to isolate himself. The self in interpersonal subjectivity can be aware of the need and necessity to relate his relationship with another to further sets of relationships; but he can also wall it off as a private preserve.

The "destiny" of the experience which persons have of themselves is a wholeness and a coherence. But this is not simply given; it must be constructed and continually maintained in being. If reality is "the synthesis of the self and other in the experience of on-going relationships," and if that synthesis is created by the free initiative of persons, then reality is continually brought into being anew.

However, reality—the synthesis of self and other—is not simply in continual creation because it is the work of freedom. It is also in continual re-creation: experience is in constant need of "reconstruction, . . . the effort to reshape experience, give it a new mold, a new direction."[19] It needs such reconstruction because the process of growth toward synthesis continually falls into alienation from reality. The self, instead of entering into interpersonal relationship, seeks to secure itself in its apartness. "Failing to recognize that only through participation in the other as other can its own radical insufficiency as an isolated, individual self be overcome and the wholeness of life restored, it may seek a spurious kind of self-sufficiency by destroying in practice the otherness of the Other and subordinating it wholly to itself."[20]

In so doing the self and the other lose the relationship whereby they are themselves; the intersubjectivity whereby they are each constituted persons is destroyed and the structure of all other relationships with things, with community and with the absolute Other are endangered. The structural lines of experience are distorted and erased. The wholeness is mutilated. The "quality of life," says Johann, becomes "anaesthetic." It loses or never attains "aesthetic" quality: "the pattern, structure, quality of making complete sense [in which] all the phases that can be discriminated . . . are grasped in their interconnection and seen as contributing to the final outcome."[21]

Johann introduces the idea of "quality of life," a phrase from John Dewey, for the first time in his essay, "The Pragmatic Meaning of God." This quality is not one property among the many which are accidental modifications of a being. It is rather the distinctive property which pervades the whole reality as the very manner in which all its qualities are conjoined. It designates:

> the sort of process that is going on, the characteristic way in which all the multiple elements in the process are conjoined. Since this process is both life and reality, the quality of a person's life will also be the quality of the real itself—the sort of sense it makes or fails to make, the sort of unity it has or fails to have, depending on the particular way the person goes about relating himself to his overall environment.[22]

Since quality in this sense is a matter of a relationship of ingredient parts, Johann speaks of *aesthetic* quality, in which all parts are rightly ordered, as opposed to *anaesthetic* quality, in which the parts are indistinct or confused.

It is the work of reflective thought and thoughtful action to overcome alienation and to restore the aesthetic quality of life by the reconstruction of experience. This reconstruction

consists, first, in seeking to recognize the possibilities for wholeness and coherence which are inherent in life. It then proceeds
to criticize the misconceptions which prevent the realization
of this wholeness. It finally involves the actualization of the
possibilities, so that the relations inherent in reality are actually
guiding and explicitly determining one's conduct. The other
is thus known and appreciated as unique, inviolable other, not
as a function of myself. The self is known as interiority demanding intersubjectivity. The other and the self are engaged
by their free initiative in a community of persons which is
open to respond to a transcendent Person. Johann writes that
this reconstruction of experience requires:

> a basic commitment to concrete life and a confidence in its
> possibilities . . . by no other strategem than the cultivation of
> a new responsiveness to this appeal (of the Other) can experi-
> ence be successfully transformed. To find himself, a man must
> ultimately go out of himself. To find the real, he must finally
> consent to let the Other be and disclose itself and to let him-
> self be transcended by it; he must finally be willing to achieve
> his own meaning and sufficiency in what is distinct from him-
> self.[23]

ETHICS OF RESPONSIBILITY

We have heard Johann say, "The ontology of the person implicit in the notion of responsibility leads us immediately into
the realm of morality." We have stated his notion of responsibility; we have tried to make explicit the ontology of the person
implicit therein. What then can be said about the "realm of
morality"?

Johann has said that responsible action is action which
meets the exigencies of the situation, which responds to the
objective demands of the occasion. He has also said that it is a
response to being, an answer to man's fundamental vocation to
promote being. In the light of his ontology of the person, we
can see that these apparently diverse statements are in fact

synonomous. The exigencies and objective demands of any moral situation are the exigencies and demands of Being itself.

Every "situation or occasion" is a complex of experienced elements: the self, faced with other selves and with objects, in a particular configuration. None of these elements are mere facts, significant in themselves, abstracted from the potential relationships which they have with one another. They are known in terms of their potentialities. All of them are involved in the potential transcendence of their mere facticity, which results from their being brought into real relationship with one another. All of them are ultimately potential elements in a whole and coherent experience.

But as Johann has indicated, experience is reality: "that synthesis between the self and the truly Other which each man must achieve for himself and which is born of his free response to that which never ceases to come to him . . ."[24] To meet the exigencies of the situation far transcends the facticity of the situation itself. Indeed, it is doubtful that facticity could have any exigencies at all. It is the dynamism of the self toward transcendence and of all selves in intersubjectivity toward Being itself that constitute the exigencies of the situation. To meet the exigencies of the situation is to meet the exigencies of Being itself. Thus, Johann can make the statement which we read above: "Man is by vocation Being's agent, called to promote its full presence in each situation in which he finds himself."

It should now be clear that the promotion of Being consists in the continual reconstitution of the communion between self and other. This communion grows out of the continuing free response to the presence of the other, who continually presents himself in new revelations, making new demands, in the light of new conditions. The promotion of being is precisely the effort to work toward the wholeness and coherence of experience, in which self is known as self, other as other, self and other in intersubjectivity which transcends itself.

"To be moral," says Johann, "is to be for Being itself, to live in its light, to seek always in all situations to promote its reign."[25] But this is precisely what love does; it is devotion to Being itself, the intention to promote being by enhancing the quality of life, and more fundamentally, by entering and deepening that communion in which each person is most fully and uniquely a self. To love is to respect and promote the uniqueness of self and other; a uniqueness that is rooted in their existence, a uniqueness that comes to be only in intersubjectivity. Thus Johann can say that the sole norm for moral action is love: "The morally right is not what conforms to a determinate nature but what conforms to the dictates of a reason enlisted in love's service."[26]

A love which enlists reason in its service is "discerning love." If love is the respect for being and the intention to promote its possibilities, then being must be known for what it is and the possibilities must be recognized as they present themselves. This is the work of intelligence. Intelligence is sometimes reflective: it stands back from the immediacy of experience in order to sort out the proper relationships inherent therein. Intelligence is also discerning: it seeks out in the particularity and immediacy of situations those features and courses of action which seem best to promote being, to contribute to the communion of self and the other. It will discover, as it goes about these two tasks, certain kinds of action which are fundamentally compatible with the promotion of being and others which are incompatible. Thus the fundamental distinction between the order of persons and the order of things grounds the moral prohibition against the exploitation of persons as means.

Still, the relationships between beings, in the concrete, is non-systematic; that is, beings enter into relationship with one another in a diversity of contexts and under extremely diverse conditions. They do not encounter one another and operate according to systematic, lawful patterns. In every encounter of self with other, either personal or objective, there is a certain newness. The proper response is the one which takes this into account. Furthermore, in this non-systematic encounter there are not only unforeseen events but contradictions and conflicts. In certain of these, some detrimental elements arise which may have to be accepted into the synthesis that is made to solve a particular problem. It is the work of discerning intelligence to seek out the possibilities which will best promote the predominant value, the promotion of being, to eliminate as far as possible and, when impossible, to mitigate the destructive courses which would ruin this moving and growing synthesis.

On the basis of these "general principles of responsibility" Johann attacks several concrete ethical problems. He treats the relation between authority and subject by noting that "the individual's response to the action of authority should be such that, all things considered, it promotes rather than hinders the advance of genuine community."[27] He counters the central issue in the Catholic problem of birth control—intervention in natural processes—by affirming that: "Man is called to a rational [responsible] work of loving enhancement—a genuine promotion of being. His intervention in natural processes is always justified when its issue is enlargement of human meanings and possibilities."[28] In short, the principle of responsibility is, "Be steadfastly heedful of the personal Other and genuinely responsive to the exigencies of communion in each situation."[29] And because in all relation with the other there is implied an ultimate relation with the absolute Other, who is the center of communion and the ground of the self, responsibility is "service of the Infinite in and through the finite, man's part in promoting and expanding God's presence among men."[30]

RESPONSIBILITY AS NORMATIVE ETHICAL PRINCIPLE

Johann is not loath to admit that his ethics of responsibility is "a natural law position." He means that his ethic, like the natural law ethic, is "thoroughly ontological in character, refusing to make the separation between the is and the ought. . . ."[31] But it is a transposed natural law position, since the ought is not grounded in the structure of specific natures but in the nature of man *as a person* open to the Absolute and called to promote it. Like natural law ethics, it maintains that morality is both objective and absolute. The moral realm is objective because there are certain exigencies which are independent of the individual and which impose themselves upon him; but these exigencies are those of Being itself. The moral realm is absolute in that moral value does not depend on individual valuation but upon Being itself: "the presence of the Infinite to the finite and man's presence to the Infinite through the finite."[32]

This is a thoroughly ontological ethic. Ontology means the disciplined and reflective analysis of experience through which its necessary structures, its inherent potentials and its dynamic exigencies are revealed. But experience is identically the real, in the sense explained above. Thus, to reveal the structures of experience is to reveal the structures of being. However, being is not itself structure, potential or exigency; it is the continuing revelation and self-revelation of actual beings which are structured, which possess potentialities and which are driven by exigencies.

This continual revelation is unsystematic: beings do not interact according to predetermined patterns, like the unfolding of the genetic code, but meet each other at different stages of development and under divergent conditions.

Ethics arises from the recognition of the structured, potential and exigent nature of the real, but only because the potentials are unactualized and the exigencies unmet in each recurring experience. It is recognized that human action can contribute to the actualizing of potential and fulfilling of the exigencies and thus work toward the wholeness and coherence of experience, that is, of being. Ethics, then, in a sense, is ontology in reverse: it is the reflection which issues in action that actualizes the potentiality of being along the vectors of its exigencies and within its structures. It issues in action only because of the free involvement of the person, on the one hand,

and only because there is room for action in the field of continually recurring non-systematic experience, on the other.

We maintain that Johann employs the notion of responsibility within this ontological ethics as a first normative principle. We mean that responsibility is the conception which expresses the most fundamental imperative of the moral life (promote being) and the justification thereof (because in the immanent dynamism toward self-transcendence present in interpersonal communion there exists the insistent call of the Infinite and Absolute). To be responsible means to employ the resources of discerning love in order to discover how the potentialities of being can best be realized in accord with its exigencies. If the ethical imperative is "promote being," the ethical response to this imperative is "responsiveness to being as it reveals itself in experience." This responsiveness consists in a discernment of the structure, potentialities and exigencies of being, a devising of patterns of action which will, in this situation, realize these potentialities and exigencies, and committed action to do so.

Responsibility is a normative principle for two reasons. First, it expresses the origin of obligation, that is, the Infinite present to the finite. Obligation derives from perceived value; value is being as ordered toward the Transcendent. Value is that which ought to be realized; but that which ought to be realized is the communion of persons and it is in this communion that the Infinite, whose nature is love, becomes present in finite experience. Second, the conception of responsibility directs man to discover those forms of life and action which are most consonant with the promotion and enhancement of personal communion, and therefore of being. It condemns undiscerning, indiscriminate, uncritical conduct.

As we have seen in the former authors, responsibility moves into a central place with ethics. It moves away from the patterns of appropriation and attribution insofar as these are particular considerations for the solution of partial ethical issues into the role of first normative principle. Still, features of the philosophical patterns remain. Johann's remarks remind one strongly of the pattern of appropriation: he is concerned about the identity of self as agent, about discernment and engagement and about the formation of character. However, he goes beyond these formal considerations to specify that the identity of the self is achieved only in intersubjectivity, that engagement and discernment is precisely the work of making the real, and that character is the formed approach to the problems of making the real through the disposition of discerning love.

If we consider the centrality of the notion of responsibility and the role that it plays in Johann's thought, we can perhaps speak of the "natural law of responsibility." In doing so, however, we encounter a problem: like all natural law theories, its relationship to the transcendent, and especially to Christian revelation, is problematic. By problematic I mean that the relationship between immanent natural norms and values and the transcendent is not self-evident and requires theological and philosophical explanation. The history of the doctrine of natural law is strewn with attempts at such explanations: the pantheism of the Stoics, the voluntarism of the Nominalists, the rationalism of the Deists. The famous phrase of the great seventeenth-century jurist, Grotius, *etiamsi daremus non esse Deum*, though only faintly heard today, remains a real challenge to those who wish to construct a comprehensive and coherent theory of theistic natural law. Furthermore, the "inruption of the Gospel" has appeared to many as a challenge to theories of natural law. Its command to love seems to overwhelm the demands of justice and right; its "hard sayings" seem incompatible with a natural law of ordered self-realization; its "other-worldliness" a contradiction to the present natural world. And perhaps above all for many Protestant theologians its form as law seems to undermine the gracious and unmerited righteousness which comes to man from God alone.

We have seen our first three authors adopt and centralize the language of responsibility within a definite theological context. For Haering the meaning of responsibility was intrinsically tied to a word-response theology; for Bonhoeffer, to a theology of incarnation; for Niebuhr, to a theology of revelation. Johann, however, makes no explicit mention of theology. His is, as we have said, a religious ethic, but it is not theological. While there is evidence of reflective Christian experience in such ideas as the "conversion" required for the reconstruction of experience, in the acceptance of a creationist ontology and the interpretation of the Absolute as love, responsibility itself appears to be adequately defined in ontological terms. We may ask, then, whether it is necessary to turn to the revealed word in order to understand responsibility or, if one does read responsibility in the revealed word, what significant contribution this word makes to our understanding of "natural responsibility." We shall return to this issue in the following and final chapter. We conclude with a rather theological word from our philosopher, which hints at his answer to the question.

> It is the recognition of our responsibility to God, of the fact that intelligence is our responsive encounter with Being itself, that puts our whole life and all our deeds under judgment and prevents us from ever giving our final allegiance to anything finite, be it ourselves or the work of our hands. In God's presence we are never so just that we are not also sinners, never so sinful that the path to redeeming our past is closed. Thus, instead of being antagonistic to our humanity, God is its deliverer, its liberator.[33]

5

The Ethic of Responsibility: Two Propositions and a Prospect

We wish to conclude by stating two propositions, sketching a prospect and posing some problems. We have documented the emergence in religious ethics of what we believe to be a rather special meaning of the term responsibility. We saw that this emergence was attended with some confusion in current Christian ethical literature: sometimes responsibility seemed to be only a contemporary refurbishing of the traditional ethics of obedience; at other times it heralded the autonomy of moral choice without (or beyond) norms and laws. But in every instance which we examined it seemed to carry connotations which distinguished it from the more or less settled meaning it carries in moral philosophy. In that discipline responsibility occurs in the discussion of two particular questions: the attribution of praise and blame and the appropriation of moral principles. Both of these "patterns of ideas" abstract, wholly or in part, from the more central issues of moral philosophy, the nature of the good and the right.

Analysis of the four major authors began to reveal more precisely the unique connotation which the general literature expressed confusedly. Each of these authors moves the language of responsibility from its place on the periphery of ethics, as a prolegomenon to the central issues of the good and the right, to a place of primacy. Each author intends to design an ethic of responsibility.

We will attempt to express in two propositions the nature of this primacy. These propositions are generalizations from the materials. But they are not merely a summation or abstract statement of what each author has said in his particular way. They are also intended to state as clearly as possible the underlying concern which attracts our four moralists to the language of responsibility and the change which that language undergoes due to their concern.

The two propositions are these: 1) the centrality of the language and notion of responsibility is due to its use as a principle of unification within a total ethical doctrine; 2) there is a significant shift in its meaning due to its employment not only as a unifying but also as a normative principle. These propositions are stated in the formal language of ethics. After we have discussed them in these terms, we will attempt to describe in a more concrete way what the use of responsibility as a first unifying and normative principle implies for the shape of a total ethical system. We shall at the same time point out some of the problems which face those who hope to mold such an ethic.

TWO PROPOSITIONS

1. *The four major religious ethicians use responsibility as a principle of unification within their total ethical doctrine.*

Ethics, whether done as moral theology or moral philosophy, is reflection upon human life as it is and ought to be lived in virtue of intelligent choice. This reflection is dignified with the title Ethics insofar as it is systematic. The system need not be the rigorous *Ethica modo geometrico* of Spinoza. But it must have, as Aristotle said of the well-made play, a beginning, a middle, and an end: it must begin with certain ideas which are taken as basic and irreducible, proceed through other ideas which expand, clarify, mediate, and finally come to some conclusions which are relevant to the guidance of choice and action. Thus, a coherent ethical doctrine ought to comprehend in some logical order a conception of the nature of man and of his world, together with general and specific precepts which are in some sense congruent with this conception.

A system of this sort will contain many elements. Some of these will be descriptive of human actuality and possibility. Some will be preceptive, indicating certain forms of action which are incumbent upon man. There will be discussion about values and their mode of perception; about rules and their force; about moral character and its assessment. If all of this is to be a system, there must be some conception which unifies all of the elements, which makes it possible to see how they are related. For example, in Aristotle's ethics, there is a view of the constitution of man as essentially *nous* in conjunction with body and *psyche*; there is a conception of virtue and its relation to choice; there is a conception of happiness. The conception which unifies these descriptive and prescriptive elements is the conception of the end. The idea of finality makes it possible to interpret the constitution of man as having a function ordered to a certain end, and the virtues as partial realizations of that end. Choice and action are moral insofar as they flow from and produce virtue, which itself is productive of the good and happy man.

A conception of this sort can be called a first principle of the ethical system: a basic, irreducible conception which serves as a starting point for the development of a coherent and comprehensive ethical doctrine. It is a *principle* insofar as it is a source or origin for intelligibility. It is *first* insofar as it is taken as primary and irreducible. It is our opinion that the four authors whom we have studied employ the idea of responsibility as a first principle in this sense: a basic conception which draws into systematic unity the various elements of their ethical doctrine.

While we have noted that each author introduces the

language of responsibility within the context of a particular theological or ethical problem, all of them do so because their problem involves the unification of disparate elements. Haering's problem is the disparity between nature and grace in the ethical order; Bonhoeffer's is the dualism of law and gospel. Niebuhr attacks the polytheism of multiple value centers in the name of monotheism; Johann desires the enhancement of being which comes only with communion and community. In each case, the problem is specifically different, but generically the same: the search for some conception which will draw into conceptual unity elements of an ethical system. The notion of responsibility appears as an appropriate principle of unification.

But it is possible to go further: behind the specific problems which exercise each author, there is a problem intrinsic to the very nature of religious ethics. Each of the authors gives evidence of his awareness of this problem. It too is a problem of unification: the problem of the relation between a transcendent God and human morality. Any serious consideration of the issues of human morality which claims that human morality is somehow a matter of divine concern must explain and justify that claim.

"Religious ethics" is a somewhat paradoxical business. It is probably true that for most of human history and in most cultures the moral life has been lived in an atmosphere of belief and has been sanctioned by the divinities who rule the lives of men. "God wills it!" has long been the final ethical justification. However, as Plato pointed out in the *Euthyphro*, and as many modern moral philosophers are fond of repeating, it appears that we must not say that something is good because God approves it: rather God approves it because it is good. For this reason it has appeared unlikely to many philosophers that morality can be deduced from or based upon religion. Howsoever one might respond to this assertion, "religious morality" does seem to involve a most peculiar problem.

Morality is a very human business. It concerns itself with

the concrete and experienced good for man, with specific rules which ordain specific procedures, with actual conformity to or deviation from the "right way." It must look to the character of men, as it is understood in a particular time and place; it must hope to form or to correct this character. Morality, and the study of morality called ethics, is deeply embedded in concrete human experience.

Religion, on the other hand, implies a certain separation from experience. Of course, religion is experience in the sense that it consists of beliefs, emotions, activities of prayer, asceticism, and so forth. But all of this experience includes a reference to a "Beyond," to a God whose ways are not our ways. The voice of God is not heard like other voices; the action of God is not experienced as we experience all other action; the presence of God is a mysterious presence. Thus, to the extent that religion designates not simply one among other human experiences but an experience involving explicit transcendent reference, it must be asked what this transcendent reference, and above all its object, God, has to do with the human experience of values and rules, desires and commands, emotions and principles, which is called morality.

It is my opinion that our four authors are attempting to deal with this most fundamental question. Each one comes at it from the perspective of the theological and philosophical positions of his tradition, as he interprets them. Each one is attentive to the voices of his time. But each struggles with the basic question, which might be called the problem of the unification of God and morality. They each have found in the term and notion of responsibility a helpful conception for the pursuit of this question.

It is not difficult to see why the language of responsibility, as developed in the philosophical patterns of attribution and appropriation, can be used so suitably to express this issue. As we noted in the conclusion of chapter 3, responsibility is an analogous notion, being used in two distinct ways which have a common center of reference. On the one hand it conceives of moral action as taking place in the public forum, as it were, as being open to public appraisal. Thus, in the pattern of attribution certain elements of the agent's act which are of importance for this sort of judgment are brought to the fore. Responsibility means the condition of an agent whereby he is liable to another's judgment. On the other hand, in the pattern of appropriation responsibility conceives of moral action as issuing from the properly human resources of the moral agent, his ability to consider conscientiously and to commit himself to a task. It refers to the very condition of moral agency itself, the formation of moral character. But as we noted also in our conclusion each of these notions, while involving quite distinct ideas, involve each other. Human morality is not simply an agent acting conscientiously nor simply an affair of public appraisal: it is, as Marcus Aurelius wrote, an affair of "those rational beings who, although unique, are constituted for community" (Meditations 7, 13).

It is this two-fold reference of the language of responsibility which makes it so suitable for the religious use which we have seen. On the one hand it refers to the inner constitution and development of a proper moral agent. On the other hand it refers to the self-other context in which the individual's moral action takes place. Since religious ethics is essentially, to borrow Niebuhr's phrase again, "man's existence as lived in relation to God," it must deal both with the forming of the moral constitution of man's existence and with the relation to the Other.

Furthermore, while the language of responsibility enables the religious ethician to hold together the presence of the Other and the moral formation of the subject, it is also aptly suited to express the relative independence of the subject. Traditionally, in moral philosophy and theology an agent would be accounted responsible, that is, a true moral agent and subject to praise and blame, only if he were free. This freedom was metaphysical freedom, the intrinsic, native ability to act or not to act. However, the evolution of the modern notion of responsibility has taken place in an atmosphere of social and political freedom. The moral subject must be one who not only can obey but who can recognize, accept, perform the tasks of a responsible citizen in a free society. The responsible citizen is (like Luther's Christian) the perfectly free man subject to none and the perfectly dutiful citizen subject to all. The task set to him is a responsibility rather than a duty. It is discretionary, filled with problems left to his ingenuity and moral sensitivity. The norm is not simply a law to be obeyed but a job to be well done.

Now, it is true that the ideas of the pattern of attribution have long been enshrined in Christian theological ethics. As we noted in the introduction to chapter 3 man's accountability before God designates both his state of original sin before God's condemning and justifying judgment and his liability for his particular deeds. The expression of Christian ethics in terms of the command and the law of God made it easy to adopt the pattern of attribution to religious use.

But the pattern of appropriation, with its emphasis on the moral maturity and autonomy of the agent, adds a new dimension to the meaning of man's responsibility before God. It is quite clear that each of our authors has this in mind in his choice of the language of responsibility. For Haering, responsibility calls man to his terrestrial task of cultivating created values; for Bonhoeffer, responsible man is commissioned by divine mandate to responsibility for the world. Niebuhr and Johann see the world of human interaction as the field of responsibility to God.

Thus, all of our authors adopt the language of responsibility because they see in it a principle of unification. It can unify nature and grace, law and gospel, the multiplicity of response and the diversity of personal existence. It can, more importantly, draw into a unity the transcendent Lord and the

human moral experience. But in performing the latter unification its meaning changes significantly: it becomes, in this use,
a first normative principle.

2. *There is a significant shift in the meaning of responsibility
due to its use as a first normative principle.*

The centrality of the language and concept of responsibility is due, first of all, to its appropriateness as a unifying
conception. It can draw together both the particular elements
of an ethical doctrine and the most fundamental terms of
religious morality, God and human morality. It can in this use
be properly called a first principle of religious ethics.

The use of responsibility as a first principle sets it apart
from its use in moral philosophy, where it is limited to two
quite specific issues, attribution and appropriation. However,
it is distinguished from these philosophical patterns in a
second, more important way. When it is used to express the
fundamental relationship between God and man it becomes
a first *normative* principle.

By normative principle I mean a conception having to do
with choice which, when adopted by a moral agent, allows
his action to be qualified by the moral predicate "right" and
his person by the predicate "good." It is a conception having
to do with choice; that is, it is an understanding of a manner of
acting which can be effected by the agent's deliberate choice.
It must be adopted by the agent; that is, he can choose to
formulate and design his action in accord with this conception.
It allows the application of the moral predicates good and
right; that is, the agent's action can be identified by himself
or by others as the sort of action which is correctly judged
right and on account of which the agent is judged good.

"Do not lie" is a normative principle. Lying is an identifiable pattern of action; it can be adopted or rejected by the
agent; the agent and the action are, in consequence of this
adoption or rejection, subject to predication "right and good."
"Act according to reason" is also a normative principle, although

more abstract. When the concept "according to reason" is identified as a certain pattern of action—for example, discerning the potentialities of nature and actualizing them—an agent can choose so to act and can be qualified as good and his action right.

Responsibility, in the philosophical patterns of appropriation and attribution, is not a normative principle. In both cases it describes certain conditions which must exist either, as in attribution, for just praising or blaming, or as in appropriation, for proper moral agency. True, the pattern of appropriation may be considered normative insofar as we desire the development of true moral agents. We do exhort people to act with consideration, conscientiously and committedly. But except in the most extreme existentialism, one who so acts is not called good nor his action right unless he does in fact observe the norms and realize the values whereby good and right are defined. Even a thief can be a thief considerately, conscientiously, committedly: responsibility in this sense, like St. Paul's *prudentia carnis* (Rom 8, 7), can be a sin.

However, each of our four authors treats responsibility as a normative principle. Haering defines it as response to values; Bonhoeffer specifies the mandates, the "natural," and vocation as the limits and guides of responsible action. Niebuhr sets down the rules for responsible response; Johann specifies the formation of community as the object of responsible action. In each case the imperative, "act responsibly," is explained by specifying the kind of values and norms which are to guide choice and action and by indicating the manner in which these values and norms are known to the agent. They are in every case known by man's natural moral perception. For Haering, the intuitive apprehension of value, enhanced by grace, bears upon created value. For Bonhoeffer, reason ("the faculty of the natural") discerns the limits and needs of the world. Niebuhr and Johann both locate value in the experience of actual and potential interrelationships. All four authors attribute a different role to the word of revelation and to the effects of grace, but essentially they agree that norms and values, the criteria of moral choice, can be found within the realm of human experience. For each of them responsibility means looking to these norms and values for guidance and acting accordingly.

However, "normative" implies something more than a conception which can determine choice. It also implies that the conception has a certain authority, a certain gravity. It is a conception not only of what *might* be done, but of what *ought* to be done.

It is quite impossible to enter the tangled controversies about the meaning of obligation. Suffice it to say that Christian faith, and in fact religious ethics in general, has felt that obligation derives in some sense from the will of God. Because each of our authors is Christian, there is no question that the ultimate norm of the moral life is the will of God. The question is only how the will of God is manifested to man.

All four authors choose to see the will of God manifested in the concrete moral experience of man. Whether they describe this moral experience in terms of value response or in terms of the perception of exigencies inherent in the nature of things and in the structure of being, they insist that the ultimate oughtness derives from the One source of good and right.

In taking this position they reject any claim that God's will is manifested to man in a way distinct from man's concrete moral experience. Of course, this moral experience itself includes the influence of grace, the example of Christ, and so on. But these expand, illuminate, empower human moral perception and response; they do not cut through it, destroy it or substitute for it. Whatever appears in man's moral experience as normative does so because of its own quality, for example, as value or as exigency. Yet, while it presents this quality to man's moral perception, it does so not simply on its own, but because it is authorized by God's will in creation and redemption.

There is nothing astonishingly original in the idea that the will of God is the ultimate norm for morality. Nor will anyone familiar with "natural law" ethics of Roman Catholicism or the "orders" of Lutheranism be surprised to hear that the will of God is manifested in the realm of man's moral experience. Still, the language of responsibility contributes to an important shift of emphasis.

The ideas of the pattern of attribution fit perfectly into a command-obedience form of ethics. They allow for the fact that the judge might also be the lawmaker. Thus God, who is author of the natural world, lays upon men the obligation of obedience to its intrinsic laws and judges their motivation and intentions. But as we noted in the previous section, our authors employ the ideas of the pattern of appropriation as well, stressing the autonomy of the moral agent. Here also the conception of God is shifted from lawmaker and judge to designer of a task to be done: God does not only impute responsibility, he imparts responsibility. God sets up a task to be done. Like any task it has a specific outline and a specific goal, but its details must be worked out by those who have the responsibility. They must, out of their skill and alertness, expedite the task in terms of the continually changing situation and of the exigencies which emerge in the doing. The concern which God has for human morality is the concern of one who commissions a certain work. He gives responsibility to do the work and expects it to be carried on responsibly, that is, with respect for the dimensions and the goals he has set and with alertness to new elements which emerge in the doing.

We contend, then, that these four authors use the notion of responsibility as a principle unifying the diverse elements of their ethics. In general, responsibility means that man responds to God by responding to the values, exigencies, actions and persons within the real world of his experience. In this response the person, graced, justified, redeemed, meets a world reconciled and elevated. This world is the locus in which God's work is done by man's agency. The moral response is a religious response, for each act directed to the ordering and bettering of the human world is an answer to God's call, command, action, summons. Likewise, this moral-religious response is rooted in the nature of being, which is essentially the communion between God and man. Karl Rahner, speaking directly of freedom, provides a most apt description of an ethics of responsibility:

> Freedom is the self-achievement of the person, using a finite material, before the infinite God. . . . Without freedom a man could not stand before God as a responsible agent, in dialogue and partnership with God; without it he could not be the subject of guilt before God nor of the proffered and accepted redemption and pardon.[1]

We also contend that our four authors conceive of this principle of conceptual unification as a normative principle. It can be stated as an imperative: be responsible! This is a directive to follow a certain pattern of choice and action, which each author defines somewhat differently but which essentially involves attention to certain features of experience that carry obligatory force: values and the exigencies of nature and being. The final authorization of this imperative derives from God, who designs human life as a task to be fulfilled and imparts to man the freedom and responsibility to fulfill it. Responsibility is a normative principle on two counts. It is a conception of action in accord with certain particular values and norms; it is a conception of action authorized by ultimate authority. The normative character of the principle of responsibility is expressed by Niebuhr: "for the ethics of responsibility, the fitting action . . . is alone conducive to the good and alone is right." Again, he writes:

> The action we see in [the responsible life] is obedient to law, but goes beyond all laws; it is form-giving but even more form-receiving: it is fitting action. It is action which is fitted into the context of universal, eternal, life-giving action by the One. It is infinitely responsible in an infinite universe to the hidden yet manifest principle of its being and its salvation.[2]

THE PROSPECT

The ethic of responsibility which our authors design is appealing. It has that openness and flexibility which is required in order to deal with the ethical issues of a culture in rapid change. It accords with the deepening appreciation of the freedom and creativity of man, as presently experienced in political, artistic and scientific life. It recognizes the dimensions of history and community which are so prominent in contemporary thought.

Moreover, our authors propose this ethic of responsibility as a religious ethic; three of them propose it as a theological ethic based upon explicit theological affirmations: a theology of incarnation, of reconciliation, of revelation. All four design this ethic so as to hold in conceptual unity God and human morality: responsibility implies both the presence of the Other and of a fully formed moral agent. As we have noted, this religious conception, as distinct from the philosophical one, sees the Other not only as judge, but as the creative source of value and being. It also sees the moral agent as having his own creative autonomy before God's creativity. It can say, in the words of a commentator on Teilhard de Chardin, "there is a double freedom at work in shaping man's future on earth, that of man himself and that of God."[3]

Such, in general, is the design of a religious ethic of responsibility. More particularly, we have suggested that the four authors employ the idea and the language of responsibility as a first normative and unifying principle of their ethic. This suggestion, which may at first seem to be a technicality for the appreciation of ethicians only, is in fact an important indication of the direction which Christian ethics seem to be taking today. We shall, then, sketch the prospect which lies before us if Christian ethics does in fact follow this path. These prospects have been glimpsed before. Many Catholic and

Protestant authors in recent years have proposed the shape which that renewal ought to take. I shall be content to indicate here what the adoption of the unifying and normative principle of responsibility implies, theologically and ethically, for the future of Christian morality.

Until now our discussion and analysis of the idea of responsibility has been, of necessity, quite abstract. Perhaps it would be well to focus on the prospects by means of a concrete example. It is a trivial example, if compared with the grave issues which confront Christian ethics; but it expresses, succinctly and directly, the spirit of an ethic of responsibility.

The students of a large Roman Catholic seminary were aggravated by the rules and the regime of their institution. They considered them repressive, paternalistic, and detrimental to maturity. They summed up their complaints in a frequently heard phrase: "Let us be responsible men." After numerous confrontations, the director of the seminary conceded their point. He told them that henceforth the bells that signaled each exercise in the daily order would be turned off and the constant checking by authorities would be discontinued. "You can be responsible," he said. "It is now up to you to follow the daily order and fulfill your duties on your own."

One of the student leaders immediately challenged the director: "Father Rector, being responsible does not mean following the rules without being reminded and warned and punished for failures. It means letting us design our own order and way of living here, an order which we find suitable for living together as human beings and as brothers in Christ and suitable for doing the job we are here for, acquiring the skills necessary to be effective priests."

Clearly the rector and his seminarians hold quite different views of responsibility. True, the rector does not think of responsibility merely in terms of the pattern of attribution. He does not say, "Don't tell me that you *want* to be responsible! You *are* responsible: there is a law, and you are accountable to me for your failure to observe it." Rather, he describes responsibility in terms of the pattern of appropriation. He understands the responsible man as one who has appropriated the existing law, who has made it his own, who obeys it on his own initiative and recognizance.

The seminarians, however, mean much more. They think of the responsible man as one who not only appropriates the law, but who partakes in the creation of the laws which he appropriates. He creates the law, makes himself responsible *for* the law, not out of a pure, totally uncommitted freedom but in view of a distinct task to which he commits himself, the creation of a human community and the attainment of a specific excellence.

If we listen again to their conversation, we shall hear one final statement which is of vital importance for the ethic of Christian responsibility. The rector responds, "You must remember that the rules and regulations which have been established by legitimate superiors are God's will for you." The seminarian again disagrees: "Father, there may be some sense in which these rules and regulations can be called God's will, but we think it makes more sense to say that God wills us to use our freedom and intelligence to work toward the accomplishment of the job he has given us. His will is really that the job be done: living humanly and Christianly."

This conversation contains, imperfectly and inchoatively, all of the elements of an ethic of Christian responsibility. The young man's argument lacks philosophical elaboration and theological grounding, but it sketches the outlines of an ethic of responsibility, as it seems to be taking shape in the attitudes of many thoughtful Christians. Our four authors have sensed this attitude coming into being and have attempted to offer the philosophical and theological considerations which form it into an ethic, a reflective understanding of morality suited for the intelligent direction of life.

An exegesis of the young seminarian's statements, done in the light of our authors' more profound reflections, may yield the prospect of an ethic of responsibility. In Chapter 2 the random sample of Christian moral literature revealed some confusion about the precise meaning of responsibility. This confusion was due, we suggested, to carelessness in distinguishing several areas of moral discourse.

An adequate ethical system ought to contain statements about the nature of the moral agent, about the principles and rules which affect this agent's choice and action, about the values which this agent should aim to realize and, if it is a religious ethic, about the way in which this agent is related to God. Thus, while in ordinary moral language these topics are often mingled, a reflective ethic should treat them distinctly, for each raises quite distinct issues. There are, then, at least four distinct but related areas of moral discourse: the area of the moral self, the area of norms, the area of values, and the area of theological affirmations. The literature examined in Chapter 2 seemed to waver uncertainly between these areas (we did not explicitly mention the area of values). On the other hand, it appeared upon analysis that our four authors rather consistently employed responsibility in the area of norms as a first unifying and normative principle.

Our seminarian also proclaims the primacy of responsibility. In his unsophisticated way he is invoking this idea as a first unifying and normative principle of morality. He claims that the idea of responsibility should be the rule of life and the rule of all other rules. He, like our authors, is placing responsibility in the area of norms. It does not directly describe a characteristic of the moral agent; nor does it directly state a value to be attained; nor does it directly make a theological affirmation. It does, however, imply something about each of these other areas. We will speak first about what it directly says as a norm, then about what it implies for the moral agent, about values and about God.

The Area of Norms The area of norms comprises the discussion of the principles and rules which affect an agent's choices and action. We have defined a principle as a conception having to do with choice which, when adopted by a moral agent, allows his action to be qualified by the moral predicate "right" and his person by the predicate "good." By "conception having to do with choice," we mean that it is the understanding of a manner of acting which can be effected by the agent's deliberate choice.

Furthermore, we indicated that a normative principle was authoritative; it lays a certain imperative claim upon the agent. Thus, a person aiming for Manhattan can be told, "Turn left before the George Washington Bridge or you will end up in New Jersey." If the person chooses to execute this conception of action, he will be "right" and go in the "right direction" to Manhattan. This advice is a principle guiding the choice of action. However, "Love your neighbor as yourself" seems to be more than practical advice. It seems to have an authority, an imperative force. It is more than helpful direction: it is an order.

Precisely how and why practical principles differ so significantly from moral principles is the subject of great controversy. Some moralists deny that they do, but most have been impressed with the difference and have endeavored to express in their own way what Kant expressed so forcibly in his doctrine of the Categorical Imperative: there is an unconditional necessity about moral principles which is lacking in hypothetical practical advice.

Thus if responsibility is a normative principle it is, first of all, a conception of action, and second, it is an imperative. If it is a first principle, it is the norm for the interpretation of any other principles or rules which the ethic involves. To say that it is a conception of action means simply that it is the idea of a certain procedure of acting, a manner of behaving which the agent can choose to adopt. The manner of acting must be rather clearly described. For example, Augustine said, "Love and do what you will," only after he had written many a page describing what loving actions looked like. To be told to love without being told how a lover proceeds is not to be given a principle but only a slogan, which any party can use to promote its own program.

Of course, the description of action may be quite general or rather detailed. If a conception of action is general, describing in a broad way a form of life, it is the kind of norm which is called a principle. Thus, the golden rule in its many formulations and "treat all men as brothers under the Fatherhood of God" are principles. They point out a stance, a general posture, which a man should take toward his life as a whole. If a conception of action is more detailed, describing a quite specific form of action, it is the kind of norm which can be called a rule. "Do not lie," "do not steal" are rules: the word "lie" evokes in the morally educated a quite specific conception of action, namely, making a public statement which is not in accord with what one knows to be the fact.

Every known morality "in lived life" contains principles and rules. In most known moralities the principles are few and usually implicit, and the rules are many and quite explicit. So a Catholic, questioned about his morality, may enumerate the ten commandments and the six precepts of the church, and usually forget "love, mercy and good faith." A Baptist or Methodist is just as likely to mention drinking and smoking, and forget the inner law of the Spirit.

Our seminarian and his patrons, our authors, certainly think of responsibility as a principle, as a general norm of action. "Be responsible" is an imperative commanding a certain manner of life. The philosophical pattern of appropriation provides a first description of that manner of life when it proposes considered, conscientious, committed action. "Be responsible" means: "In all that you do, exercise careful deliberation, stay with your deliberations, act decisively, accepting the consequences of your decision."

We have seen some of the authors examined in Chapter 2 describe responsibility in this way. It is a principle prescribing a consistent pattern of deliberate, conscientious, committed behavior. It is sometimes suggested that if responsibility is adopted as a first principle in this sense, this pattern is itself moral behavior. Morality consists in acting in this way and only in acting in this way. There are no other rules.

The primacy of the principle of responsibility, however, does not entail the disappearance of all other principles and rules. Our four authors, on the contrary, expect that there will be and in fact must be other rules and principles. Responsibility is the first principle, not the only principle; it is a unifying, not a unique principle. They intend the principle of responsibility to rule, and hence to draw into order all other norms. In fact, the principle of responsibility does not simply describe a pattern of action similar to the pattern of appropriation. It performs a much more important task for our authors: it describes a specific form of life insofar as it refers to a definite source of values and to a definite structure of the moral subject. In so doing, it indicates implicitly a whole realm of rules and principles, for rules and principles arise when a moral subject of a certain sort seeks to realize values of a certain sort.

The principle of responsibility, then, does much more than command conscientious, considered, committed action. It commands this manner of acting within a specific context of rules which are relevant to a certain moral subject and to definite values. In other words, first and foremost it commands that the total moral order—the structure of rules, values and agent—be taken seriously. It directs that the moral agent quite deliberately assume a moral order. He is asked to make himself responsible. This has a double meaning: he becomes responsible before other men by allowing himself to be judged in the light of his performance; he becomes responsible for the moral order by engaging himself to make its values and rules effective.

The former sense is familiar to all morality as the pattern of attribution; the latter sense is a rather unique conception. In attribution it is assumed that the moral agent is subject to the moral order, that is, that its rules and values imperatively determine his behavior. However, when the principle of responsibility requires that a man make a morality effective, it places the moral agent in charge of the morality itself. He is not only ruled, but ruler. He engages himself to bring into effective reality the norms and values which he accepts. This requires that he accept the task of understanding them, of bringing them to clarity of conception, of cultivating them and criticizing them.

An ethic of responsibility begins with an engagement to a moral order, something akin to the "conversion to the good" which St. Thomas posits as the inauguration of the moral life. It begins with the "fundamental option" which contemporary moralists require as the basis of morality: the free—though implicit—self-disposition in favor of or against one's finality. It begins with what other contemporary ethicians call "a decision of principle," the deliberate choice whereby man allows a moral order, with its rules and values, to become effective for himself. In this initiation into morality the agent seriously submits himself to a rule and at the same time undertakes the care of the rule he accepts.

In other words, if we may paraphrase Socrates, unexamined rules are not worth having. There is, in our opinion, no incompatibility between responsibility and rules. Indeed, it is difficult to think very seriously about responsibility in total abstraction from rules. All sorts of questions begin to arise: responsible for what, to whom, to what extent? On the other hand, it is not only easy but apparently it is one of the endemic diseases of morality to conceive, impose, and obey rules without responsibility.

There seems to be a deeply rooted tendency in the ethical animal to canonize rules. The holy rule of a religious order, the statutes of a church policy, custom, convention and rubric can all assume an imperative majesty which dictates, "Scrutinize not, nor question: simply obey!" Even quite properly moral rules can become detached from the values they once protected and promoted, and which are their *raison d'etre*. "Thou shalt not steal" has, in human history, justified the death or mutilation of the starving man who dared snatch bread from the prince's table. Put less picturesquely, it has prevented land reform, just taxation, fair wages. There is something about the definiteness and specificity of a rule which attracts and assuages the human conscience.

The principle of responsibility requires that whatever rules exist as defining a moral order be subject to scrutiny, revision and sometimes repeal. The criterion for the propriety of a rule is its effectiveness in promoting and protecting a value. A rule has no validity unless it commands action that realizes a value or prohibits action that endangers value.

The kind of norms we have called principles may in fact be direct expressions of values and are usually stated positively: for example, "love your neighbor" is an imperative to exercise that form of life which constitutes the value of community. Rules, on the other hand, seem to refer only obliquely to values and are very often stated negatively: "do not steal" prohibits a specific action in order to protect the value of private property.

If a norm has no obvious reference to a value, if it obstructs value-realization, it has gone awry. Either it is formulated improperly, and must be reformulated in such a way as to resume its proper function; or it has lost its validity, because the value no longer seems important or relevant. In either case, it is incumbent upon the responsible man to find the cause and remedy it. Revision or repeal of a long standing moral rule may be as necessary—though not as easy—as revision or repeal of an obsolete traffic law. However, unlike traffic laws, some moral norms have been proposed as "absolute": they lay claim to validity everywhere and always. In Antigone's oft-quoted words, they are the "unwritten, unalterable laws of God and heaven . . . not of yesterday or today, but everlasting." If there are such, they would resist repeal and be recalcitrant to revision.

We shall defer discussion of absolutes to our remarks on value. For the moment we shall only suggest that responsibility requires that norms *which are proposed as absolutes* should all be subject to examination in order to determine whether they do in fact have this dignity. As we mentioned above, ethics is constantly being deformed by the human bent to eternalize the temporal, to magnify the trivial and to absolutize the conditional. Without prejudice to the complex question of the existence and nature of absolute moral norms, it is still possible to test the claims of any norm to be absolute. This, we suggest, is not impertinence but responsible ethics.

Responsibility for the effectiveness of a moral order not only requires the reasonable criticism of principles. It also moves in to fill the gap where there are no rules. Ethicians have always recognized that principles and rules are abstract, universal propositions. As such, they cannot cover all contingencies in the actual, living reality of the moral decision. The medieval scholastics provided a rich store of moral concepts to supply for the insufficiency of rules: the doctrines of prudence, *epikeia,* dispensation, excuse, and so forth. These usually referred to the moment when an individual had to make a decision in a particular case.

However, today we find whole areas of life which are not "covered by the rules." The ethical problems of modern business and of modern warfare arise from the fact that these enterprises have vastly outgrown the relatively simple plan of moral principles which once provided guide-lines. The expansion of trade and the invention of investment, on which modern business is based, broke open the simple and formerly reasonable prohibition of usury which was a basic moral norm for mercantile transactions. The emergence of the national state, with its complex network of national interests, began to put severe strain on the doctrine of just war, for it became extremely difficult to discern the "just cause." The possibilities of mass destruction finally cracked that doctrine; it became too easy to expand the "just limits." Again, modern medical research is discovering immense possibilities of controlling not simply disease but the very physical and psychic structure of the person. Our meager stock of norms in medical morals is quite insufficient to deal with the ethical questions which this advance poses.

Clearly, the ethician cannot simply tell the advertising man, "be honest," nor the general, "attack only combatants," nor the physician, "do not mutilate." The complexity of their problems far surpasses the utility of such rules. This seems to leave vast areas of human endeavor without moral principle, and when an ethic which has emphasized rules has nothing to say, it appears to approve "laissez faire." Too familiar is the sight of the pious Catholic who is an unscrupulous politician, of the devout Baptist who is an unscrupulous businessman.

The principle of responsibility requires that the responsible man, salesman, general, politician or physician carry the spirit of the ethical principles which they adopt into those areas where no clear rules exist. He is asked to reflect upon the fundamental values which he espouses in the light of the actual facts of his work. In this context he must be a moral entrepreneur, bearing the responsibility of devising procedures which will, even if remotely, reflect the general stance which he takes toward human life. Responsibility not only requires considered, conscientious commitment to principle, not only the careful critique of principle, but also a moral creativity. The responsible man assumes the responsibility of taming, rationalizing, and humanizing every area of life in which he is engaged. We shall return to the subject of moral creativity when we discuss the moral agent.

We seem to have left our young seminarian far behind in this abstruse discussion of rules. However, he is still with us. In his request to be allowed to design his own order of life, he is asking not only to be responsible for observing rules, but to be responsible for the rules themselves. He and his companions have deliberately adopted a manner of life; they have made a decision of principle. They have, of course, chosen to be Roman Catholic priests, but in so doing they have intended to adopt one specific form of the Christian life.

The Christian life has been described in many ways. Every articulate man who has attempted to follow Christ, from Paul and Augustine through Martin Luther and John Calvin to Albert Schwietzer and Pierre Teilhard de Chardin, has tried to express the manner of life which this following requires. But in every description certain principles constantly reappear: the law of charity, of forgiveness, of humility, of fidelity, of trust in God's loving mercy and care. These principles are constitutive of a form of life. While their specific description can differ and their concrete realization vary, they stand as the indispensable characteristics and the essence of Christian moral life.

The seminarians are aware that they must undertake this form of life. They know that they must discern the meaning of these principles and realize these values—and, in concert with most Christians, admit that this discernment and realization is due to God's gracious action as well as their human effort. Within the context of this Christian life they have chosen a certain specific style and task, the priesthood as it is defined by Roman Catholic doctrine and by the discipline of that church. Their adoption of the priestly vocation, in an explicit act, and their adherence to the Christian life, which was probably more implicit, exemplify the first act in accord with the principle of responsibility. They have engaged themselves, considerately and conscientiously, to a form of life.

Having made this step, they now assume responsibility for the way of life they have adopted. They must employ their intelligence to clarify its principles; they must discern which of these principles are indispensable, defining features of the Christian life and of the priesthood, and which are but secondary. They must, in the light of this discernment, reform any deformed rules, abandon any useless ones, and create procedures for responsible action where none exist. They must use intelligence and discretion to modify the existing order in such a way that its real purpose can become effective.

Such responsibility by no means denies the presence and validity of principle and rule, for without these any manner of life loses its distinctive form. It only claims to deal with principles and rules responsibly. There may be, for example, a long standing seminary rule requiring silence during the day. It may have its origin in an ascetical doctrine which is no longer convincing. The seminarians, by a decision of principle, may determine to keep the rule for practical purposes: to maintain an atmosphere of study and reflection without which their expressed purpose, preparation for the priesthood, cannot be attained. But they may at the same time modify the rule so that it does not obstruct the formation of a community of friends and brothers in Christ. In this very small way they take responsibility for the form of life which they have deliberately chosen. They invoke in practice the first unifying and normative principle of responsibility.

But we must not be naïve: a seminary is not the world. Critics of such places, those who live in them and those who look in from without, will confirm this in detail: they are isolated, idealistic, introverted. A seminary might be called a world, but it is a very small one. Yet this is not the real problem. We are using the seminary as a sort of Plato's cave, as an image to evoke certain essential features of the morality of responsibility. It succeeds in evoking the features of commitment to and criticism of principle. It highlights the creativity which responsibility encourages. But precisely at this point the image is insufficient. Strangely enough, the moral world is often much smaller, much more confined than the seminary. The seminary, like any human institution, can be taken apart and put together again in any number of ways. An imaginative designer can think of a variety of arrangements, all of which will perform the same basic function, with the emphasis placed on different aspects. An order of the day, a regime of life, a plan of studies, these can be transformed in rich variety, to suit the needs of the time, the place, the individual.

The moral way, however, is strait and its gate is often narrow. Many moral situations do allow for a creativity which can evoke a variety of solutions. Such is often the case when a new and complex area of human enterprise opens up. But very frequently the moral problem is the "either/or." A man must often ask the one question, "Is this act right or wrong?" An ethic of responsibility widens the horizons by urging creative approaches to the moral problem of abortion, or of overpopulation: how many resources can be brought to bear on the solution of these problems? But in the last analysis the question remains: is abortion right or wrong? are we who practice contraception good or bad? The moral world consists of norms which need criticism and creative implementation, but it also consists of norms which pose the urgent and single question of the good and the right.

The Area of Value　　This urgent question, sharp and precise as it is, conceals a tangle of most difficult issues. We have seen our authors' attempts to untangle some of them. Their efforts seem to center on the question of value: the determination of the right action depends on adherence to the right rule, but the rule is itself right only when it protects and promotes a value. Moral action always involves reference to values. Turning onto the West Side Drive to reach lower Manhattan can be called "right action" but no one is called "good" because he does it. Moral philosophers will probably never explain why, but in some way the "right actions" and the "goodness of men" are intrinsically related. It is necessary to find the values which are at stake if the rules of morality are to remain valid and effective.

Finding value is just as much, perhaps more, the work of ethics and morality as obedience to rules. In fact, the word "creative" which we have used to describe responsible action might be replaced or supplemented by the word "inventive." To invent is to discover after investigation that one method, that one instrument, that one combination of elements which will do the job. Thus, it is morally necessary to find by the means proper to ethics—reason in conjunction with affection —the one value which will humanize this or that area of life.

Our four authors have provided a principle of responsibility which not only dictates a manner of action, but indicates the values, the "goods" which this action and the rules guiding it should realize. Our seminarian expresses quite simply what our four authors have stated much more elaborately. He and his companions ask to design an order of life which will bring about a community of friends and brothers in Christ and which will facilitate the task to which they are devoted.

This is the dominant value: a true human community living effectively in its environment. We have heard this proposed again and again by our authors. They call for the cultivation of true and full human life. They advocate the discovery and the implementation of the potentiality of human reality. The human good, the goal and the criterion of ethical rules and actions, is growth in humanity, in the use of intelligence and in the union of love. This basic value is attained only as it is refracted into a concern for all of the conditions necessary for human existence and progress: the improvement of physical, economic, social and cultural life.

A commitment to realize the basic value of full humanity involves a devotion to the study of the actual, concrete factors which contribute to richer and deeper human life. Thus the basic value summons to a philosophical reflection on the nature of man, to psychological and psychosocial research, to economic and sociological and biological study. It summons also to political action, to involvement in social crisis and, perhaps, to forms of social revolution.

There is considerable interest today in the nature and function of value. But neither the social scientists, who have investigated value function, nor the philosophers, who have

reflected on the nature of value, are satisfied with their understanding of this elusive subject. We cannot here enter into their
discussions. It is sufficient for our purpose to define value
as a state of the person or the community which it is desirable
to achieve and maintain. There are interminable debates
about whether "desirable" means "*able* to be the object of
desire" or "*ought* to be the object of desire." We shall avoid
them by simply saying: to the proponents of a morality of
responsibility certain states of the person and of the community are *de facto* desired goals. They are the objectives
of action and the criteria for the validity of rules and the
propriety of behavior.

These values are all refractions of the basic value: a true
human community of persons living together effectively in its
environment. The states of person and community which
constitute this or which are its conditions are diverse. Physical
health, comfort, emotional stability and satisfaction, intellectual
attainment, friendship, trust, openness and reciprocity, economic progress, social order and justice, peace, and so on.
Indeed, perhaps it is impossible to define the human good
except by specifying its numerous constituent elements. However, insofar as a generic definition is possible, it can be said
that all of the values of an ethic of responsibility center on
the attainment and preservation of the human person living
easily and effectively in a community of persons.

Should this be surprising? Does this not say precisely
what the best forms of contemporary humanism are saying?
This is exactly what *is* surprising. The ethic of responsibility
is a humanism, and as such is in need of vindication in the
Christian community. We have seen our four authors struggle
to overcome in theory the dualities which, in their judgment,
have vitiated Christian ethics. Are these dualities, however
they may be expressed in one or another Christian tradition,
merely figments of their imaginations? After all, the Christian
Church has always had before it the words of its Lord: "I
was hungry and you gave me to eat, thirsty and you gave me

to drink. . . ." And the Church has always sought to do this "to the least of his brethren." Even in the worst of times, Christian care for the poor, the sick, the ignorant, has gone on. Furthermore, for most of its history the Christian Church —Catholic, Protestant and Orthodox—has been deeply involved for better or worse in politics and culture. Finally, Catholic and Protestant theologies have adopted ethical theories for action in the world: Catholic natural law, Lutheran orders of creation, Calvinist stewardship. Is not all this proof enough that the Christian Church has always advocated a humanistic ethic, centered on the good of man?

Yet there is some reason why Pope Paul VI had to say, in his closing address to Vatican II, "The Church looks at the world with profound understanding, with sincere admiration and with the genuine intention not of dominating it but of serving it; not of despising it but of appreciating it; not of condemning it but of strengthening and saving it." His words counter the deep and widespread conviction, among Christians and non-Christians, that the domination, despisal and condemnation of the world are inextricably woven into the substance of the Christian viewpoint. The Church has also had before it the words of its Lord: "I pray not for the world, but for those you have given me out of the world . . . they are not of the world, as I too am not of the world." It has heard the words of his disciples: "Be not conformed to the world," "True religion is to remain unspotted from the world."

It has been much too easy to interpret "world" as the culture in which one lived, the human life with which one was surrounded and was forced to share. The mission to save the world became in the minds of many Christians the task of saving it from itself, from its humanity. This humanity was identified in diverse ways: sexuality, the need for friendship, the use of money and possession of property, the production of art, of artifacts, or weapons. At some time in Christian history, each of these and other human endeavors has been identified as "the world," as a sign of the weakness of the flesh and the effect of sin. They were, then, to be eradicated, or neglected, or repressed.

Many scholars have noted that Thomas Aquinas, the first Christian theologian to develop systematically the ancient stoic and patristic idea of natural law, transformed it in a most interesting way. Although he retained and used an earlier definition of the natural law as a participation in the divine law, he avoided another traditional definition which identified it as the law of the gospel. He concentrated on the way in which the divine law, the ordering wisdom of God in creation, is manifested in the nature of man. He specified its site in the most radical human inclinations or instincts: self-preservation, procreation, the need to know truth and to live in society.

Some commentators have called this the "desacralization" or "secularization" of the moral law: human morality does not consist of rules which break into human life from without, but of rules meant to promote and protect that very life itself, growing out of its most concrete manifestations. Scholars have not, to my knowledge, noted that Thomas wrote this at a time when orthodox Christianity was faced with the most extreme dualistic heresy, Albigensianism. Thomas' fundamental precepts of the natural law counter the fundamental ethical doctrines of the Albigensians, who extolled suicide, condemned procreation, and hid the truth about God in an esoteric society. Thomas affirmed, more clearly than any earlier Christian theologian, that Christian morality was a humanism: that it commanded men to live in their world as men.

But if the Church and its teachers have strongly condemned the extreme dualisms, as Augustine did Manichaeism and Thomas did Albigensianism, it has never overcome the more muted dualisms. Orthodox Christians have, by invoking the dualistic language of heaven and earth, spirit and flesh, sacred and secular, preached a subtle condemnation of human life and its progress. Two worlds of value exist: human, natural values and supernatural, divine values. The former must, of course, be respected, but they are always to yield to the latter.

The latter are characterized usually by a negation of natural instincts, effected by ascetical practice and iron will, and by invoking in crisis a divine aid wholly beyond human experience. These values are not expected to exhibit themselves in any empirical way that gives evidence of a deepening or an enrichment of the person. They constitute a wholly other ethic, a superior ethic, which parallels the natural ethic of human life.

This is, perhaps, a bit of a parody. But it is what many Christians seem to believe. Our four authors take it seriously enough to launch a vigorous attack against its various forms. Indeed, many Christians live comfortably enough with this dual ethic. For some Catholic Christians, the supernatural ethic is a specialty to be practiced by monks and nuns. Some commentators observe that the Protestant abolition of convent life threw Lutheran and Calvinist ethics into confusion: every man was faced with the excruciating problem of being in the world but not of it.

But while many Christians live fairly easily with dualism by ignoring it or mitigating it, it has been responsible for serious aberrations. Among individuals, it has led to the "Sunday Christianity" of the good churchgoer who would do his grandmother out of her pension check any (other) day of the week. More seriously, it has led to the belief that a practice like clerical celibacy was an "other worldly" value, which somehow could be lived outside the realm of human emotions, physical reactions, affection. Celibacy is as much a human moral stance as marriage—though it owes its status in Christianity to the words of its founder—and can be elected and lived in precisely the same way, with the same resources and with the same responsibility as marriage.

In the social sphere, dualism has also deformed Christian ethics. In the nineteenth century certain moral theologians objected to social reforms on the grounds that if there were no more poverty, the specifically Christian or supernatural virtue of charity could not be practiced: to whom would one give the cup of cold water if every man had his own faucet? The two most vigorous and telling criticisms of Christianity in the nineteenth century bear precisely on this point. Both Marx and Nietzsche condemned a teaching which turned men away from the task of being human and toward a future reward gained by an asceticism that denied the value of this world and a supernaturalism that absorbed them in spiritual duties to the detriment of human work. Both critiques are perhaps extreme, but they have had their effect. Nietzsche's analysis set the theme for subsequent intellectual critiques of Christianity; Marx's has been convincing enough to draw to his side countless men who have despaired of finding their humanity within the Christian faith.

Thus, while there is a proper theology of the supernatural and a proper Christian asceticism, the ethic of responsibility insists that there is no place for an "other-worldly" ethic running parallel to and above the ethics of this world. Human morality exists precisely to foster the human good, and the human good is the creation and protection of human personality in community. No action can be called "right" and no agent "good" unless this value is in view.

While it is impossible ever to guarantee results in the moral order, human behavior must be motivated by the hope that it will effect this goal. The ethic of responsibility refuses to offer as a motive for moral behavior, "you will go to heaven and save your soul." This, hopefully, is the consequence of good Christian action, but the agent must look to the good effected in the world by his action. Likewise, it is not enough simply to say, "God wills it" in order to sanction a moral rule. God may indeed will it, but the responsible man believes that God's will bears on the empirical human good. If he can find no human value involved, he suspects that God's will might in reality be someone's whim.

The rules which constitute a morality come, not out of the blue nor from the fancy of an authority, but from looking for, discovering, "inventing" human values. Values are not discovered by looking into the blue, but by looking at man living in the world. This looking is much more than sight-seeing: it requires anthropological expeditions, sociological surveys, psychological interviews. But it requires something much more complex and perplexing: it requires the philosophical look, the reflection upon our own humanness and the a priori conditions for its attainment and preservation. We must know not simply that men like to be free and that they struggle to be free, but that they *must* be free if they are to be human. We must know not simply that men love company and seek out friends, but that they *must* find communion if they are to be human. Our moral norms, principles and rules are the rational attempt to formulate ways and means of reaching that which we must have in order to be human.

We can discover value only where it lies, in the reality of man. A rule is morally valid when it directs us back to the reality from which it was drawn and focuses our attention and decision upon the values demanded by the reality. A precise moral "situation," a here-and-now for decision, is by no means the total moral reality. It is a limited sector, ontologically and epistemologically. It needs to be informed about the wider moral reality, the fuller scope of the human person in community. Rules provide this service: they expand the morally relevant issues, they reveal the extent of value at stake. In the last analysis, the norms, rules and principles are not "extrinsic" to the situation, imposed upon it from without, but drawn from the wider realm of moral value, of which the situation is but a sector. It is not always easy to say what rules are applicable, but if we find one that is, its applicability rests on its function as a pointer to the values at stake in this actual decision.

The Area of the Moral Self   When we hear our seminarian call for a form of life which will be conducive to a community of friends and brothers and will facilitate the job of learning to be effective priests, he echoes the values which our four authors specify as determining the shape and scope of an ethic of responsibility. He also seems to be recalling a statement which he had recently read in the great charter of the ethic of responsibility, *The Constitution on the Church in the Modern World* of Vatican Council II. The Council bishops declare:

> In every group or nation, there is an ever-increasing number of men and women who are conscious that they themselves are the artisans and the authors of the culture of their community. Throughout the world there is a similar growth in the combined sense of independence and responsibility. Such a development is of paramount importance for the spiritual and moral maturity of the human race. . . . We are witnesses of the birth of a new humanism, one in which man is defined first by his responsibility toward his brothers and toward history.[4]

Our seminarian can quote from reputable sources. He may not realize all of the implications of his request. He most probably has little fear that his humanism poses the serious theological problem which is today discussed under the rubric of secularism. He simply feels that the form of life to which he is devoted should be defined by human criteria, and that the Christ to whom he is devoted sanctioned such a definition. We shall discuss in turn the problem of the human criteria and then, finally, the theological assumptions of an ethic of responsibility.

An ethic which claims to be a "humanism" must supply its adherents with some understanding of the human reality. This is not a simple task. It requires profound philosophical reflection, constant attention to empirical evidence, acute sensitivity to the breadth and depth of human experience. For the Christian, it includes as well the awareness of a message about man which does not come from man, but from his creator and redeemer. Further, the understanding of man does not simply reach a final Q.E.D., like the understanding of a geometrical figure. It grows philosophically and empirically as the race lives longer and individuals live more expansively. We are only beginning to appreciate the role of man's history in the formation of his reality; we have hardly begun the exploration of the depth of his personality. Whatever "human nature" might mean, it certainly does not denote, as some seem to have thought, a metaphysical skeleton, untouched by time and experience, about which a long chain of clear and certain propositions can be listed.

An ethic, then, needs an anthropology. The anthropology for the ethic of responsibility begins to coalesce, drawing on many sources: existentialism, personalism, phenomenology, the sciences of man, even literature and art. It will suffice for our purposes to focus on one of the central and characteristic features of the understanding of man in an ethic of responsibility. As Niebuhr suggested in his *Responsible Self,* it is possible to elucidate the basic image of man which underlies a particular form of ethics. In the light of his suggestion and those of our other authors, we might propose that the image of the moral agent which dominates an ethic of responsibility is that of the decision maker.

But is this not terribly trite? Does not every ethic necessarily picture man as a decision maker? The very idea of an ethic presupposes that man is faced with alternatives, one of which he must choose. Aristotle's ethic pivots on the *proairesis,* selective choice; Aquinas insisted that without an adequate notion of free choice the notions of right and wrong, good and bad, praise and punishment were nonsense. How can the image of man as decision maker be unique to an ethic of responsibility?

The image of the responsible man as decision maker brings into view an aspect of moral choice which the traditional ethics either neglect or de-emphasize. It concentrates on the confusion and on the creativity of moral decision. By "confusion," I mean that moral decisions are sometimes more complex than a choice between clearly discerned good and bad: they are often agonizing dilemmas about where the good lies. There is very often a challenge to discern precisely what *is* the just, the honest, the courageous course of action. Moral men are often torn between obedience and honesty, or between justice and mercy. Thus, the ethics of responsibility stresses that many a moral decision involves a confusion that cannot be dispelled by getting more information, nor by good will and pure intention. The information is in, the good will is abundant, but the right way remains uncertain. Still, lest nothing happen at all—not an unusual escape from such dilemmas—action must issue from the confusion: this takes place only by decision.

Many traditional images of man as decision maker seem to imply that the decision is a simple yes or no, uttered in the presence of definite alternatives. The popular moral image which borrows, quite improperly, the scriptural language of "flesh and spirit," insinuates that the moral alternatives can be clearly identified. The things of the flesh can be listed, whether they be wine, women and song for the baser sort, or self-satisfaction, creature comforts, and the mere stirring of desire for the more advanced. Even the much more sophisticated Kantian alternatives, duty and inclination, suppose that in any moral situation the path of inclination is clearly marked. The moral decision is in essence a choice made at a cross-road, where the signpost can be read. Indeed, how often has Christian moral literature used that very image!

Admittedly the serious ethicians, Christian and non-Christian, have always been aware of the complexity of moral decision. Elaborate systems of "probabilism, equi-probabilism, probabiliorism, and so on, devised by moral theologians, attest to that fact. Even more, the Pauline struggle between "the good that I would do and the evil that I do" has cast its shadow over all Christian ethics. Still, few ethicians and even fewer preachers seem able to resist the temptation to point out the way. They grant that the matter is difficult and complex, but they are confident that this way or that way is in fact the right one and will lead to the good.

The ethic of responsibility hopes to be much more modest. While it is often possible to dispel the confusion which besets a man faced by a decision, just as often that confusion arises not from simple misinformation nor from profound conflicts of desire, but from the complexity of the issues or from the density of the matter. The usual ethical signals are scrambled: the inextricability of undesirable and desirable consequences, the uncertainty of results, direct contradiction between rules, an obedience that seems to impede value, and value achievement that seems to defy obedience, all this and much more can contribute to the confusion surrounding the moral decision. The responsible man must resign himself to enter into this confusion, to make his decision, not only in the light of values and principles, but in the darkness of actually experienced pain and joy, desire and revulsion, love and hatred.

But if the responsible decision is condemned to confusion on many important occasions, it is also privileged to be creative. Responsibility seeks to bring values into "lived life." It struggles to bring a new and better situation out of the confusion. It seeks a fresh vision of values that inspire a way of life and a more effective statement of the rules that are meant to promote those values. The ethic of responsibility, like man himself, is in the making.

Once again, the responsible man and the more traditional moral man can be thought of as travellers. But the more traditional image allows the traveller to have a map and a well-posted road. The newer image pictures him as an explorer. Time and again he will meet in a relatively open moral landscape an unsuspected obstacle. A chasm to cross or a mountain to climb presents the peril of the unknown. He must decide whether to continue ahead or to return, and if he continues, which path to take.

Less romantically, the image of the moral man must comprehend within itself the actual men of modern politics, business, science, industry. These men are, in fact, faced with new situations, for which there are no precedents or rules of procedure. These must be devised, designed. The design of the procedures will be shaped to further the goals of the company, the party, the nation. These are the real men whom we hope will be moral men. If a morality is offered them in which all eventualities are foreseen and solved, they can hardly judge it useful for their lives. If a morality is closely tied to the relatively patterned life of the individual, it can say little of relevance about the more rapidly evolving life of industry, communication, commerce, defense.

Thus the responsible man as decision maker is one who, while he admits that in great part established principle and rule suffice to order life, is aware that he will meet new situations, with new exigencies. He is aware that the values which he accepts must be realized in new situations, amid new difficulties, with renewed energy and resourcefulness. He knows that he must continually endeavor to draw out of his personal and communal experience a new appreciation of the values. But he is also aware that his experience is unfinished and often deceptive. He attains new insights into his own reality and achieves new expression of those insights, but always by experiment, risk, trial and error. His moral creativity is more that of the apprentice than of the master: his strokes are tentative and often need to be retouched.

Human moral creativity is far from divine. Many Christian authors have maintained that man participates in a limited way in God's creativity. But unlike God, man never summons being from nothing. So this moral creativity draws on human experience as its material. Moral experience is by no means limited to moral trials and tribulations, victories and achievements of the individual. Moral experience is the experience of the human community. Moral discussion and decision are effected in a particular society whose form of life is defined by certain values. This society inherits the cumulative experience of its ancestors.

The efforts of many men to live humanly, aided by the

reflection of some few great men and many minor moralists on these efforts, have yielded certain constants. They have recognized that certain ideals are indispensable for human life and growth. The protection of life itself, the cultivation of physical conditions for its thriving, the distribution of good, the promotion of fidelity, of honesty, of impartial justice: these have, through long experience, emerged as constant demands, as a priori conditions for human life in community. They reflect "human nature," and the rules formulated in their regard constitute, as St. Thomas pointed out, the first precepts of the natural law. Man's moral creativity inherits all this material. Here man is more the inventor, the discoverer, than the creator.

Ethicians have debated much about "absolutes." Usually they have asked whether any laws or rules were absolute, that is, imperative always and everywhere. This is a valid question, but it must be preceded by a discussion of whether *values* are absolute. In this question "absolute" means something rather different; it is to be taken in its etymological sense of "removed, in abstraction from." Thus the question is, are there certain states of the person and the community which are to be desired and promoted (for which are values) regardless of where or when men are living? If there are values *absoluta a circumstantiis et particularibus,* then whatever rules (that is, directives for action) devised for their promotion and protection are also "absolute" in the former sense (that is, to be observed everywhere and always).

Perhaps some of the confusion in moralists' debates could be dissolved by recognizing that "absolute" can mean two quite different things. However, we do not pretend to solve with this comment the difficult issue of absolutes in ethics. We wish to point out that man's moral creativity inherits certain constants which moral reflection has disengaged from experience. These constants or values do not impede his creativity, for they come to it precisely to be realized in action, in the particular time and place where he is, to resolve the concrete issue with which he is faced. As many philosophers from Plato to Hartmann have suggested, values, though found in human reality, seem to live in a timeless conceptual world. They must be born into the time and space of human action. As soon as a situation calls for the birth of a concrete act of fidelity or justice, man's creativity must be exercised. The medieval scholastics called this creativity prudence; many today call it responsibility.

Assuredly our young seminarian was not thinking of all this when he asked to design his own life. The enthusiasm of youth makes such a project seem easy. But he does appreciate himself in the role of one who must make decisions and whose decisions must be allowed to enter into the substance of his life. Moral education and moral exhortation must prepare responsible men. Many a priest and minister has bemoaned the fact that his parishioners do not know what to do, or even that there is something to be done, unless he tells them. They complain that there are so many Christians who measure out the modern forms of mint and cumin, but neglect the weightier things of the law, justice and mercy and love. In essence they are complaining that they do not find responsible men among their people. Perhaps they are unconsciously admitting that they have not formed responsible men. Perhaps it is, above all, God's will and God's work that those beings to whom he has given the potential for responsibility, freedom and intelligence, become in fact responsible men.

The Area of Theological Affirmation   With the words "God's work and will" we approach the final and possibly the most difficult category of moral discourse: theological affirmation. We must ask about the theological assumptions which underlie the ethics of responsibility. The responsible man is a creative moralist, a decision maker, devoted to the promotion and protection of human values within the context of certain rules because he believes that this is God's will for him and for his world. He believes that his responsibility is the agency for God's action in the world.

While theologians struggle over the epistemological problem of how man can conceive God or make affirmations about him, moralists have selected images of God which support or substantiate their presentation of ethics. Scripture and Christian tradition provide them with a rich store of such images. But moralists have usually chosen one or another of these to suit the purposes of their moral system. If they preached a rigorous ethic of duty, they chose to speak of God as ruler and judge. If they preached of morality of love, their God appeared as redeemer and savior. The ethic of natural law needed a creator of nature; an ethic of otherness and separation required God as deliverer. Asceticism displayed the incarnate, suffering Lord; enthusiasm invoked the Holy Spirit. Some few great figures in Christian ethics endeavored to draw much of this together in more comprehensive images: Augustine's creator, the beginning of all things, was also object of desire, the end of all things; Luther's God is creator, source of the orders of nature, and redeemer, source of saving faith and love. Thus, while the God of Christian faith is all of this, theological ethicians must find in this superabundance of divine names one or several which best serve to identify the Lord of their lives.

With this in mind, we shall mention here those aspects of the Christian understanding of God which seem most suited to serve as the basis for a theology of responsibility. We cannot, of course, even begin to construct such a theology here. We recognize that the theological concepts to which we refer and their sources in Scripture and tradition may not support the interpretations which the ethic of responsibility wishes them to bear. Furthermore, some may be incompatible with others. Finally, even if they can be rightly interpreted and rightly integrated, it is not certain whether they do in fact give theological support to the ethical positions. It is not easy to say precisely how a theology supports an ethic. All of these questions we leave for future consideration. We will here try to describe the God of responsibility, Father, Son and Holy Spirit.

Our seminarian concludes his argument by asserting that God wills us to use our freedom and intelligence to accomplish the job he has given us, living humanly and Christianly. In saying this, he assumes that God's will is manifested in the form and function of the human being as he finds himself. He finds himself with a reasoning power and with the ability to choose; he finds himself faced with the problem of living humanly. This "given data" is a revelation of God's will. His will is revealed in his work. This is, of course, the basic assumption which underlies any ethic which looks to the created world for its signals about the right and the good. It is the fundamental assumption of natural law ethics and of the ethics of the orders of creation.

This assumption performs two important roles for Christian ethics. First, it declares that the creation is good; that, hence, man can live and work in its realities without fear of contamination or condemnation. This is the resounding condemnation of the radical Gnostic dualisms. Second, it provides a theory for the source of ethical norms. Values are basically linked to the things men find necessary and pleasing: life in community and its prerequisites, marriage, property, government, justice, and so on. Rules are drawn from the perception of the necessary safeguards for these human goods. The values and the rules are "words of God," for creation is the manifestation of his will for man. Even the great "Ten Words," the Decalogue, which men do not read in their world but hear directly from God himself, do not add to the sum of the commands which man knows from his nature. They reaffirm with the majesty of direct divine sanction, and state with lapidary conciseness, the law of man's nature. In this manner Christian theologians from the very beginning have depicted the role of God the creator, one who designs a world which utters his intention and command.

The ethic of responsibility accepts and re-affirms the centrality of God the creator as a basic ethical affirmation. Its emphasis on human values requires this. It is, like the natural law ethic, not world-denying but world-affirming, to use Troeltsch's terms. In more modern language, it is a secular ethic, in the sense of an ethical system which values the created world and which finds its values in that world. But it is a secular ethic which is part of a secular theism: it contends, on ontological as well as theological grounds, that the world and its values are marked with the evidence of transcendence. This is a world which in its origin, its present and its purpose is the work of God.

It is the conception of the work of God which differentiates ethics of responsibility from the older ethics of creation. The more traditional forms, natural law and order of creation, have been accused of static conservatism. Whether or not this is intrinsic to these conceptions, it is historically true that both of them have been invoked to defend institutions which were no longer humanly functional on the grounds that these were "natural" to man and, hence, manifested the immutable will of God. Thus monarchy, the subjection of women and social inequality, have been defended in terms of the ethics of creation. True, revolutionary social change has also been justified by natural law, but strangely, the most dramatic of such changes, the revolutions of the eighteenth century, were effected by non-theistic or deistic practitioners of natural law.

The doctrine of creation which appeals to the ethicians of responsibility conceives of God as still at work, as presently acting in the universe to bring new being into existence. *Creatio continuata* refers not simply to the divine action sustaining all things in existence, but to God's present activity effecting the evolution of all things. Such a conception reflects the contemporary understanding of physical evolution and of history. Growth and progress are not simply waves on the surface of a quiet creation, but constitute its deepest current. This growth and progress are by no means independent of the divine creativity. God is at work in and through all of this, drawing all things to himself.

Creation is not only actuality, but potentiality waiting to be realized. Man is the agent of that realization. His own constitution, as potentiality which can actualize itself, in self-reflection and freedom, is directed toward the actualization of the world in which he is placed. Morality consists in the self-direction with which man sets himself to the task of his own realization within the realization of mankind and the world. It is a self-direction because he must, on his own initiative, accept and undertake the task. It is a direction, because the task itself is not random play, but a work to be accomplished within the context of definite dimensions and limitations. These are not arbitrarily imposed like the rules of a game, but are the reflection of the inner potential of the beings which make up the world. They will grow and develop only if their own potential is tapped; they can be destroyed or retarded if it is ignored.

This description of a doctrine of creative evolution that might be congruent with an ethic of responsibility is stated very generally. But the theological doctrine of creation is itself in evolution. Certainly we see today that it is possible to reconcile creation and evolution, but we do not yet know the precise conditions for that reconciliation. Even less clear are the moral implications of a doctrine of creative evolution.

The ethic of responsibility would maintain that man's moral life cannot be the constant rehearsal by successive generations of the same simple patterns. Indeed, there is a pattern, constituted by the very structure of the potentiality of man and the universe. But the pattern undergoes rearrangement, reformulation and renewal. Man's ethical creativity is not God's creativity, but it is linked to it and involved in it. Both divine and human freedom are creative and are engaged in a cooperative creation. God creates in such a way that the created world—not merely the physical universe, but all finite reality, history, culture, experience—is designed as a task, with certain dimensions and goals. This task is then committed to human agents for implementation. The human agents are created and constituted with the freedom and creativity which enable them to recognize, accept and realize the task set for them by God. In a very real sense, man is a providence unto himself, as St. Thomas Aquinas said. But in this new theology man's own providence enters effectively into the victory or failure—even if only relative failure—of the divine providence.

Within this perspective, it is possible to imagine that man's moral activity may move toward levels hitherto unsuspected, that new exigencies may arise in his moral experience, that fresh values may emerge. It is also possible that this progress may so widen and deepen moral experience that former exigencies lose their force and values their appeal. If God and man are engaged in creative cooperation then, behold, all things can be made new! God's activity and man's activity continually bring into being and into sight new values.

The history of morality can be read as the history of the emerging and receding importance of values. Certainly the subordinate place of women in the western world for so many centuries was considered a moral matter. It was defined by clear rules for behavior, was strongly sanctioned, and reflected definite values. Within the social, cultural and economic structure it was a functional system. But for a variety of reasons the values it reflected and the rules which supported them receded in meaning and importance. Today one reads with amusement the serious arguments of some nineteenth century moralists who were attempting to reinforce a system of values and rules already crumbling under the emergence of new and more significant ones.

Likewise, we seem to be witnesses today of a growing sensitivity to the destruction of human life. At a time when the ability to destroy extensively and swiftly increases enormously, many people, in word and action, demonstrate that the inviolability of life is a value more important than self-defense and the interests of a nation. Where this fluctuation of value might lead is yet unsure, but it dramatically reveals the emergence and recession of values. There are many more such examples.

The ethic of responsibility wishes to associate this history of the emergence and recession of values to man's moral creativity and his moral creativity to the continuing creation which God is effecting in the present and for the future. Such a theology is most appealing to the contemporary mind. But despite its *prima facie* appeal it raises many theoretical problems. The language in which I have described it is unclear. The vocabulary of cooperative creation, potentiality, realization, task, progress, needs insofar as possible to be chiseled into clarity. There are still, as there have always been, profound metaphysical problems. To speak of cooperative creation does not solve the ancient difficulties about *concursus*, the congruence of primary and secondary causes. To speak of progress, the emergence of new values, and so on, does not dispel the old questions about mutations of natures. There are serious ethical problems as well. On what grounds is it justifiable to say that what becomes present to human experience as a "new value" or as a "new exigence" does in fact represent the creative action of God? Is it possible to indicate any fixed points in human life in relation to which progress or deterioration can be recognized? In what sense can that progress or deterioration, if recognizable, be related to the fulfillment of God's will? It is easy to assert that man's creative moral evolution represents cooperation with divine creativity; it is much less easy to point to this or that moral stance as an example of creative evolution.

There are, then, theological, metaphysical, and ethical problems surrounding the assumptions about God the creator in the ethics of responsibility. Still, many Christians today are convinced that their moral life must be lived under the eyes of such a God. They believe that human history, filled though it is with sin and destruction, does manifest a growing appreciation of man's humanity. They believe that this growth itself reveals God's desire to lift to higher actuality the human potentiality he has created. They believe that they are called to be cooperative agents in this work. The ethical life, for such Christians, is the human, limited, tentative, but real participation in this desire of God.

Ethicians of responsibility should recognize the problems involved in adopting a theology of creative evolution. But their theological commitment is not limited to the doctrine of creation. Roman Catholic moral theology has been accused of restricting its theological view to the doctrine of creation—and even of seeing this doctrine only in philosophical terms —and of neglecting to find a significant place in Christian morality for the doctrine of redemption. Lutheran ethics, on the other hand, has been accused of accepting both doctrines without integrating them. The ethic of responsibility looks to both doctrines and hopes to integrate them.

The natural and human world is affirmed as good and valuable because it is the object of God's creative action. But clearly that world is marked by sin and death. In particular, man's moral life carries brutal, often self-inflicted wounds: it is vacillating, vicious, weak, lethargic, self-deceptive. Yet is not all this within the ambit of God's creation? Indeed it is: it is precisely the world of sin and death which he has seen fit to redeem. This is the world which he so loved that he sent his only Son for its salvation. The incarnation, life, death and resurrection of Jesus Christ manifest the Father's intention to draw a fallen world to himself, to integrate it again into the revelation of his glory.

Theologians have explored at length the profound theological significance of the redemption, but they have seldom dwelt upon its ethical significance. Perhaps it is one of the historical misfortunes of theology that having once vanquished Pelagianism, a heresy which overstressed the ethical significance of the redemption, theology did not seriously pursue the elements of truth embedded in the rejected doctrine. Thus, beyond the common agreement that one principal effect of the redemption is to render man's action pleasing to God, Christian theology —with a few outstanding exceptions—has not exploited the ethical meaning of God's redemptive action.

Even the few exceptions have been strangely ineffective. Aquinas, taking up a clue from Augustine, asserts the primacy of charity, which means that the supernatural virtue of charity, the created participation in the divine love, informs and vivifies all human virtue. But this doctrine has neither been developed by dogmatic theologians nor applied by moral theologians until very recently. Luther, though he violently rejected the doctrine of "informing charity," stressed the invasion of God's love into the justified man, a love which flowed down to the believer and which the believer was to pass on to his brethren and neighbors. But the over-rigid interpretation of Luther's doctrine of the Two Kingdoms ultimately excluded any real effectiveness for this love in the world.

The ethic of responsibility must seek the ethical significance of the redemption. This doctrine can teach first of all that Christian ethics is an ethic for men wounded by sin, and that it is thus an ethic which accepts limitation, weakness and failure as part of the human reality. It cannot develop into a thorough-going, uncritical optimism. We shall speak of this matter briefly at the end of this chapter.

Second and more important, the doctrine of redemption teaches that the moral life must be a life which not only avoids sin but which destroys sin. Christian morality has long centered on the avoidance of sin; it must turn its energy to the more positive task of destroying the marks of sin and death, insofar as these can be attacked by human effort. Although many theologians in recent times have restricted their notion of sin to individual acts and their understanding of original sin to the effects in the individual person, there is a long Christian tradition which sees in the hatred, destructiveness, disorder and exploitation of men in society the most profound inroads of sin in the world.

One reaction to this "sinful world" was escape: the formation of the community of saints who lived apart, neither touching nor touched by the affairs of men. The reaction of the ethic of responsibility is to turn toward the world of human affairs and to engage in healing the wounds. This healing comes not from the kindly word and the friendly gesture (though these are often badly needed), but from engaging in political, social and economic action and reform. The redemption reconciles God and man, and consequently, as St. Paul realized, reconciles man and man. The ethics which seem to flow from this redemption must be directed to the reconciliation in the most concrete way: the endeavors to close the rifts which divide men, to build a viable human community.

The redemption means Jesus Christ. Christian responsibility lives in the presence of the one whom the Father sent to redeem the world. The person of Jesus has entered into human life so strikingly that he has forced a re-evaluation of what man is and how he stands before God. Even if one sees only the man, Jesus of Nazareth, his words and example can have profound moral impact. He can be the hero of the secular non-theistic humanist because of his call for men to attend to their lives. But if he is confessed as eternal Son of the Father, his presence in human history must be an overwhelming revelation of what God means man to be.

It is very difficult to define the human reality. We who have the power to reflect upon ourselves can never comprehend the totality of what we are. We are, in fact, a perpetual question to ourselves. We are, despite the vast amount of information and the profound insights, mysteries to ourselves. But it has always seemed to Christian thinkers, and now to ethicians of responsibility, that there is light shed on that mystery by looking at the man whom we confess as eternal Son of the Father.

Christian ethics has chosen a certain picture of Jesus, just as it has selected a certain image of God. The gospels present a poor and humble preacher, an ascetic, a sympathetic friend and healer, an imperious prophet, an insightful teacher, a suffering victim, an obedient son, a victorious Lord. All of these pictures have served as models for a Christian ethic. (Interestingly, the standard manuals of Roman Catholic moral theology seldom mention Christ as more than new lawgiver!)

We cannot discuss in detail the role of Christ in the ethics of responsibility. However, we will mention two points which are of particular importance. The total picture of Jesus which the gospels present puts a strain on our conception of what the good man ought to be. When tempted to think of ourselves as men of simple moderation and good sense, we see Jesus uttering the hard words about abnegation and suffering. When satisfied that we have worked out an ethic of enlightened self-interest, we see him give his life for his brethren. When extolling the primacy of human liberty, we find him obedient unto death. When defining the human reality only in terms of evident growth, we are recalled to the mystery of failure. The presence of Jesus Christ in our history must inevitably put pressure upon our self-understanding. Human beings are more than they know themselves to be; their behavior has repercussions beyond the evident ones. Jesus Christ reveals in the most concrete way that which philosophers and theologians most abstractly name the transcendence of man.

Thus, Jesus Christ enters the Christian ethic of responsibility as a teacher about the reality of man and of human life. He does not teach men about "another life": he teaches them that "this life" has depth and height which they do not recognize. His words to abandon self call men to abandon the smallness of their self-conception and to discover the wide reality of their possibility and their destiny. He confirms the hope that human endeavors are not doomed to total destruction—a fear that saps the strength of many a good man—but have an everlasting reality. He summons men to find their real source and goal in the midst of mundane concerns. The words and work of Jesus, for an ethician of responsibility, do not justify the elaboration of another, supernatural ethic beside that of natural life. They verify and deepen the ethic of natural life, revealing its full scope.

Jesus also enters into the ethic of responsibility in a second way. The gospels conclude with his appearance as victorious Lord, as the one who conquers death. St. Paul speaks of this victorious Lord, who conquers death because he is from all eternity, as the one who will "hand over the kingdom to God the Father" (I Cor 14, 25). He has brought all things to life, destroyed death, subjugated all things to his benevolent power. All of this he hands over to the Father that "God may be all in all." Christ wins back that which was his from the beginning, for "through him all things come and in him we exist" (I Cor 8, 6).

The victorious Lord is the prototype of Christian responsibility. He, who is Lord of creation in his eternal Sonship, by his obedience and love, is raised up and made Lord, firstborn of many brethren. His life, and the Spirit whom he sends, will win men to obedience of faith and love. These men, in turn, are called upon to enter into the world, as he did, and by working and suffering in that world draw it toward the Father. The Christian is to follow his Lord, not only in his earthly pilgrimage, but in his final action of "handing over the kingdom to the Father." Thus the ethic of responsibility finds in Jesus Christ both an exemplar and a prototype. He is exemplar in his human life, presenting not simply a model to be followed literally but an image of the reality of man, of the depth and heights of human life. He is prototype because he is the first, both temporally and ontologically, to do that which all Christians and all men must do: bring themselves and their world to perfection in God.

Once again, there is no lack of theological questions. Is it legitimate to interpret the incarnation and the redemption in such a way? Are these doctrines concerned essentially or even accidentally with the empirical betterment of the human condition? If so, how is this related to the "supernaturality" of the redemption? Does sound exegesis support this picture of Jesus? Is there solid ground for interpreting the "hard sayings" as promotion rather than denial of human life? These and many other questions are posed for theologians by the ethic of responsibility, which is in need of an ethical theology of the redemption. They are posed by many Christians who, heedless of the theoretical difficulties, wish to follow Jesus in a way which is significant in the modern world.

Finally, the ethic of responsibility finds in the doctrine of the Holy Spirit further confirmation that God is at work in the world. The sources of faith proclaim that the Spirit, sent to the world by the risen Lord, will teach and encourage. The Spirit joins man's life and action to the life and action of God. Roman Catholic theology has insisted that the elevation of man's life to the supernatural through the Spirit's presence, sanctifying grace, has ramifications in man's mind and will. The theological virtues of faith, hope and love are immediate effects of the presence of the Spirit. Furthermore, many theologians added that the presence of the Spirit also "infused" moral virtues, habitual sources of action which draw the entire moral life into the ambit of the love of God. Aquinas proclaimed that the New Law *is* the Holy Spirit.

These traditional doctrines provide the seeds for understanding the role of the Holy Spirit in an ethic of responsibility. The Spirit is the agent of God's intention to draw the world to himself. His presence sensitizes the conscience to the direction of God's action. His presence empowers hesitant man to move forward, to enter into the progress toward humanity. His presence accuses those who destroy and obstruct. His presence gathers into communion of purpose and sympathy those who love the Father and the world he has created and redeemed.

Again, a flock of theological questions is stirred up. Can the sources of faith confirm these claims? How do they, in fact, advance the traditional doctrines? But above all, how is the presence of the Spirit discerned? It is vitally important for an ethic which believes God is at work in decision and action to develop and explain the criteria whereby that action can be recognized. Certainly the ethic of responsibility does not rely on private revelations; it affirms its dependence upon the human sources of ethical knowledge, perception of value and critical, constructive intelligence. Still, in some way it affirms that value perception and use of intelligence share in the gracious presence of the Spirit.

The tradition speaks of the illumination of intellect and inspiration of will as the effects of the Spirit's action. How are the bright idea and the poignant desire to be distinguished from the work of the Spirit? Or are they the work of the Spirit? These are some of the questions which contemporary theology must answer if the ethic of responsibility is to stand on solid ground. Yet even while these questions await answers, many Christians deeply feel that their conscientious decisions, taken seriously and unselfishly, bear the marks of the powerful presence of the Holy Spirit. Many Christians are certain that the moral conscience which takes form in the Christian community, living in faith and love, vividly manifests the vital indwelling of the Spirit of love and truth.

The ethic of responsibility develops even while its theology and its metaphysics are incomplete. It develops despite the theoretical problems which it evokes. But there are two problems which, while theoretical, have particularly pressing and troubling urgency. They are the problem of sin and the problem of the Church as moral magisterium. We cannot discuss them here, for they are too extensive for what pretends to be a conclusion. However, we must note their place in the developing ethic of responsibility.

An ethic which stresses the importance of personal decision, the indispensable use of intelligence, the discernment of the Spirit, must hesitate before the strong insistence in the sources of faith on the sinful condition of man. The ethic of responsibility places great confidence in man's resources to discern and decide. Yet the tradition insists that it is precisely here that man is most deeply divided. True, grace is said to have a healing function, but human experience reports most convincingly that the healing is yet unfinished. Deep theological reflection on the scriptural and traditional doctrine of sin must accompany and temper the growth of the ethic of responsibility.

In like manner, the role of the magisterium, so much stressed in Roman Catholic theology, so absent in most Protestant theology, must be clarified. As responsibility calls for personal deliberation and decision, it inevitably poses the problem of the conflict between the teaching of the magisterium and the "conscience" of the Christian individual or community. The Roman Catholic church is undergoing a most traumatic crisis in this matter today, not only over the painful issue of contraception, but over the much more radical one of obedience and authority. Yet this is not the first crisis. In the oft-cited usury question, in the complicated church-state matters, in the positions on socialism and communism, in certain medical questions, many Catholics have faced the agonizing moment of a decision "in good conscience" against the teaching of a Church they accept as divinely founded and aided.

It is safe to say that the Roman Catholic church does not yet have an adequate theology of the moral magisterium. Protestant churches rejected the practicing magisterium and hence did not develop a theology of magisterium. The Roman Catholic church continued to act as magisterium with a self-assurance that perhaps made a developed theology seem unnecessary. But today that self-assurance is challenged. Challenges come from within and without. Long accepted theological formulae are questioned by theologians and scripture scholars. Discipline and morality are doubted and rejected by a laity which still considers itself as faithful. In this situation, it is not enough for the magisterium to insist on its authority to teach. It is necessary to rediscover, reexamine and reveal, with clarity and convincing reason, the sources of its authority. In the view of many serious theologians, this source is not simply a mandate from its divine founder to teach, but also is found in the living Spirit and in the living consciences of the community. Thus, the theology of the magisterium must clarify its claim to authority by an explanation of how the Spirit teaches teachers and faithful alike, how the New Law —which, as Aquinas says, is the Holy Spirit—and the law of man's inner potentialities, and the law of the institutional church are related; how the church, teachers and taught alike, both instructs and learns from the world. These are crucial issues which face theologians, if they are to help authority commend itself. If God's first imperative is, "be responsible," it is uttered to all human creation: the magisterium, insofar as it partakes in that creation, is bound by that imperative. The magisterium fulfills its responsibility by making men responsible.

This, then, is the prospect of an ethic of responsibility: the human person, essentially a decision maker and creative moralist, working in community to find those forms of rules and principles which will best promote and protect the growth of human life in depth and breadth, doing all this as a participation in God's worldly activity to accomplish cooperatively God's purposes. Our young seminarian hardly comprehends all this: he only wants to make a practical point about living in a seminary. But he implies all this as he senses himself as seeking responsibility, as searching for ways to become a responsible man. He may read our four authors for suggestions; he may look to living examples of responsible persons. He may also reflect on the difficulties which such a form of life poses, both practically and theoretically. But in the last analysis he and his companions are faced with the challenge: be responsible! They are called to accept a manner of life and to accept the care for its effective expression. They are called to discern value and creatively implement it. They are called to the most difficult task, to live humanly, in awareness of their communion with man and with God.

We have only sketched these prospects. We have drawn on our authors for the elements of the sketch, but have omitted further reference to the details of their thought. We have indicated most briefly the basic premises upon which we think such an ethic must rest and the underlying assumptions about the moral agent, rules, values and God which are operative in those premises. We have mentioned, without development or precision, the problems which are involved in these premises and assumptions. The ethic of responsibility, as a critical and reflective system of ideas, is still in the future. The morality of responsibility, as lived life, is daily becoming for many Christians a present reality.

In conclusion, we suggest that an ethic of responsibility and its success in meeting the theoretical and practical problems of contemporary religious ethics will contribute greatly to the human experience of living in the world seriously, energetically, and creatively. We suggest as well that this responsible life in the world will itself contribute to the human experience of transcendence, of sharing in something more than our limited present and our limited nature. We believe that this ethic and the manner of life it inspires is the inevitable result of reflection upon the Christian doctrines of God as the God of the living and of his creation as the recapitulation of all things in Christ. We feel that the development of such an ethic can further the realization of Père Teilhard de Chardin's hope:

> May the time come when men, having been awakened to a sense of the close bond linking all the movements of the world in the single, all-embracing work of the Incarnation, shall be unable to give themselves to any one of their tasks without illuminating it with the clear vision that their work—however elementary it may be—is received and put to good use by a Center of the Universe.[5]

REFERENCE MATERIAL

Bibliography

This bibliography consists of suggestions for further reading rather than of the sources of the matters discussed in this book. I have limited these suggestions to a few of the most important and interesting books and articles. I have also listed, for the most part, only English references, but many of these provide bibliographies of the European literature.

Chapter One. At the outset recognition should be given to an author who, although we cite him only once and in passing, inspired much of the contemporary discussion of responsibility. We refer to the renowned Jewish philosopher, the late Martin Buber. Almost everything he wrote is in some way relevant to this subject. Rather than list his works, I refer the reader to the brief selections gathered by N. N. Glatzer, *The Way of Response: Martin Buber. Selections from His Writings* (New York: Schocken, 1966).

There is little need for bibliography for the rest of Chapter 1, unless the reader wishes to pursue the intriguing subject of moral language. There is a survey of the contemporary discussion in B. Williams and A. Montefiori (eds.), *British Analytic Philosophy* (London: Routledge & Kegan Paul, 1966). Patrick Nowell-Smith approaches ethical problems from this standpoint in his *Ethics* (London: Penguin Books, 1954). R. M. Hare, *The Language of Morals* (New York: Oxford University Press, 1964) is a significant contribution to the discussion. Much Anglo-American moral philosophy is concerned with the meaning of moral words; two valuable histories of this trend are Mary Warnock, *Ethics Since 1900* (New

York: Oxford University Press, 1960) and G. C. Kerner, *Revolution in Ethical Theory* (New York: Oxford University Press, 1966). Some of the essays in Ian Ramsay (ed.) *Christian Ethics and Contemporary Philosophy* (New York: Macmillan, 1966) treat these questions as they affect Christian ethics.

Chapter Two. Literature on Vatican Council II is enormous and easily available. The best English edition of the text, edited by Walter Abbott (New York: American Press, 1966), contains essays in comment. The series *Concilium,* published regularly by Paulist Press in the United States and by Burns and Oates in England, is devoted to the theology subsequent to the Council. Volume V, which has appeared in three numbers, May 1965, 1966, 1967, specializes in moral theology.

The best introduction to the World Council of Churches is Edward Duff, *The Social Thought of the World Council of Churches* (New York: Association Press, 1956). Paul Abrecht's "Christian Action in Society," appears in *Ecumenical Review* 2 (1950), which is the journal where one can find discussions of the theological and social issues current in World Council circles. A recent collection of essays on such issues is John C. Bennett (ed.), *Christian Ethics in a Changing World* (New York: Association Press, 1965), which contains H. D. Wendland's "The Theology of the Responsible Society."

There has been an avalanche of literature on the contraception problem. A bibliographical review can be found in *Concilium* 5 (May, 1965). Of prime importance is John Noonan, *Contraception* (Cambridge, Harvard University Press, 1965). The opposing positions are represented by Germain Grisez, *Contraception and the Natural Law* (Milwaukee: Bruce, 1964) and by G. Egner, *Contraception vs. Tradition* (New York: Herder and Herder, 1967). R. P. O'Neil and M. A. Donovan, *Sexuality and Moral Responsibility* (Washington: Corpus Books, 1968) pertains directly to our topic. The Anglican position stated at Lambeth and a lengthy commentary can be found in Ian Ramsay's *Christian Ethics and Contemporary Philosophy,* cited above.

Finally, a survey of Christian situation ethics can be found in Giles Milhaven and David Casey, "Situation Ethics," *Theological Studies* 28 (June, 1967). Two most acute critical articles are James

Gustafson, "Context vs. Principle," *Harvard Theological Review* 58 (1965), reprinted in Martin Marty and D. Peerman (eds.), *New Theology* III (New York: Macmillan, 1966), which has specific reference to the Anglo-American and Protestant discussion, and J. Fuchs, "Morale théologique et morale de situation," *Nouvelle Revue Théologique* (1954), abstracted in *Theology Digest* 2 (1954), which is particularly relevant to the European and Catholic scene. Most current discussions can be found in Paul Ramsey and Eugene Outka (eds.), *Norm and Context in Christian Ethics* (New York: Charles Scribner's Sons, 1968) and in Charles Curran (ed.), *Absolutes in Moral Theology?* (Washington: Corpus Books, 1968). Paul Ramsey reviews much of the most prominent literature of the situationist bent in his *Rules and Deeds in Christian Ethics* (Edinburgh: Oliver and Boyd, 1965), which contains an acerbic comment on the Quaker view of sex, entitled "On Taking Sexual Responsibility Seriously Enough." Finally, we call the reader's attention to two recent books devoted to the topic of Christian responsibility: one, *Christian Responsibility* (New York: Sheed and Ward, 1964) is by a Catholic, Rosemary Haughton, the other is by a Protestant, Victor Obenhaus, *The Responsible Christian* (Chicago: University of Chicago Press, 1957).

Chapter Three. The third chapter spans all of moral philosophy. However, introductions to the philosophical view of responsibility can be found in William Frankena, *Ethics* (Englewood Cliffs: Prentice-Hall, 1963), in Richard Brandt, *Ethical Theory* (Englewood Cliffs: Prentice-Hall, 1959) and the companion volume of readings, *Value and Obligation* (New York: Harcourt, Brace and World, 1961). Vernon Bourke, *Ethics* (New York: Macmillan, 1956) treats responsibility in the tradition of Catholic scholastic ethics.

There are two volumes of important essays devoted to the topic: Carl Friedrich (ed.), *Responsibility: Nomos III* (New York: Liberal Arts Press, 1960) contains a stimulating essay by George Schrader, "Responsibility and Existence"; the volume of papers presented to the International Congress of Philosophy in 1956, published in *Revue internationale de philosophie* 11 (1957) includes a valuable essay by Richard McKeon, "The Development and Significance of the Concept of Responsibility," which provides a historical perspective on the use of the language of responsibility. A.

W. H. Adkin's *Merit and Responsibility* (Oxford: Clarendon Press, 1960) also provides a history of the idea, but limited to Greek classical culture.

Several of the Supplementary volumes of *The Proceedings of the Aristotelian Society* contain symposia on the various aspects of responsibility: "Intention, Motive and Responsibility," Supp. vol. 19 (1945); "Guilt," Supp. vol. 21 (1947); "Motives and Causes," Supp. vol. 26 (1952). Sidney Hook (ed.) *Determinism and Freedom* (New York: Collier, 1961) contains a number of essays dealing with the controverted question of responsibility and freedom. This topic is treated thoroughly in Moira Roberts, *Responsibility and Practical Freedom* (Cambridge University Press, 1965).

The psychological issues involved in responsibility are discussed in H. Schoeck and J. Wiggins, (eds.), *Psychiatry and Responsibility* (New York: Van Nostrand, 1965) and in the issue of *Journal of Religion and Mental Health* 2 (1960), which is devoted to this question. A reader wishing to pursue the philosophical discussions of responsibility is advised to thumb the pages of the journals, *Philosophy, Mind, Ethics, Review of Metaphysics,* and *Philosophical Quarterly,* which contain numerous articles, some of which I cite in the text.

Chapter Four. The text of this chapter contains references to the principal works of our four authors. A few which were not cited, as well as some helpful secondary materials, might be mentioned here.

Bernhard Haering has produced an immense volume of literature in several languages. The following among them contain materials relevant to our subject: *Toward a Christian Moral Theology* (South Bend: University of Notre Dame Press, 1966); *Christian Renewal in a Changing World* (New York: Desclee, 1964); *The Time of Salvation* (New York: Herder and Herder, 1966); *The Liberty of the Children of God* (Staten Island: Alba, 1966). One book which shows Haering doing the concrete work of a responsible moralist is his study of religious sociology, which has not been translated into English, *Macht und Ohnmacht der Religion* (Salzburg: Müller Verlag, 1956). F. Bourdeau and A. Danet have prepared *An Introduction to the Law of Christ* (Cork: Mercier Press, 1966). The theological question of nature and supernature, which is the background of Haering's problematic, is discussed in magisterial fashion by Henri de Lubac, *The Mystery of the Supernatural* (London: Chapman, 1967) and by Karl Rahner, *Nature and Grace* (London and New York: Sheed and Ward, 1963) and "Concerning the Relationship between Nature and Grace," *Theological Investigations* I (Baltimore: Helicon, 1961).

Dietrich Bonhoeffer's *Cost of Discipleship* (New York: Macmillan, 1963) presents positions rather different from those found in the *Ethics* and in the *Letters and Papers,* but is still most illuminating for understanding his view of the Christian life. The final chapter in particular sheds light on the idea of imitation of and participation in Christ. His commentary on the first chapters of Genesis, entitled *Creation and Fall* (New York: Macmillan, 1966), discusses the "knowledge of good and evil." The major secondary work on Bonhoeffer is a four volume collection of essays, *Die Mündige Welt* (Munich: Kaiser Verlag, 1956-1961). In English, there is a multitude of periodical literature and several helpful books: Martin Marty (ed.), *The Place of Bonhoeffer* (New York: Association Press, 1962); John Godsey, *The Theology of Bonhoeffer* (Richmond: John Knox Press, 1960); with particular reference to his Christology, J. A. Phillips, *The Form of Christ in the World* (London: Collins, 1967). The problem of the theology of law and gospel stands behind Bonhoeffer's ethics. There is a great deal of literature on this problem, but the reader would be well advised to start with a good summary of Luther's teaching, such as that found in Paul Althaus, *The Theology of Martin Luther* (Philadelphia: Fortress Press, 1966). The short treatment found there is expanded in Althaus' volume on Luther's ethics, *Die Ethik Martin Luthers,* presently being translated into English. Fortress Press also publishes small essays by prominent Lutheran theologians in their series of Facet Books; those on this subject are H. Bornkamm, *Luther's Doctrine of The Two Kingdoms;* P. Althaus, *The Divine Command;* W. Elert, *Law and Gospel.* A carefully detailed study of Luther's thought is given by T. M. McDonough, *The Law and The Gospel* (London: Oxford University Press, 1963).

We have cited most of H. Richard Niebuhr's writings that are relevant to our theme, with the exception of *The Meaning of Revelation* (New York: Macmillan, 1944) and *The Purpose of the Church and Its Ministry* (New York: Harpers, 1956). A complete bibliography of Niebuhr's work is given in the collection of very helpful essays, presented as a Festschrift, Paul Ramsey (ed.), *Faith and Ethics* (New York: Harper Torchbooks, 1965). James Gustafson's introduction to *The Responsible Self* is an indispensable aid to understanding Niebuhr's approach to ethics.

Robert Johann's writing is spread through many journals. We recommend checking the issues of *America,* where his "Philosopher's Notebook" has appeared quite regularly since 1963 (volume 108). Many of these essays, together with several longer articles, are collected in *Building the Human* (New York: Mentor-Omega, 1967). His first book, *The Meaning of Love* (Glen Rock, N. J.: Paulist Press, 1968) states in terms of neo-thomistic philosophy the basis of the idea of intersubjectivity.

Chapter Five. The final chapter touches on many aspects of the renewal of moral theology and of Christian ethics in general. A bibliography on the renewal of moral theology can be found following the first chapter of Haering's *Law of Christ.* More recent general statements are Enda McDonough (ed.), *Moral Theology Renewed* (Dublin: Gill & Son, 1965) and Charles Curran, *Moral Theology Today* (Notre Dame, 1966). The 5th volume of *Concilium,* mentioned above, is dedicated to the subject of the renewal of moral theology. The best survey is the Latin article of J. Fuchs, "Theologia Moralis Perficienda Votum Concilii Vaticani II," *Periodica* 55 (1966).

Scriptural issues involved in the development of Christian ethics are treated in R. Schnackenburg, *The Moral Theology of the New Testament* (London: Burns and Oates, 1965); W. Crotty, "Biblical Perspectives in Moral Theology," *Theological Studies* 26 (1965); T. W. Manson, *Ethics and the Gospel* (London: SCM, 1960); W. Lillie, *Studies in New Testament Ethics* (Edinburgh: Oliver and Boyd, 1961). Charity as the basis of a renewed moral theology is the theme of G. Gilleman's important *Primacy of Charity in Moral Theology* (Westminster: Newman Press, 1959); Karl Rahner makes an important contribution to this discussion in "The Commandment of Love in Relation to the Other Commandments," *Theological Investigations* V (Baltimore: Helicon Press, 1966). James Gustafson discusses the role of Christ in Christian morality in *Christ and the Moral Life* (New York: Harper and Row, 1967). On the crucial issue of discernment of the Spirit, see Karl Rahner's *The Dynamic Element in the Church* (New York: Herder, 1964);

A. Müller deals with the problem of obedience and authority in *Obedience in the Church* (London: Burns and Oates, 1966).

Several recent books deal with the problem of sin, M. Oraison, (ed.), *Sin* (New York: Macmillan, 1962) and P. Schoonenberg, *Man and Sin* (London: Sheed and Ward, 1965). L. Monden, *Sin, Liberty and Law* (London: Chapman, 1966) takes up many of these themes with special reference to the problem of evolving morality. This latter subject is treated by A. van Melsen, "Natural Law and Evolution," *Concilium* 6 (June, 1967). The other numbers of the 6th volume deal with the much-discussed relation of the Church and the world and the problem of secularity, although a survey article on this subject appears in volume 5 (May, 1967), C. van Ouwerkerk, "Secularism and Christian Ethics." Among the more recent works on secularity, are R. G. Smith, *Secular Christianity* (New York: Harper and Row, 1966) and Brian Wicker's brilliant *Culture and Theology* (London: Sheed and Ward, 1966).

Notes

CHAPTER ONE

1. André Lelande (ed.), *Vocabulaire technique et critique de la Philosophie* (6th ed.; Paris, 1951), 426-427. "Responsibility" appears neither in the *Dictionnaire des Sciences Philosophiques* (1851), nor in the *Wörterbuch der philosophischen Begriffe und Ausdrücke* (1899). It does appear in the *Dictionary of Philosophy and Psychology* (1902).

2. Walter Abbott (ed.), *Documents of Vatican II* (New York: America Press, 1966), 269, 261.

3. Emil Brunner, *The Divine Imperative* (Philadelphia: Westminster Press, 1947), 487.

4. Bernhard Haering, *The Law of Christ* (3 vols.; Westminster, Md.: Newman Press, 1964-67), Vol. I, 51.

CHAPTER TWO

1. W. A. Visser 't Hooft (ed.), *The First Assembly of the World Council of Churches* (New York: Harper and Brothers, 1948), 77.

2. Paul Abrecht, "Christian Action in Society," *Ecumenical Review* 2 (1950), 143.

3. The Roman Catholic Hierarchy of the United States, "On Individual Responsibility," Annual Statement, November 19, 1960, reprinted in *Catholic Mind* 59 (1961), 557-562.

4. *The Lambeth Conference of 1958* (London, 1958).

5. *Constitution on the Church in the Modern World,* II, #50-51, in Abbott, *op. cit.,* 254-256.

6. *Ibid.,* 256.

7. Richard Fagley, *The Population Explosion and Christian Responsibility* (New York: Oxford University Press, 1960), 221.

8. Abbott, *op. cit.,* 256.

9. "Responsible Parenthood and the Population Problem," Report of a Commission meeting at Mansfield College, Oxford, April 12-15. Reprinted in Fagley, *op. cit.,* 231.

10. Pope Pius XII, "Allocution to Italian Midwives," October 29, 1951, *Acta Apostolicae Sedis* 43 (1951), 845-846.

11. F. Cardegna, "Contraception, the Pill and Responsible Parenthood," *Theological Studies* 25 (1964), 611.

12. C. Curran, "Christian Marriage and Family Planning," *Jubilee* 12 (August, 1964), 11.

13. G. Kelly, "Responsible Parenthood," *America* 107 (May 5, 1962), 205-207.

14. St. T. Aquinas, *Summa Theologiae,* II-II, q. 47, a. 15.

15. George Woods, "Situation Ethics," in Ian Ramsay (ed.), *Christian Ethics and Contemporary Philosophy* (New York: Macmillan, 1966), 330.

16. J. A. T. Robinson, *Christian Morals Today* (Philadelphia: Westminster Press, 1964), 44-45.

17. J. Fletcher, *Situation Ethics* (Philadelphia: Westminster Press, 1966), 80.

18. *Op. cit.,* 82.

19. *Op. cit.,* 83-84.

20. *Op. cit.,* 98, 127.

21. Alastair Heron (ed.), *A Quaker View of Sex* (London: Friends House, 1963), 41.

22. *Op. cit.,* 40.

23. *Op. cit.,* 45.

24. *Op. cit.,* 20.

25. These distinctions of areas of moral discourse are borrowed from J. M. Gustafson's "Context versus Principle," *Harvard Theological Review* 58 (1965), 172-202.

CHAPTER THREE

1. G. E. M. Anscombe, *Intention* (Oxford: Blackwell, 1957), 1.

2. *Op. cit.,* 18.

3. J. Dewey and J. Tufts, *Ethics* (New York, 1914), 247.

4. *Nichomachean Ethics* III, 3, 1112ᵇ20.

5. R. M. Perkins, *Criminal Law and Procedure* (Brooklyn: Foundation Press, 1959), 973.

6. *Black's Law Dictionary* (St. Paul, West Publishing Co., 1951), 947.

7. *Nichomachean Ethics* III, 1, 1110ª35.

8. *Ibid.*, III, 1, 1111ᵇ21.

9. *Ibid.*, III, 4, 1113ª10.

10. *Ibid.*, III, 5, 1113ᵇ20.

11. J. L. Austin, *Philosophical Papers* (Oxford, 1961), 129.

12. H. L. A. Hart, "The Ascription of Responsibility and Rights," in A. Flew (ed.), *Logic and Language* I (Oxford: Blackwell, 1955).

13. J. Feinberg, "Action and Responsibility," in M. Black (ed.), *Philosophy in America* (Ithaca, 1965), 140-141.

14. *Nichomachean Ethics* II, 4, 110ª30.

15. D. Hume, *Concerning Human Understanding* VIII, 2.

16. P. Nowell-Smith, *Ethics* (London: Penguin Books, 1954), 304.

17. J. S. Mill, *An Examination of Sir William Hamilton's Philosophy* (London: Longmans, Green, 1867), 571.

18. *Ibid.*, 585.

19. W. Frankena, *Ethics* (Englewood Cliffs: Prentice-Hall, 1963), 3-4.

20. F. H. Bradley, "The Vulgar Notion of Responsibility in Connection with Free Will and Determinism," *Ethical Studies* (Oxford: Oxford University Press, 1876), 33.

21. *Nichomachean Ethics* III, 2, 111ᵇ5; *De Malo,* q. 6, art. unc., Summa Theologiae I, 83, 1.

22. R. Brandt, *Ethical Theory* (Englewood Cliffs: Prentice-Hall, 1959), 469.

23. A. Farrar, *Freedom of Will* (New York: Scribner's, 1958), 263, 278.

24. *Nichomachean Ethics* II, 2, 1103ᵇ15.

25. J. P. Sartre, *Being and Nothingness* (New York: Philosophical Library, 1956), 554.

26. J. Dewey, *Theory of The Moral Life,* 169.

27. *Ibid.*, 170.

28. Laurence Sears, *Responsibility* (New York, 1932), 182.

29. *Freedom of the Will,* 274.

30. We shall only pause to remark that just as praise and

blame pertain to the pattern of attribution, so guilt and remorse would seen to belong to the pattern of appropriation. These phenomena are, in a sense, the recognition that one's action falls short of full integration into one's being, although they imply the judgment of another on one's action as well, just as praise and blame imply the actual guilt or merit of the agent. Philosophers, however, have not often discussed guilt and remorse. This is not the case with the idea of freedom, which is regularly associated with the idea of responsibility; their relationship is hotly debated.

While admitting the great importance of this issue, we apologetically relegate it to this extended footnote because it is in one sense rather a different question than the one we are pursuing, that is, the philosophers' use of responsibility. All the authors from whom we have abstracted the patterns of ideas affirm the existence and significance of responsibility, although they hold quite different ideas about freedom. If after hearing them say, "here is what I mean by responsibility," one were to inquire, "but can responsibility in your sense be possible if there exists or does not exist freedom?" one moves into a new issue, namely, is freedom a presupposition of responsibility.

We feel that we can prescind from this very important question, given the purpose of our present study. However, we shall state summarily the principal sorts of answers which have been suggested. A great many moralists in the scholastic and in the Kantian traditions, and some contemporaries, clearly insist that responsibility, in the sense of being subject to praise or blame, must presuppose the existence of a free cause, in the sense of being self-determining and able to choose otherwise than he actually does choose.

The predominant view today, however, seems to be determinism, which justifies responsibility on the utilitarian grounds that praise and blame serve to effect change in the character of the agent. Some of these determinists insist that responsibility is meaningful *only* if determinism is true, since otherwise the agent could not be designated the cause of his action, nor would praise and blame effect any change in the agent. Finally, some have asserted that, in the last analysis, because determinism is true, responsibility has no real meaning at all. There is no proper sense in which man is the cause and author of the actions that issue from him.

A great deal has been written on this subject and the issues are complex and challenging. Ultimately, the British philosopher W. D. Ross may be right: "A philosophical genius may some day arise who will succeed in reconciling our natural thought about freedom and responsibility with acceptance of the law of causality;

but I must admit that no existing discussion seems to be very successful in doing so" (*Foundations of Ethics* [Oxford, 1939], 251).

31. *Ethics,* 257.

CHAPTER FOUR—BARTH

1. Karl Barth, *Church Dogmatics* (Edinburgh: T. & T. Clark, 1957), II/2, 511.

2. *Ibid.,* 641.

3. *Ibid.,* 632-633.

4. *Ibid.,* 641.

5. *Ibid.,* 655.

6. *Ibid.,* 662.

CHAPTER FOUR—HAERING

1. Bernhard Haering, *Gesetz Christi* (7th ed. rev.; Freiburg im Breisgau: Eric Wewel, 1963), I, 87. *The Law of Christ* (translated from the 5th German edition, Westminster: Newman Press, 1961). I shall cite the English edition, except for passages which I translate or for material found only in the 7th German edition.

2. *Law of Christ* I, 38.

3. *Ibid.,* 36, 51.

4. *Ibid.,* 47.

5. *Ibid.,* 35.

6. *Ibid.,* 36.

7. *Ibid.,* 37, 46.

8. *Ibid.,* 47.

9. "Religion and Morality: Fellowship and Responsibility," in *Personalism in Philosophy and Theology,* 12.

10. *Gesetz Christi* I, 113-114 (*Law of Christ* I, 76).

11. *Law of Christ* I, 227.

12. *Ibid.,* 233.

13. *Gesetz Christi* I, 293 (*Law of Christ* I, 259).

14. *Ibid.,* 295 (*Ibid.,* 261).

15. "Fellowship and Morality," *Personalism in Philosophy and Theology,* 14.

16. *Ibid.,* 12.

17. *Law of Christ* I, 146-147.

18. K. Rahner, *Nature and Grace* (London and New York: Sheed and Ward, 1963), 5-6.

19. Y. Congar, "Review of H. Davis, *Moral and Pastoral Theology*," *Revue des Sciences Theologiques et Philosophiques*, 24 (1934), 709.

20. *Law of Christ* I. 52.

CHAPTER FOUR—BONHOEFFER

1. Dietrich Bonhoeffer, *Ethics* (New York: The Macmillan Co., 1955), 202.

2. *Ibid.*, 144.

3. *Ibid.*, 150.

4. *Ibid.*, 191.

5. *Ibid.*, 286. O. Dilschneider, *Die evangelische Tat* (Bertelsmann, 1930), 87.

6. *Ethics*, 291.

7. *Ibid.*, 63.

8. *Ibid.*, 191.

9. *Letters and Papers from Prison* (London: SCM, 1953), 137-138.

10. *Ethics*, 142. (In the revised German 6th edition, this section, "The Love of God and the Decay of the World," is the opening chapter.)

11. *Ibid.*, 150.

12. *Ibid.*, 56.

13. *Ibid.*, 8.

14. "The Challenge of Dietrich Bonhoeffer's Life and Theology," *Chicago Theological Seminary Register* 51 (1961), 8.

15. *Ethics*, 17.

16. *Ibid.*, 89.

17. *Ibid.*, 10.

18. *Ibid.*, 63-64.

19. *Ibid.*, 60-61.

20. *Ibid.*, 56.

21. *Ibid.*, 24-25.

22. *Ibid.*, 57.

23. *Ibid.*, 78.

24. *Ibid.*, 192-193.

25. *Ibid.*, 204.

26. *Ibid.*, 192.

27. *Ibid.*, 251. For Barth's doctrine, see *Church Dogmatics* II/2, 583-613.

28. *Ibid.*, 254.

29. *Ibid.*, 212.

30. *Ibid.*, 205.

31. *Ibid.*, 206.

32. *Ibid.*, 103.

33. *Ibid.*, 217.

34. Max Weber, "Politics as a Vocation," in H. Gerth and C. Wright Mills (eds.), *From Max Weber* (New York: Oxford University Press, 1958), 127.

35. *Ibid.*, 121.

36. *Ethics*, 211.

37. *Law of Christ* I, 143.

38. *Ethics*, 211.

39. *Ibid.*, 212.

40. *Ibid.*, 214, 216.

41. *Letters and Papers from Prison*, 138.

42. *Ibid.*, 125.

43. *Ethics*, 165.

CHAPTER FOUR—NIEBUHR

1. H. Richard Niebuhr, *The Responsible Self* (New York: Harper and Row, 1963), 122-123.

2. "Center of Value," in *Radical Monotheism and Western Culture* (New York: Harper and Brothers, 1960), 105.

3. Paul Ramsey, "The Transformation of Ethics," in *Faith and Ethics* (New York: Harper and Row, 1965), 165.

4. *Christ and Culture* (New York: Harper Torchbooks, 1956), 192, 195.

5. Hans Frei, "The Theology of H. Richard Niebuhr," *Faith and Ethics*, 66.

6. *Radical Monotheism*, 32.

7. *The Responsible Self*, 126.

8. *Radical Monotheism*, 16.

9. *Ibid.*, 43.

10. *Ibid.*, 47.

11. *Ibid.*, 48.

12. *The Responsible Self*, 46.

13. *Ibid.*, 48.

14. J. M. Gustafson, Introduction to *The Responsible Self*, 8.

15. *The Responsible Self*, 61.

16. *Ibid.*, 65.

17. *Ibid.*, 73.

18. *Ibid.*, 93.
19. *Ibid.*, 87.
20. *Loc. cit.*
21. *The Responsible Self*, 97.
22. *Ibid.*, 100.
23. *Ibid.*, 106.
24. *Ibid.*, 107.
25. *Ibid.*, 112.
26. *Ibid.*, 116.
27. *Ibid.*, 121.
28. *Ibid.*, 126.
29. "Center of Value," in *Radical Monotheism*, 103.
30. *Ibid.*, 107-108.
31. *Ibid.*, 110.
32. *The Responsible Self*, 88.
33. *Ibid.*, 126.

CHAPTER FOUR—JOHANN

1. Robert O. Johann, "Authority and Responsibility," *Catholic Mind* 63 (1965), 12.
2. "Responsible Parenthood," *Problems of Population* III (South Bend: University of Notre Dame Press, 1965), 86.
3. *Ibid.*, 79-80.
4. *Ibid.*, 82.
5. *Loc. cit.* Cf. "Philosopher's Notebook," *America* 109 (Nov. 9, 1963), 568.
6. "Philosopher's Notebook," *America* 108 (May 25, 1963), 761.
7. "Responsible Parenthood," 85-87.
8. "Philosopher's Notebook," *America* 111 (August 1, 1964), 111.
9. "Return to Experience," *Review of Metaphysics* 17 (1963-1964), 325. Cf. "Philosopher's Notebook," *America* 108 (Jan. 5, 1963), 21.
10. "Philosopher's Notebook," *America,* 109 (Aug. 17, 1963), 160.
11. "Return to Experience," 327.
12. *Ibid.*, 337-338.
13. "Knowledge, Commitment and the Real," *Wisdom in Depth* (Milwaukee: Bruce, 1966), 115.
14. *Loc. cit.*

15. "Subjectivity," *Review of Metaphysics* 12 (1958-1959), 207.

16. *Ibid.*, 232; cf. "Philosopher's Notebook," *America* 108 (Jan. 5, 1963), 21.

17. "Subjectivity," 232.

18. "Return to Experience," 330.

19. *Ibid.*, 332. Cf. "Knowledge, Commitment and the Real," 121-122.

20. *Ibid.*, 334.

21. *The Pragmatic Meaning of God* (Milwaukee, 1966), 28.

22. *Ibid.*, 25.

23. "Return to Experience," 337.

24. *Ibid.*, 338.

25. "Responsible Parenthood," 87.

26. "Philosopher's Notebook," *America* 112 (April 10, 1965), 487.

27. "Authority and Responsibility," 14; "Natural Law and the Person," 9.

28. "Responsible Parenthood," 92.

29. "Philosopher's Notebook," *America* 108 (May 25, 1963), 762.

30. "Philosopher's Notebook," *America* 111 (Aug. 1, 1964).

31. "Responsible Parenthood," 89; "Natural Law and the Person," 10.

32. "Responsible Parenthood," 90.

33. "Creativity and Unbelief," *Building the Human* (New York, 1967).

CHAPTER FIVE

1. "The Freedom and Dignity of Man," *Theological Investigations* II (Baltimore: Helicon, 1963), 246-247.

2. *The Responsible Self*, 61, 145.

3. Christopher Mooney, "Teilhard de Chardin on Freedom," in J. C. Murray (ed.), *Man and Freedom* (New York: Kenedy and Sons, 1965), 103.

4. W. Abbott (ed.), *op. cit.*, 54, 261.

5. *The Divine Milieu* (London, 1960), 67.

Index